VERNON PRESS

SERIES IN BUSINESS AND FINANCE

Selflessness in Business

EDITED BY

DOMINIKA OCHNIK
UNIVERSITY OF OPOLE, POLAND

www.vernonpress.com

In the Americas:
Vernon Press
1000 N West Street,
Suite 1200, Wilmington,
Delaware 19801
United States

In the rest of the world:
Vernon Press
C/Sancti Espiritu 17,
Malaga, 29006
Spain

Series in Business and Finance

Library of Congress Control Number: 2019936422

ISBN: 978-1-62273-846-5

Also available:

978-1-62273-639-3 [Hardback]; 978-1-62273-756-7 [PDF, E-Book]

Cover design by Vernon Press.
Cover image: "Ambition", acrylic. Barbara Zofia Ochnik, Vienna, Austria.
barbarazofia.ochnik@gmail.com

Table of Contents

Preface

Dominika Ochnik,
Institute of Psychology, University of Opole, Poland

This volume undertakes interdisciplinary perspective on comprehensive understanding of selflessness in business. The authors deal with a controversial and seemingly paradoxical relationship between selflessness and business. It depicts the primary and lasting controversy between the *selfish* (egoistic, competitive) and *selfless* (prosocial, collaborative) behavior in view of social, organizational and individual benefits.

It is noteworthy that selflessness is not understood here as an idealistic purity, requiring the Kantian criterion of a duty emerging from moral imperative causing no personal gain. Selflessness is understood from a social perspective as related to self-transcendence (Levenson et al., 2005; Frankl, 2000) and connectedness to others (Dambrun, 2017). Considering this, it is worth noting, that both, selflessness and business pertain to relation. Those relations may occur and interact at different levels: individual, organizational, and social. The relations can be found in interactions of a person-work environment fit, employee collaboration or participating in corporate voluntary or organizational altruism. On an individual level, authors discuss motivation behind those actions and psychological consequences, like subjective wellbeing. Selfless actions like charity or corporate voluntary are great challenges for organizations in a contemporary business world. Arising literature (Bolino & Grant, 2016; Clarkson, 2014; Li et al., 2015) revealing positive implications of prosocial behavior in organizations for productivity and effectiveness, calls for action to be taken by organizations and business.

The Fourth Industrial Revolution shows the prerequisite for cooperation with others (World Economic Forum, 2016). It seems that it is more valuable for companies to include rather prosocial than self-interested employees. This change is also visible at social level. The research has shown that young adults, surprisingly and in contrary to previous findings, are less narcissistic compared to earlier generations (Wetzel et al., 2017). Furthermore, the idea of a human being driven by self-interests and selfish reward: the *Homo economicus* — "Economic man" model of human behavior (Fehr, Sigmund, & Nowak, 2002) has not been confirmed in the study in 15 societies (Henrich et al., 2005). Is it a fall of the *Homo economicus*? And if so what should be the next step?

The strain between selfish and selfless motivation translates to basic inquiry about motivation of a human being, and has been undertaken from biological, philosophical or psychological point of view for decades or even centuries. Nevertheless, the aim of the book was to explore this issue in a contemporary business-related context. Therefore, it takes a step into finding a solution to the challenges of the twenty-first century.

The volume consists of four parts. Part I deals with the aspects of selflessness in business in the twenty-first century. In Chapter 1 *Finding an Equilibrium between seeking-profit and Work-Life-Balance: The Challenge of Entrepreneurs within their SMEs* by Claudia Nelly Berrones-Flemmig, Francoise Contreras, Utz Dornberger, and Yonni Angel Cuero Acosta, authors aim to develop a framework about how this new ventures that are small and medium-sized enterprises (SMEs) can achieve an effective balance between the profits and the personal life of the firms' personnel. Around the world, there is a massive loss of jobs due to the industrial and technological revolution. This revolution contents the common understanding of the entrepreneurship phenomenon, what creates an urgent matter to generate the optimal foundations to be a better entrepreneur that enables not only to make profit and maximizing the shareholders' wealth (as economic theory instructs managers), but also to take into consideration the human being and the resources available in the planet. To find this balance is not easy; nevertheless, it is fundamental to search for developing suitable innovative models that promote this balance. In this context, the main research question of this chapter is: Which elements can be taken into consideration to propose a conceptual framework and methodology for SMEs with the objective to assess the balance between profit and personal life? According to the proposed model, the balance between the worker's personal life and the firm's profits can be achieved through tangible and intangible resources, the latter being the main source of sustainability for SMEs.

Chapter 2 *Social Entrepreneurship: Blending prosocial Motivation and Self-interests in Business* by Andreana Drencheva, pertains to rarely undertaken subject of motivation in social entrepreneurship. This conceptual book chapter proposes that both prosocial and personal motivations fuel social entrepreneurship at the same time or over time and provides examples from the extant research. The chapter examines how prosocial and personal motivations interact with each other to create synergies or tensions that influence the wellbeing of both social entrepreneurs and social ventures. It proposes that meaningful synergies between prosocial and personal motivations can enhance the wellbeing of social entrepreneurs and social ventures, while unmanaged tensions can hinder the wellbeing of social entrepreneurs and their ventures.

Chapter 3 *Personalist Economics: Caring, Justice, and Christian Charity* by Edward O'Boyle presents a philosophical perspective. The Author thoroughly examines the meaning and interaction of caring, justice, and Christian charity from the personalistic economy perspective. The limits on gain seeking behavior are also explained. As a consequence of a literature review, the Author presents an interactive model of the *Person of Action*, who may act virtuously or viciously. The *Person of Action* challenges the machine-like and passive *Homo economicus* model.

Part II of the book relates to dimensions of selflessness at the work environment. In this part, the idea of organizational altruism, quantum leadership and issue of employee's loyalty will be undertaken.

In Chapter 4 *Dimensions of Selflessness at Work: Typology of organizational Altruism* by Joanna M. Szulc, a novel approach to organizational altruism is presented. The chapter replies to increase of scholarly call to examine workplace behaviors which are clearly other-oriented (e.g., Bolino and Grant, 2016; Grant and Patil, 2012; Li et al., 2015). The Author presents insightful literature analysis and examining organizational altruism and how it reflects the idea of selflessness in modern business. A typology of organizational altruism has been developed. Building on organizational and socio-psychological research, the Author consider a variety of dimensions of organizational altruism that relate to the: a) beneficiaries of such behaviors, b) associated costs, c) level of the actor's commitment, d) intuition and rationality involved, e) consequences of such actions, f) actor's initiative, and the g) type of help involved. The Author demonstrates how the development of a comprehensive taxonomy can advance the existing theory and research on organizational altruism and selflessness in business and how it generates a number of important directions for future research.

In Chapter 5 *Quantum Leadership: Toward Ethical Selflessness* by Michael A. Piel, Karen Putnam, and Karen K. Johnson present a novel idea of quantum leadership and its benefits toward overcoming corruption. Ethical selflessness is one immunogenic mechanism which has the potential to transform organizational cultures and mitigate the corruption infection. Authors claim that quantum leadership opens businesses to the powerful potential capabilities of ethical selflessness. After briefly introducing the concepts and principles of quantum leadership, this chapter leads the reader to exploring the value dynamics of ethical selflessness. In examining several standard ethical theories, the selflessness construct is described in detail within the context of quantum leadership principles and practices. Further comparing the concept through a range of various philosophical and literary perspectives, the reader can ultimately decide whether to accept, reject, or sustain judgment on whether to implement this leadership approach within their organizations. The power of selflessness transcends and is far greater than the impotence of selfishness. Any individual or organization currently plagued by any form of corruption would benefit from the ethical selflessness actualized in exercising quantum leadership. The ethical wave of possibilities is unlimited for those organizations and individuals who embrace selflessness.

Chapter 6 *Type of Obligation to the Company and the Loyalty of an Employee* by Renata Rosmus is dedicated to an empirical examination of the employee's loyalty. The author analyses the factors of employee loyalty in the situation of deteriorating working conditions. Various individual and situational factors were taken into account when deciding about remaining loyal towards the company such as formal obligation, attachment, conformism, standards, norms, as well as personal factors (e.g., locus of control, Machiavellianism). The paper-pencil research plan was used. In order to collect the data ($N = 125$), the specially designed survey questioning participants' opinion on their level of moral duty (obligation) and their level of acceptance of the new deteriorating working conditions have been used. The results confirmed the hypothesis on the relation between the type of obligation, personal characteristics and loyal behavior. The conclusions can be applied in explaining the social behavior of people as members of organizations and also in working out the strategy for creating the loyal behaviors of the company.

Part IV of this volume relates to dimensions of selflessness and gender. The chosen subject is rarely tackled.

In Chapter 7 *Selfless Women in Capitalism?* by Luka Boršić and Ivana Skuhala Karasman deal with selflessness in the context of traditional and contemporary understanding of the role of women in society and personal identity from a philosophical approach. Personal identity is a direct consequence of social roles that individuals have in society. When it comes to women in business, there is a conflict between different systems of values and the roles women are expected to take. To what extent is the social expectation of women's behavior paired with the socially acceptable role of women in collision with the corporate expectation that is imposed upon the same women? Selflessness appears here as a value that connects and bridges over these two different social roles. Involvement of selflessness in corporate ethics opens up new dimensions of the problem. Moreover, authors deal with the question of how selflessness as a value is matched to the value system that dominates liberal capitalism. When questioning the consistency of selflessness with the dominant system of values in liberal capitalism, there is the gap between the proclaimed values in business, which are based on maximizing profits based on rational egoism, compared to the moral imposition of selflessness as an altruistic attitude towards the other. Authors systematically challenge syllogisms leading to the conclusion that "capitalism is not suitable "habitat" for women." This discussion contributes to a deeper awareness of the social role and situation of women in business. The Authors propose social perception of capitalism less selfish or perception of women less selfless, as to provide equal opportunities.

In Chapter 8 *Prosocial vocational Interests and Gender in the Labor Market* by Dominika Ochnik empirical approach is introduced. The author shows research on prosocial vocational interests with regard to gender in the age of entering the labor market and the highest vocational activity within the framework of *Contextual model of vocational interests*. The so-called *vocational social clock* as the key factor of the model – reveals the dynamics of vocational interests in view of social expectations with regards to age and gender. The prosocial vocational interests were measured by an original tool — Vocational Potential Inventory (Ochnik, Stala, & Rosmus, 2018). The number of 9359 persons, including 5364 women (57%) and 3995 men (43%) in the age of entering labor market (20-24 years), the highest vocational activity (30-34 years) and the age of 40-44 and 50-54 years, took part in the study. Research results revealed a significant effect of gender and age interaction of pro-social vocational interests. Men, both in the youngest and the oldest group, scored higher than women, whereas in the group of 30-34 years women scored higher, and in the group of age 40-44 years, the gender differences were irrelevant. Therefore, in the age of decreased professional activity (the youngest and the oldest group) both men and women preferred non-stereotypical vocational interests. Whilst the period of the most intense professional activity and also undertaking new social (family) roles – was related to stereotypically gender-based prosocial vocational interests. The phenomenon of non-stereotypical vocational interests referring to interpersonal relations emerging in such a large sample of women and men of various ages may be significant for breaking stereotypes in society.

Part IV has been dedicated to the aspect of selflessness in practice. The authors in this part showcase studies and discuss selflessness from a practical point of view.

In Chapter 9 *Selflessness in Business – Theory vs. Practice* by Monika Jakubiak, the motivation behind and types of philanthropic initiatives undertaken by the employees of the companies in the financial sector are revealed. The subject matter of the study pertains to issues associated with the significance of selflessness in business. The chapter outlines theoretical concepts and results of own studies connected with activities undertaken by a socially responsible entrepreneur. Results indicated that the owner and the company's employees undertake numerous activities in the area of corporate social responsibility, especially as far as charity is concerned. The following constitute the driving force behind these activities: values, cultural orientation, interest in raising awareness regarding healthy lifestyles. Such activities result in positive models of behavior and norms for functioning becoming rooted, and the brand becoming more recognizable (higher reputation).

Chapter 10 *Donations from Ecuadorian Firms: A quantitative Analysis* by Hector Alberto Botello Peñaloza presents empirical analysis. This phenomenon of the selfless actions of Ecuadorian companies is analyzed by observing the amounts of donations they make and the endowments they provide to their workers. The author reveals the relationship between these behaviors, satisfaction and productivity of companies. The database corresponds to the 2010 economic census along with administrative records and industrial surveys. This is one of the first quantitative studies in the country. The contribution of this research is to use firm and worker-level data to observe the disinterested behavior of companies and psychology at work. This area of research has always been one of the scientific literature associated with Latin American developing countries such as Ecuador.

In Chapter 11 *Prosocial Motivation and Selflessness in Cultural Institutions. A Case Study of CAC Málaga* by Lucía Pérez-Pérez and Miquel Banstons Prat, the authors relate to prosocial motivation. The chapter examines the communication strategy aligned to the mission for XXI century museums and cultural institutions. The authors propose the Prosocial Model applied to communication, which builds on the opportunities offered by the Information and Communication Technologies (ICTs). Authors propose a management model that brings the idea of communication closer to the idea of service (*prosocial motivation*) and aligns it with the fulfillment of the own mission of the institution. According to this model, the organization develops its strategy of communication starting not from the information that you are interested in giving but of the communication oriented to what interests the public. This makes possible to achieve competitive efficiency in the current environment of globalization; and starts from the point of the fact that the museum is, above all, a community of people that relates to each other and to other people from abroad. Authors defend that the person, not only should be treated accordingly the dignity of the human being, rational and free but also, the knowledge of their motivations is essential for the communication management in order to reach the true objective of the institution —its mission. The methodology combines the CAC Málaga case study, focused interview and documentary analysis. The study revealed the benefits of applying a Prosocial Management Model in the communication strategy for effective interaction with the public and how this reinforces the effectiveness, attractiveness and unity of the institution.

The academic discussion presented in this book presented non-obvious relations between widely understood selflessness and business. Interdisciplinary perspectives shed new light on various aspects of relations between selflessness and business and showed new directions for future research in the theme.

Acknowledgments

At this point, I would like to show appreciation to all contributors and reviewers for their dedicated work. I would also like to express my gratitude to prof. Zofia Ratajczak for inspiration to undertake the topic of *Selflessness in Business*.

References

Bolino, M. C., & Grant, A. M. (2016). The Bright Side of Being Prosocial at Work, and the Dark Side, Too: A Review and Agenda for Research on Other-Oriented Motives, Behavior, and Impact in Organizations. *Academy of Management Annals, 10*, 1, 599-670. DOI 10.1080/19416520.2016.1153260

Clarkson, G. P.(2014). Twenty-First Century Employment Relationships: The Case for an Altruistic Model. *Human Resource Management, 53*(2), 253-269.

Dambrun, M. (2017). Self-centeredness and selflessness: happiness correlates and mediating psychological processes. *PeerJ*, 5:e3306. DOI 10.7717/peerj.3306

Frankl, V. E. (2000). *Man's search for ultimate meaning*. New York: Perseus Publishing.

Grant, A. M., & Patil, S. V. (2012). Challenging the norm of self-interest: Minority influence and transitions to helping norms in work units. *Academy of Management Review, 37*(4), 547-568.

Henrich, J., Boyd, R., Bowles, S., Camerer, C., Fehr, E., Gintis, H., ... Tracer, D. (2005). "Economic man" in cross-cultural perspective: Behavioral experiments in 15 small-scale societies. *Behavioral and Brain Sciences, 28*(6), 795-815. https://doi.org/10.1017/S0140525X05000142

Levenson, M. R., Jennings, P.A., Aldwin, C. M., & Shiraishi, R. W. (2005). Self-transcendence: conceptualization and measurement. *International Journal of Aging and Human Development 60*, 2, 127-143. DOI 10.2190/XRXM-FYRA-7U0X-GRC0.

Li, N., Kirkman, B., & Porter, C. (2014). Toward a model of work team altruism. *Academy of Management Review, published ahead of print March 25, 2014.*

Ochnik, D., Stala, M., & Rosmus, R. (2018). Skala prospołecznych preferencji zawodowych.[Prosocial scale of vocational interests.] *Czasopismo Psychologiczne—Psychological Journal, 24(1), 151-158.* DOI: 10.14691/CPPJ.24.1.151

Sigmund, K., Fehr, E., & Nowak, M. A. (2002). The Economics of Fair Play. *Scientific American, 286*(1), 83-87.

Wetzel, E., Brown, A., Hill, P.L., Chung, J. M., Robins, R. W., & Roberts, B. W. (2017). The Narcissism Epidemic Is Dead; Long Live the Narcissism Epidemic. *Psychological Science, 28*(12), 1833–1847. https://doi.org/10.1177/0956797617724208

World Economic Forum (2016). Future of Jobs Report. Retrieved from http://www3.weforum.org/docs/WEF_Future_of_Jobs.pdf

Part I:
Aspects of Selflessness in Business in the XXI century

Chapter 1

Finding an Equilibrium between seeking-profit and Work-Life-Balance: The Challenge of Entrepreneurs within their SMEs

Claudia Nelly Berrones-Flemmig,
International SEPT Program, Leipzig University, Germany

Francoise Contreras,
Business School, Universidad del Rosario, Bogotá, Colombia

Utz Dornberger,
Director of International SEPT Program, Leipzig University, Germany

Yonni Angel Cuero Acosta,
Universidad del Rosario, Bogotá, Colombia

Introduction

The field of entrepreneurship has been widely conceptualized from a different perspective such as international entrepreneurship, social entrepreneurship, environmental entrepreneurship, sustainable entrepreneurship, among others. According to the most recent Global Entrepreneurship Monitor (GEM) —in 2017-2018, opportunity-driven entrepreneurship predominates in the world across different sectors. This global characteristic is important to see the relevance of entrepreneurship within societies today. The connection between entrepreneurship and societal goals has facilitated the emergence of the tendency of how to build and extend the prosocial motivation of entrepreneurs as well as to work on the improvement of the entrepreneurs' and stakeholders well-being (Shepherd, 2015). This represents a more holistic view of the benefit that firms create internally – for the employees – and externally – for communities.

This more humanized perspective of entrepreneurship occurs within a shifting global situation, where there are industrial and technological revolutions going on. Jensen (1993) explained that the industrial revolution represented a shift to capital-intensive production, rapid growth in productivity and living standards, and the creation of large corporates, which overpass their capacity. Around the world, the workers are facing an age of transformation, driven by new technological opportunities (Khallash & Kruse, 2012). Additionally, a recent report from PricewaterhouseCoopers (2018) shows that presently there is a fundamental transformation in the way of working: automation and "thinking machines" are replacing human tasks and jobs what also raises important challenges in the organizations and the human resource management (HRM). According to this report, the way that the human beings respond to the challenges and the opportunities will determine the world in which the future of work plays out: Collectivism versus individualism, integration versus fragmentation. Collectivism versus individualism presents the contrast between the sense of collective responsibility and the "me first" individualism trend in the world. Integration versus fragmentation discusses whether digital technology could conduce to the end for large companies. A positive outcome of the current situation is that technology has allowed small business to access a large amount of information as well as skills and financing that usually were only available for large enterprises. Besides, technology has allowed a large business to reduce substantially its internal and external costs and expenses. Now, organizations can be more productive with fewer employees and even expands their operations without investing large amounts of capital. However, the dilemma in this aspect is if the government's actions will incentive or penalize larger companies for reducing job positions for humans or if they are going to design policies to encourage small business and start-ups to bring jobs for those who are replaced by machines. According to Khallash & Kruse (2012), all these changes driven derived from the present technological transformations will have consequences in the organization of the future way of working and the concept of work-life balance.

The trends described above contains the common understanding of the entrepreneurship phenomenon in which entrepreneurs create a fit to the need of the society. However, it is important to generate the optimal foundations for a better entrepreneur who makes not only profits and maximizes the shareholders' wealth, but also who takes into consideration the human wellbeing and the resources available in the planet. To find this balance is not easy and we conceptually discuss how to achieve this equilibrium in the following sections.

Facing the Problem

Some researchers analyze the entrepreneurial process as a generator for refining potential opportunities considering building, engaging and transforming communities (Shepherd, 2015). Recent developments in the field of entrepreneurship come from scholars that concentrate on the exploration of entrepreneurial actions that at the same time benefit others, particularly, research on social entrepreneurship (e.g., Dacin, Dancin, & Tracey, 2011; Mair & Marti, 2006; McMullen, 2011; Peredo & Chrisman, 2006), environmental entrepreneurship (e.g., Meek, Pacheco, & York, 2010; York & Venkataraman, 2010) and sustainable development (e.g., Hall, Daneke, & Lenox, 2010; Shepherd, Patzelt, Wiliams, & Warnecke, 2014), among others. In this regard, we can observe the tendency to develop different forms of analysis about entrepreneurship, particularly, related to benefit communities. Likewise, in many small and medium-sized enterprises (SMEs), it is common that only one person (or a reduced group of persons) is responsible for different areas in the enterprise. SMEs dominate the enterprise's landscape around the world and these companies relatively present low standards in terms of accomplishment of the basic rules of HRM, including the aspect of work-life balance (WLB) (Robak & Słocińska, 2015). The analysis of WLB has been evolved from a typical female problem, related to family life, into a broader field, concerning all the employees. Several studies show that the aspect of WLB has relevant social implications that also benefit the profit of the firms. For example, Harrington and Ladge (2009) found a positive correlation between WLB and the employees and the organizational performance. In addition, WLB has another type of results for the HRM of the companies such as a low turnover intention, organizational commitment, higher job satisfaction, and reduction of inter-role conflict (Cegarra-Leiva, Sánchez-Vidal, & Cegarra-Navarro, 2012; De Sivatte, Gordon, Rojo, & Olmos, 2015). WLB experiences improve the overall psychological well-being and increase the satisfaction at work and in the family as well (Grzywacz & Carlson, 2007). There are also empirical studies that reveal that a poor WLB leads to poor job performance and higher absenteeism in the workplace (Frone, Russel, & Cooper, 1992). These negative implications exert an adverse effect on the profits of the companies. Thus, WLB is an element that contributes to the overall sustainable development of the human being and at the same time to the sustainability of the enterprises.

Theoretical Framework

Work-life balance (WLB) studies the equilibrium between personal life and profit orientation within organizations. Delecta (2011) defines WLB as the ability of an individual to accomplish their work and family commitments in combination with other non-work activities. That means WLB involves not only work and family functions, but also other roles in different areas of life.

According to Robak, Słocińska, and Depta (2016), SMEs possess a weak HRM, including the aspect related to WLB. This weakness is not only due to organizational limitations in terms of size and resources but also because of the lack of employers´ awareness of this issue. The term WLB is difficult to define. In general, it marries up from one side the work activities; on the other side, the non-professional life such as personal life, private life and family life. The term WLB has mostly been examined within a work-family relationship (Laurijssen & Glorieux, 2013). Robak et al., (2016) point out that a minority of the studies examine the phenomenon assuming that all workers have the right to expect the balance between work and private life. It is worth noting, the term "all workers" refer to not only mothers with small children —which have been a misconception within the practices of HRM – but also it implies all the personnel within a firm.

In the case of SMEs, it is quite interesting to observe how this type of companies could be able to tackle the needs of HRM as well as the WLB. The difference with large companies does not set up only in the size or the resources that the large firms possess. Even though an SME cannot devote an entire department to manage human resources, these firms are able to provide well-being within the workplace for the workers. What it is important to highlight is that SMEs' HRM is very informal sometimes, less systematic, and in the somehow more intuitive way. It is within this particular way of doing things, in which SMEs can obtain advantages or present limitations. Size constitutes an advantage to know the personnel; however, in terms of resources to develop programs, these resources can be scarce. Hence, from the conceptual point of view, it is important to understand how job satisfaction, commitment, organizational identity, loyalty and quality of personal life in the workplace can be ensured by SMEs. A significant starting point for the analysis of the WLB, it is to consider the importance of the problems and challenges in a process of building proper relation between work and personal life under the conditions of globalization, increasing competitive pressure, demographic and social changes, deregulation of the labor market, and especially in the face of a rapid technological development within SMEs.

WLB refers to the workers' ability to decide how much time, where, and when will they devote to the activities, so WLB can be understood as an equal distribution of time, energy, and engagement in all the areas of life in a way that you achieve satisfaction in all of them (Kirchmeyer, 2000). Although the employees' main goal within a workplace is to perform well the tasks for which they were hired, the WLB should be seen as the main resource to make it better. In fact, employees' well-being constitutes an important resource to improve the quality of the job. This resource can be strengthened when the SMEs are aware of the importance of WLB and the concern about employees' well-being is part of their organizational culture. In this kind of organizations do not only exist policies related to WLB but also there is a trusting work environment where the employees feel free to enjoy the possibilities provided by the SMEs (Allen, 2001). In this case, SMEs should look for employees to ensure this balance. The success of this relationship will depend on what extent employees perceive that their own needs and values are closely related to the organizational ones. Likewise, this fit between individual and organization is increasing the possibility to stay in the organization and to achieve exceptional performance (Ostroff, Shin, & Kinicki, 2005). A recent study found that the match between individuals' goals and the values of the organization can predict work-family balance (Seong, 2016) and this fit is significantly related to organizational commitment, job satisfaction, reducing the turnover intent (Fan, 2018; Pérez, Vela, Abella, & Martínez, 2017).

Moreover, WLB includes the importance of personal life. A recent international research project (Dunay, Swadzba, Vinogradov, & Illés, 2015) examined the economic awareness and working attitudes of university students. According to the findings of this project, the family, health, and friends are the most important factors of the general system of values of university students. When analyzing the values' system of work, the most important factors of work were the certainty of work and good salary, but the colleagues and the number of working hours were considered as very important as well. These results suggest that private life has a substantial motivating power for the young generation. The discussion here turns into the idea of how to idealize WLB as a process in order to create a balance between work and private life. Thus, it is reasonable to present work-life relationship as a constant process: balancing, harmonization, integration, matching, or reconciliation of the sphere of work with non - professional life. A dynamic approach to WLB also assumes that organizations must conduct uninterrupted monitoring of the needs and expectations of employees and must make changes in the organizational activities in this area (Robak et al., 2016). It should be noticed that balancing work with personal life is usually referred to the family responsibilities, especially responsibilities connected with the fact of having little children that is why the notion of WLB is mainly addressed to women. However, implement work-family practices in the SMEs is crucial for all employees, who are looking for the possibility to manage in the best way the interconnection between work and family. Their rejection from the discourse about the balancing of the discussed areas of life could be understood as discrimination. WLB assumes the possibility of realization of the needs and desires of all employees, both in the area of private and personal lives, in line with their expectations and interest and possibilities of the organization. In addition, for the candidates for a job, the declarations of the potential employers concerning possibilities of meeting these needs and expectations are a significant deciding factor in a process of employer's choosing. In the context of SMEs, Robak et al. (2016) indicated that the peculiarity of the functioning of a SMEs may be recognized as a factor fostering efficient management of WLB (greater flexibility in decision- making process, greater flexibility in terms of structural and economic matters), but at the same time size of the company can be recognized as a factor creating an obstacles in implementation of the WLB idea (ad hoc management, lack of knowledge in the area of shaping activities concerning WLB, focus on profit in a short time, lack of strategic management, lack of formal representations of the employees' interests).

Scientific literature of WLB emphasizes only general aspects such as "human being", "well-being." Dunay et al. (2015) found in their study that the health, family, and friends are the most important factors of the general system of values of university students. Kichmeyer (2000) indicates that WLB can be understood as an equal distribution of time, energy, and engagement in all the areas of life in a way that you achieve satisfaction in all of them. Although the relevant areas of personal life that should be considered as a component of WLB require more deeply examination, there is evidence that health, personal development, family, and friends among others, are important factors to be included in WLB.

Furthermore, health condition (physical and mental) is very important. A well-known folk saying expresses, "a healthy mind lives in a healthy body". The Constitution of the World Health Organization (WHO) defines health as "a state of complete physical, mental and social well-being and not merely the absence of disease or infirmity." In order to maintain good physical health, every human being should continuously take care mainly about three aspects: to have enough sleep every day, to dedicate everyday time for daily sport (and enough daily movement), and the possibility to have a daily well-balanced diet. Likewise, personal development includes time dedicated to different activities like career development and/or learn other activities non-related with professional life. Personal development includes also taking enough time for spiritual life (independently from the religion and/or believes). Finally, it is important to have enough time for family (core and extended family) and enough time to take care of the friendships. However, this enough time does not affect the working time as well as the working hours should not affect the time for family and friends. This means, besides family demands and family responsibilities, there are some other demands in work-life balance than family and this includes work live relaxation, time for vacation, sports and personal development (Delecta, 2011). These aspects exposed above are part of every individual life and if there is not a good balance between them and work activities, this can affect negatively the employees' quality of life. In the context of business, if the companies do not have "balanced" employees, this is not positive for the firm in different aspects such as organizational climate, commitment, achievement of innovation, and firm's performance. Thus, at the workplace, the balanced work-life experiences improve the overall psychological well-being (Grzywacz & Carlson, 2007). The improvement in performance, organizational commitment, and higher job satisfaction include also the efficiency, as well as the development of creativity and innovation in individuals within the firms.

Components of the proposed Model

According to the above exposed, there are some crucial factors that entrepreneurs who most of the time they own their businesses – and these businesses initially take the form SMEs – should take into account which currently is a priority to both, employees and organizations in order to increase the WLB within the firm. Even though the size of the companies could be an advantage because it allows keeping close relationships and knows the whole personnel, the resources to develop programs for the employees are limited. According to Bloom et al. (2009), the optimistic perspective of WLB practices in firms is justified with the help of tangible and intangible business benefits of good WLB. For the model proposed in the present chapter, two types of resources are recognized:

Intangible resources

The components of the proposed model are supported in intangible resources, which constitute the main source of sustainable competitive advantage for the companies (Pérez et al., 2017). Among them is an organizational culture characterized by management practices where employees perceive support, trust and a genuine concern for them. The culture of the organization and how the employees perceive the organizational climate is crucial. It is important to improve the organizational culture considering employees´ well-being, communicating the efforts of the human resources department of the company regarding WLB initiatives (Cegarra-Leiva et al., 2012). Employees need to feel comfortable as well as to trust in the firm. Likewise, it is important to have an organizational value system where the WLB is relevant to achieve organizational/personal goals. It is also relevant to recruit, select, retain and promote people that share these same values.

Tangible Resources

This component includes to implement work-family practices, understood as services offered by the companies that allow employees to have a better manage the interconnection between work and family (Thompson, Beauvais, & Lyness, 1999). These practices may include, for example, flextime or telework (using the available technology) giving more autonomy to employees for doing their job. The firm should provide the opportunity to organize and to stimulate new forms of working to help the development of work-family practices (tangible resources). Of course, it implies a careful look in the hours, payment, and time consideration for the employees. As a consequence, the sustainability of both, human being and enterprises can be fostered. Figure 1 presents the conceptual model.

For the proposed model described below in Figure 1.1, it is important to generate adequate indicators to assess the different aspects, as well as to test the model in the context of SMEs. The aspects considered in this model will be also helpful for the SMEs in order to continue monitoring the WLB in their employees. This model could constitute the base to develop relevant tools for human resource development in SMEs to assess the level of WLB, particularly to assess the balance between profit and quality of life, something that entrepreneurs have to consider when constituting their companies. Complementary to this, it is important to evaluate with the employees the reasons for the unbalance (if it is the organizational capabilities and/or due to workload and/or other reasons (for example lack of personal organization). The model presented shows as a result, the advantages that this balance can generate on SMEs. As the major goal is to achieve sustainability for both, employees and the firm itself, it is important to pay attention to those elements that contribute to creating such sustainability. For instance, there are two main areas, those related to intangible and tangible resources. Doing a good balance between the tangible-intangible resources mentioned before could have an important impact on the firm's outcomes in terms of turnover, absenteeism, employees' performance, commitment, and job satisfaction. It will facilitate that SMEs can be seen as competitive workplaces.

Figure 1.1. A conceptual model to assess the balance between profit and Work-Life-Balance in SMEs

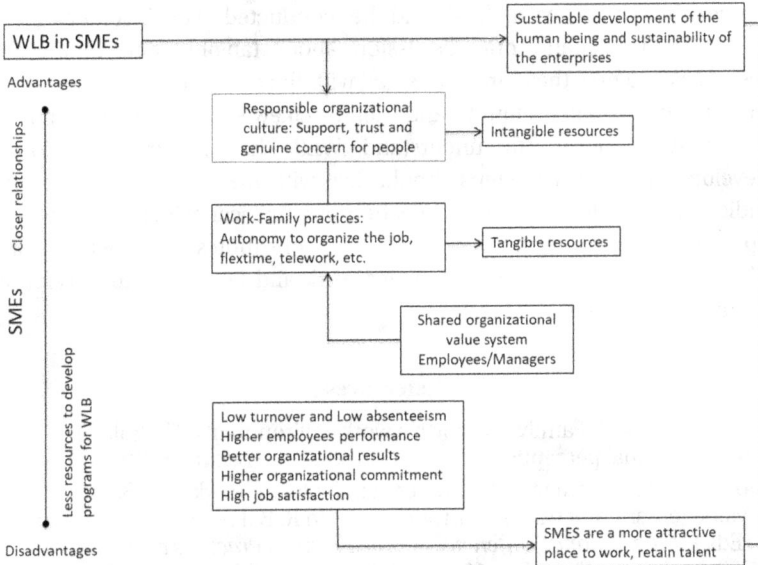

Conclusions

Overall, this paper brings the discussion about WLB and how this notion is in line with the profit-oriented of the firm. SMEs have the ability to easily connecting with the employees because of the size. This ability of the small business contributes to developing advantages that are going to influence the performance of the firm. In this regard, managers who can optimize this ability are going to create better organizational results that consolidate the sustainability of the firm. Although WLB requires investment from the companies size, the potentials benefiter in long-term is worthy enough to consider this practice. Employees with high perception and appreciation of the workplace are more willing to foster creativity and innovation within the firms' process.

Even though the performance benefits are highlighted in this paper, it is important to call the attention that better workplaces contribute to a better society. Thus, this chapter invites other scholars to contribute to this discussion within the business management schools. Educated entrepreneurs with a broader vision of the impact of the businesses in society with enhance a healthy and happy population. Of course, in this chapter, our efforts are limited to explain all the aspects of WLB and how to deal with personal life and profits within SMEs. For this reason, we would like to further this conceptual discussion by pointing out future venues in which research should be conducted. For instance, it is important to expand our discussion about tangible and intangible resources and how these are connected with the concept of gaps in health, personal development, family, and friends. Likewise, our proposed model is an initial effort to understand WLB that requires additional development. The next steps should deal with the operationalization of indicators as well as with the collection of empirical evidence about our approach. We hope that this chapter contributes to having more discussion about how people balance work and family life to develop a sustainable business.

References

Allen, T. D. (2001). Family-supportive work environments: The role of organizational perceptions. *Journal of Vocational Behavior, 58* (3), 414-435.

Bloom, N., Kretschmer, T., & Van Reenen, J. (2009). Work-Life-Balance, Management practices and productivity. In R. B. Freeman & K. L. Shaw (Eds.). *International Differences in the Business Practices and Productivity of Firms* (pp. 15-54). University of Chicago Press: National Bureau of Economic Research.

Cegarra-Leiva, D., Sánchez-Vidal, M. E., & Cegarra-Navarro, J. G. (2012). Understanding the link between work-life balance practices and organizational outcomes in SMEs. *Personnel Review, April*, 1-39. DOI: 10.1108/00483481211212986

Dacin, M., Dacin, P., & Tracey, P.(2011). Social entrepreneurship: a critique and future directions. *Organization Science, 22*, 1203–1213. http://dx.doi.org/10.1287/orsc.1100.0620

De Sivatte, I., Gordon, J., Rojo, P., & Olmos, R. (2015). The impact of work-life culture on organizational productivity. *Personnel Review, 44* (6), 883-905.

Delecta, P. (2011). Review article: Work Life Balance. *International Journal of current research, 3* (4), 186-189.

Dunay, A., Swadzba, U., Vinogradov, S., & Illés, B. C. (2015). Economic awareness and entrepreneurial attitudes of Hungarian university students. In V. Somosi & M., Lipták (Eds), *Proceedings of the „Balance and Challenges." IX. International Scientific Conference* (pp. 516-528), Miskolc: University of Miskolc.

Fan, P. (2018). Person-organization fit, work-family balance, and work attitude: The moderated mediating effect of supervisor support. *Social Behavior and Personality, 46*(6), 995-1010.

Frone, M., Russel, M., & Cooper, M. (1992). Antecedents and outcomes of work-family conflict: testing a model of the work-family interface. *Journal of Applied Psychology, 77*(1), 65-78.

Global Entrepreneurship Monitor (2017/2018). GEM 2017/2018 Global Report. Retrieved from https://www.gemconsortium.org/report/50012

Grzywacz, J., & Carlson, D. (2007). Conceptualizing Work-Family Balance: Implications for practice and research. *Advances in Developing Human Resources, 9*(4), 455-471. DOI: 10.1177/1523422307305487.

Hall, J., Daneke, G., & Lenox, M. (2010). Sustainable development and entrepreneurship: past contributions and future directions. *Journal of Business Venturing, 25*, 439–448. DOI: 10.1016/j.jbusvent.2010.01.002.

Harrington, B., & Ladge, J. J. (2009). Work-Life Integration: Present Dynamics and Future Directions for Organizations, *Organizational Dynamics, 38*(2), 148-157. DOI:10.1016/j.orgdyn.2009.02.003.

Jensen, M. (1993). The modern industrial revolution, exit and the failure of internal control systems. *The Journal of Finance, XLVIII* (3), 831-880.

Khallash, S., & Kruse, M. (2012). The future of work and work-life balance 2025. *Futures, 44*, 678-686. https://doi.org/10.1016/j.futures.2012.04.007

Kirchmeyer, C. (2000). Work-life initiatives: Greed or benevolence regarding workers' time. In C. Cooper, L. Rousseau & D.M. Chichester (Eds.). *Trends in organizational behavior* (pp. 79-93). Chichester: Wiley.

Laurijssen, I., & Glorieux, I. (2013). Balancing work and family: a panel analysis of the impact of part-time work on the experience of time pressure. *Social Indicators Research, 112*(1), 1-17.

Mair, J., & Marti, I. (2006). Social entrepreneurship research: a source of explanation, prediction, and delight. *Journal of World Business, 41*, 36–44. DOI:10.1016/j.jwb.2005.09.002.

McMullen, J. (2011). Delineating the domain of development entrepreneurship: a market-based approach to facilitating inclusive economic growth. *Entrepreneurship Theory & Practice, 35*, 185–193. DOI: 10.1111/j.1540-6520.2010.00428.x.

Meek, W., Pacheco, D., & York, J. (2010). The impact of social norms on the entrepreneurial action: evidence from the environmental entrepreneurship context. *Journal of Business Venturing, 25*, 493–509. DOI:10.1016/j.jbusvent.2009.09.007

Ostroff, C., Shin, Y., & Kinicki, A. J. (2005). Multiple perspectives of congruence: Relationships between value congruence and employee attitudes. *Journal of Organizational Behavior, 26*, 591–623. https://doi.org/d4p3fd

Peredo, A., & Chrisman, J. (2006). Toward a theory of community-based enterprise. *Academy of Management Review, 31*, 309–328.

Pérez, M., Vela, M. J., Abella, S., & Martínez, A. (2017). Work-family practices and organizational commitment: the mediator effect of job satisfaction 1. *Universia Business Review, (56)*, 52-83.

PricewaterhouseCoopers (2018). The workforce of the future: The competing forces shaping 2030. Retrieved from https://www.pwc.com/gx/en/services/people-organisation/publications/workforce-of-the-future.html Robak, E. & Słocińska, A., & Depta, A. (2016). Work-Life Balance Factors in the Small and Medium-sized Enterprises. *Periodica Polytechnica Social and Management Sciences, 24*(2), 88-95. DOI: 10.3311/PPso.8871.

Robak, E., & Słocińska, A. (2015). Work-Life Balance and the Management of the social work environment. *Polish Journal of Management Studies, 11*(2), 138-148.

Seong, J. Y. (2016). Person-organization fit, family-supportive organization perceptions, and self-efficacy affect work-life balance. *Social Behavior and Personality: An International Journal, 44,* 911–921. https://doi.org/ccfj

Shepherd, D. (2015). Party On! A call for entrepreneurship research that is more interactive, activity based, cognitively hot, compassionate, and prosocial. *Journal of Business Venturing, 30*(4), 489–507. DOI: 10.1016/j.jbusvent.2015.02.001

Shepherd, D., Patzelt, H., Williams, T., & Warnecke, D. (2014). How does project termination impact project team members? Rapid termination, Creeping Death, and learning from failure. *Journal of Management Studies, 51,* 513–546, https://doi.org/10.1111/joms.12068.

Thompson, C. A., Beauvais, L. L., & Lyness, K. S. (1999). When work-family benefits are not enough: the influence of work-family culture on benefit utilization, organizational attachment and work-family conflict. *Journal of Vocational Behavior, 54,* 391-415

World Health Organization (n.d.). Constitution of WHO: principles. Retrieved from https://www.who.int/about/mission/en/

York, J., & Venkataraman, S. (2010). The entrepreneur–environment nexus: uncertainty, innovation, and allocation. *Journal of Business Venturing, 25,* 449–463. DOI:10.1016/j.jbusvent.2009.07.007.

Chapter 2

Social Entrepreneurship: Blending prosocial Motivation and Self-interests in Business

Andreana Drencheva,
University of Sheffield Management School, UK

Introduction

In a world of grand societal challenges (George, Howard-Grenville, Joshi, & Tihanyi, 2016), the media, policymakers, practitioners, and researchers are increasingly turning to social ventures as catalysts for social change. Social ventures are organizations that use market-based activities to pursue a social objective regardless of their legal form (Mair, Battilana, & Cardenas, 2012). This means that social ventures can be legally registered as charities, limited liability companies, or any social enterprise specific form, yet at their core is improving the physical, psychological, social, and financial wellbeing of diverse individuals, communities, and environments. Commercial entrepreneurship contributes to social objectives, such as job creation and productivity growth (Van Praag & Versloot, 2007), as a byproduct (Venkataraman, 1997). However, such social objectives are a primary or equally important goal as commercial goals in social entrepreneurship, instead of a byproduct (Mair & Martí, 2006). Economic, civic engagement, law and rights, environmental, education, health, food, housing, technology, culture, and family issues are common social issues that social ventures aim to address (Mair et al., 2012).

Social entrepreneurship activities vary in scale and scope as they can address specific local community issues, build and institutionalize alternative national structures to address social issues, and build lasting structures to challenge the status quo globally (Zahra, Gedajlovic, Neubaum, & Shulman, 2009). For example, social ventures have addressed social issues, such as drug addiction recovery (Perrini, Vurro, & Costanzo, 2010), homelessness (Tracey & Jarvis, 2007), poverty (Mair & Schoen,

2007), and high barriers to labor markets (Hockerts, 2015) in different institutional settings. Common beneficiaries of the work of social ventures are civic engagement organizations, the public, children, farmers, women, youth, families, teachers, disabled individuals, people living in poverty or who are homeless, students, governments, and businesses (Mair et al., 2012).

Grameen Bank is an established and prominent example of social entrepreneurship that demonstrates the phenomenon. It was founded in Bangladesh to provide microcredits, which are small, unsecured loans for starting or expanding a business, to the poorest rural individuals, predominantly women, who did not qualify for loans from traditional banks due to lack of collateral. The underpinning logic of Grameen Bank was that affordable loans could reduce extreme poverty while also improving health and education attainment levels. A recent meta-analysis provides strong evidence that microcredits reduce poverty and increase nutrition, education, and female empowerment (Chliova, Brinckmann, & Rosenbusch, 2015), while Grameen Bank ensured its financial sustainability by developing a system to support borrowers in repaying loans (Yunus, 1998). Financially sustainable from the early stages, as of 2006, Grameen Bank had supported 6.6 million borrowers with an unprecedented repayment rate above 95% (Giridharadas & Bradsher, 2006).

Social ventures emerge from the work of social entrepreneurs – the individuals who intend to, start, lead, and manage organizations that pursue a social objective through market mechanisms and do so on their own account and risk (Stephan & Drencheva, 2017). Individuals are driven to engage in such actions to express their motivations – the broad and specific values, motives, and interests that express what individuals find important and thus energizing their behavior. While it is often assumed that social entrepreneurs are driven by prosocial motivations, that is desire to benefit others and expand effort out of concern for others (Grant, 2008), in this chapter I argue for a more nuanced understanding of their motivations and the consequences of these motivations. Indeed, the evidence challenges the taken-for-granted assumption that social entrepreneurs are energized only by prosocial motivations. Social entrepreneurs are also motivated by self-interest as desire to benefit and protect oneself and expanding efforts to do so, as I explain and demonstrate in the rest of the chapter. Thus, in this chapter, I present a nuanced perspective on the prosocial motivations and self-interests that energize social entrepreneurs during their entrepreneurship journeys and how these motivations interact in conflicting or synergetic ways to influence the wellbeing of social entrepreneurs and social ventures. Indeed, social entrepreneurs' wellbeing is an important factor to consider in relation to the impact, effectiveness, and sustainability of social ventures, yet the autobiographies of celebrated social entrepreneurs present multiple issues related to personal health and burnout (Dempsey & Sanders, 2010).

Social Entrepreneurs' Motivations

Social entrepreneurs are driven to start, lead, and manage social ventures by diverse prosocial motivations and self-interests.

Social Entrepreneurs' prosocial Motivations

Theoretical and empirical research supports the intuitive assumption that social entrepreneurs are driven by prosocial motivations in relation to their values, motives, interests, and emotions. Indeed, motivations broadly related to helping others are vividly described with qualitative accounts of the experiences of social entrepreneurs and tested with quantitative methodologies. I summarize the evidence on social entrepreneurs' prosocial motivations in this section.

Social entrepreneurs are characterized by prosocial values as abstract and enduring life goals. Social entrepreneurs express high self-transcendence values, this is universalism and benevolence. They also attribute less importance to self-enhancement values, this is achievement and power (Bargsted, Picon, Salazar, & Rojas, 2013; Diaz & Rodriguez, 2003; Egri & Herman, 2000; Sastre-Castillo, Peris-Ortiz, & Danvila-Del Valle, 2015).

Social entrepreneurs are characterized by specific prosocial motivations and interests. Their motivations are based on altruism as a broad prosocial motivation and vocational interests in service, helping and nurturing others, and providing care (Almeida, Ahmetoglu, & Chamorro-Premuzic, 2014; Bargsted et al., 2013; Braga, Proença, & Ferreira, 2014; Chen, 2014). However, social entrepreneurs also express specific prosocial motivations relevant to their communities and are motivated by addressing unmet community needs (Ross, Mitchell, & May, 2012; Yitshaki & Kropp, 2016). For example, they are motivated by preserving the heritage of their communities, community improvement, national development, promoting sustainable lifestyles, and protecting nature (Allen & Malin, 2008; Bargsted et al., 2013; Koe, Omar, & Majid, 2014; Yitshaki & Kropp, 2016). Social entrepreneurs are also characterized by a sense of responsibility (De Hoogh et al., 2005), moral obligation to support marginalized groups (Hockerts, 2017), and anticipation of the effects of one's actions on future generations (Allen & Malin, 2008).

Social entrepreneurs are characterized by relational prosocial motivations. They express affiliation motives as the need to relate to others in positive ways (De Hoogh et al., 2005) and start social ventures to strengthen local ties with the community (Allen & Malin, 2008). This affiliation motive can be expressed in relation to different communities based on the identities of social entrepreneurs. For example, social entrepreneurs with a communitarian social identity aim to support their local community and belong to this community, while social entrepreneurs with a missionary social identity view society at large as their reference group (Fauchart & Gruber, 2011). Social entrepreneurs are also theorized to have a salient role and personal identities associated with social welfare and belonging to communities that value social justice, equality, and care for the environment (Wry & York, 2015).

Finally, social entrepreneurs are motivated by prosocial emotions as short-lived, intense affective experiences. Prosocial emotions include compassion, empathy, and sympathy as other-oriented emotions that link an individual with a suffering individual or community. First, social entrepreneurs' prosocial emotions, such as empathy and sympathy, are related to prosocial motivations, such as altruism, obligation, and social justice (Ruskin, Seymour, & Webster, 2016). Second, prosocial motivations can direct individuals' attention toward concern for others and their suffering, thus increasing the desirability of and commitment to engaging in social entrepreneurship (Hockerts, 2017; Miller, Grimes, McMullen, & Vogus, 2012). Prosocial emotions are also theorized to enhance the cognitive processes that enable social entrepreneurs to engage in the complex and challenging tasks associated with social entrepreneurship (Miller et al., 2012).

Thus, social entrepreneurs are driven by long- and short-term prosocial motivations, such as prosocial values, motives, interests, and emotions. These prosocial motivations are drivers for social entrepreneurs not only to start the social entrepreneurship journey, but also to continue what is a very challenging process characterized by multiple challenges related to operational status, legitimacy, and internal tensions (Battilana & Dorado, 2010; Pache & Santos, 2013; Renko, 2013). However, prosocial motivations are not the only driver for social entrepreneurs. Indeed, social entrepreneurs are also motivated by multiple self-interests in their social entrepreneurship journeys. I turn to these self-interests next.

Social Entrepreneurs' Self-interests

While prosocial motivations are prominent in driving social entrepreneurs, individuals intend to, start, lead, and manage social ventures to benefit and protect themselves as well. Indeed, prosocial motivations are combined with diverse self-interests that play a significant role in individuals' decisions to start, lead, and manage social ventures. These self-interests present a continuum from addressing social issues that affect the individual as a member of a community to an active pursuit of primarily financial gain. I summarize the evidence on social entrepreneurs' self-interests in this section.

Social entrepreneurs are motivated by personal experiences of pain and trauma. Social entrepreneurs can develop offerings that address significant social issues in institutional voids and deprived areas not only to benefit others, but also to benefit themselves as members of such communities. For example, in the United Kingdom, social ventures are more likely to be located in the most deprived areas of the country compared to commercial SMEs (Department for Digital, Culture, Media & Sport & Department for Business, Energy, Industrial Strategy, 2017; Social Enterprise UK, 2017). However, social entrepreneurs may also recognize social issues and develop new offerings because of their personal experiences of pain and trauma as service users or relatives of service users. For example, they might experience traumatic events, face specific medical challenges, or have no access to professional care for their own elderly parents (Wong & Tang, 2006; Yitshaki & Kropp, 2016). Such experiences of personal need help individuals to recognize social issues and understand what effective solutions are, while also pushing individuals to pursue social entrepreneurship to support themselves and their wellbeing.

Social entrepreneurs are motivated by authenticity. Social entrepreneurship is a pathway for individuals to express their values and identities related to social justice, equality, environmentalism, or their professions in authentic ways. Social entrepreneurs engage in social entrepreneurship to pursue personal passion (Braga et al., 2014; Tigu, Iorgulescu, Ravar, & Lile, 2015). This can include passion for the social issue, such as protecting the environment (Allen & Malin, 2008), as well as passion for the profession (Campin, Barraket, & Luke, 2013) or for their craft (Allen & Malin, 2008). Given social entrepreneurs' passion for their professions and craft, it is not a surprise that they are also motivated to engage in social entrepreneurship by the opportunity to enhance the quality of services and offerings (Chen, 2014). However, authenticity also includes expression of other values and motivations beyond passion. For example, social entrepreneurs are characterized by stimulation and self-direction values and need for achievement, power, autonomy, drive and determination motivations (Bargsted et al., 2013; Campin et al., 2013; De Hoogh et al., 2005; Egri & Herman, 2000; Seiz & Schwab, 1992; Smith, Bell, & Watts, 2014). They also exhibit high levels of creativity and risk-taking (Smith et al., 2014) and report that enjoyment is an important motivating factor (Ross et al., 2012). This is particularly relevant given their desire for less bureaucratic red tape compared to working in public services (Chen, 2014). Thus, social entrepreneurship presents a good fit for individuals to express their values, motivations, and identities with its focus on social goals, the opportunity to set personal goals and be accountable to oneself as an entrepreneur, and the multiple challenges that social ventures face that call for creativity, risk-taking, and drive. As individuals create organizations that are authentic expressions of their values and identities (Fauchart & Gruber, 2011), social entrepreneurship enables individuals to be authentic and remain true to oneself. While authenticity is beneficial for individuals in itself, it is also related to individuals' wellbeing (Goldman & Kernis, 2002).

Social entrepreneurs are motivated by professional development and dissatisfaction with prior work. Individuals engaged in social entrepreneurship activities report that they are motivated by the opportunities to learn (Ross et al., 2012) as well as increased responsibility and reputation (Chen, 2012, 2014; Greco et al., 2014). For many individuals, social entrepreneurship presents an opportunity for both professional and career development (Chen, 2014; Tigu et al., 2015). However, experiences with prior work may also motivate individuals to engage in social entrepreneurship. For example, individuals' job dissatisfaction and lack of meaning in previous jobs are important motivating factors for engaging in social entrepreneurship (Yitshaki & Kropp, 2016). Thus, social entrepreneurship benefits individual social entrepreneurs by providing them with an opportunity to learn and develop their careers. These career self-interests are also connected to the financial self-interests discussed next.

Social entrepreneurs are motivated by financial self-interests. While the financial self-interests of social entrepreneurs are often overlooked in social entrepreneurship research, they are an important motivating factor for individuals to start, lead, and manage social ventures. Financial self-interests are important for both organizational and individual reasons. Social ventures need to be financially sustainable to pursue their social objectives (Wilson & Post, 2013), while social entrepreneurs have family and personal responsibilities that require personal income. This is particularly relevant from a social inclusion perspective whereby social entrepreneurs from the most deprived communities start new organizations to support themselves and their communities. Indeed, the financial self-interests of social entrepreneurs range from meeting basic financial needs to significant financial gain. For example, some individuals are motivated to start social ventures because of layoffs or limited opportunities for employment, including due to discrimination in the labor market (Chen, 2014; Wong & Tang, 2006). Other individuals engage in social entrepreneurship due to an approach financial motivation hoping for financial independence, a better salary than in the public sector, and financial gain more generally (Chen, 2014; Ross et al., 2012; Seiz & Schwab, 1992; Tigu et al., 2015). Some individuals have enlightened social interests which allow them to pursue their self-interests through social entrepreneurship. They recognize that there are financial benefits from social entrepreneurship, such as maintaining good relationships with the community (Campin et al., 2013), fiscal advantages, and access to subsidies and donations (Greco et al., 2014). Thus, individuals may recognize and pursue social entrepreneurship opportunities (Braga et al., 2014) that allow them to obtain high income (Koe et al., 2014) due to growth potential in the market (Wong & Tang, 2006). While prosocial motivations and financial self-interests are intertwined for many social entrepreneurs, several in-depth qualitative studies demonstrate that for some social entrepreneurs financial gain is the primary motivation for their activities (Ross et al., 2012; Tigu et al., 2015; Wong & Tang, 2006).

In summary, social entrepreneurs are motivated by multiple self-interests, including addressing social issues that affect their individual wellbeing, authenticity, professional development and dissatisfaction with prior work, and financial factors.

Interactions Between Prosocial Motivations and Self-interests: Implications for Social Entrepreneurs' and Social Ventures' Wellbeing

Social entrepreneurs are motivated not only by helping others but also by helping oneself. They are neither selfless nor selfish because their prosocial motivations and self-interests are not always mutually exclusive. Indeed, social entrepreneurs demonstrate that prosocial motivations and self-interests can be blended in business because they can pursue both.

Social entrepreneurs' prosocial motivations and self-interests are not stable. Both prosocial motivations and self-interests can change over time and become more or less prominent as the needs of the social venture and of the social entrepreneur change. For example, as the number of employees and services users grows, thus making the social issue more salient for the social entrepreneur, the social entrepreneur's prosocial motivation may also become more salient. However, social entrepreneurs' personal lives also change which may enhance their self-interests. For example, when social entrepreneurs start working on the social venture full time or their family responsibilities grow (e.g., having children or elderly parents who require care), their financial self-interests may become more prominent.

Social entrepreneurs' prosocial motivations and self-interests coexist and interact to influence social entrepreneurs' and social ventures' wellbeing. While in some cases only prosocial motivations or self-interests might be salient, in the cases when both prosocial motivations and self-interests are salient, they can interact in two main ways: conflict and synergy. The ways prosocial motivations and self-interests interact can influence social entrepreneurs' and social ventures' wellbeing. At the individual level, wellbeing refers to a state "in which every individual realizes his or her own potential, can cope with the normal stresses of life, can work productively and fruitfully, and is able to make a contribution to her or his community" (WHO, 2014). At the organizational level, wellbeing refers to social ventures' optimal performance to achieve their social mission in financially and organizationally sustainable ways. As wellbeing at both the individual and organizational levels of analysis exists on a continuum, I argue that conflicting and synergetic interactions between social entrepreneurs' prosocial motivations and self-interests can enhance or hinder wellbeing across this continuum.

Conflicting Motivations and Wellbeing

Social entrepreneurs' prosocial motivations and self-interests can interact in conflicting ways. A conflict exists when the pursuit of salient prosocial motivations has a negative impact on the achievement of salient self-interests, or vice versa. For example, preserving the heritage of communities or protecting nature may be in conflict with professional and financial self-interests in the early stages of the venture development process when the social venture does not have a reputation or employees, does not offer formal learning opportunities, and is still identifying revenue streams. In such cases, the social entrepreneur is unlikely to consider their self-interests met even when their prosocial goals are achieved.

Conflicts between prosocial motivations and self-interests hinder social entrepreneurs' and social ventures' wellbeing. Conflicting prosocial motivations and self-interests create tensions, contradictions, uncertainty, and dissonance (Putnam, Fairhurst, & Banghart, 2016). Such experiences are not just unpleasant, but stressful and overwhelming (Lazarus & Folkman, 1984), thus negatively influencing the wellbeing of social entrepreneurs as individuals. Motivational conflicts deplete the attention and personal resources of social entrepreneurs (Baumeister & Vohs, 2007), thus damaging strategic decision making and negatively influencing the wellbeing of the social venture.

As such experiences are stressful, social entrepreneurs may attempt to resolve the conflict by considering prosocial motivations and self-interests as trade-offs and prioritize one over the other. However, such prioritization of prosocial motivations or self-interests can also have a negative influence on social entrepreneurs' wellbeing. When they prioritize their prosocial motivations, social entrepreneurs may face personal financial challenges and interpersonal conflict with family members, thus experiencing even more stressors hindering their individual wellbeing. When they prioritize self-interests, they may experience a lack of authenticity, again hindering their wellbeing (Goldman & Kernis, 2002). Prioritization of prosocial motivations or self-interests can also have a negative influence on the social venture's wellbeing. When prosocial motivations are prioritized, the focus on financial sustainability might be deprioritized, thus putting the venture's survival in jeopardy (Renko, 2013). When social entrepreneurs' self-interests are prioritized, the operations of their social ventures may be characterized by conflict with co-founders, employees, and volunteers, potential mission drift, and lack of legitimacy (Battilana & Dorado, 2010; Battilana & Lee, 2014; Ometto, Gegenhuber, Winter, & Greenwood, 2018).

While conflicts between social entrepreneurs' prosocial motivations and self-interests can hinder their own wellbeing and the wellbeing of their social venture, prosocial motivations and self-interests can also interact in synergetic ways.

Synergetic Motivations and Wellbeing

Social entrepreneurs' prosocial motivations and self-interests can interact in synergetic ways. A synergy exists when salient prosocial motivations can be pursued alongside self-interests with the same activities, thus prosocial motivations and self-interests can be achieved simultaneously. For example, developing innovative solutions to preserve the heritage of a community or to protect nature can also lead to developing the reputation of the social venture and providing learning opportunities and financial gains for the social entrepreneur. In such cases, the social entrepreneur can pursue both their prosocial motivations and self-interests.

Synergies between prosocial motivations and self-interests can enhance social entrepreneurs' wellbeing. Instead of considering prosocial motivations and self-interests as trade-offs, social entrepreneurs can develop synergies between them through creative integration that makes the conflict between motivations productive. Developing synergies between conflicting motivations requires cognitive and behavioral complexity (Denison, Hooijberg, & Quinn, 1995; Miron-Spektor, Gino, & Argote, 2011) and can lead to novel and creative solutions. Such synergies allow social entrepreneurs to remain authentic in pursuing their prosocial motivations while increasing the likelihood of financial security. Novel and creative solutions also create opportunities for learning due to their novelty and complexity and can establish a reputation for the venture as innovative and cutting-edge in its approaches. Thus, synergies between prosocial motivations and self-interests enhance the wellbeing of social entrepreneurs by enabling them to pursue multiple salient prosocial and self-interest motivations.

Synergies between social entrepreneurs' prosocial motivations and self-interests can also enhance the wellbeing of the social venture by enabling long-term organizational sustainability (Smith, Lewis, & Tushman, 2012) across their social and financial objectives. By pursuing their prosocial motivations, social entrepreneurs can enhance the social outcomes their ventures catalyze to benefit others. By pursuing their self-interests, they promote efficiency, innovation, growth, and reputation building. Thus, synergies allow social ventures to remain both socially focused and operational instead of facing mission drift, internal conflicts, and closure. Social entrepreneurship empirical and theoretical research supports this argument. Social entrepreneurs with innovative or successful social ventures combine identities, values, and behaviors common for not-for-profit and commercial leaders, thus representing both prosocial motivations and self-interests (Katre & Salipante, 2012; Wry & York, 2015). Sustainable social ventures also place equal importance to social and financial goals and pursue both with diverse actions that create synergies (Battilana & Dorado, 2010; Battilana, Sengul, Pache, & Model, 2015).

Thus, synergies between social entrepreneurs' prosocial motivations and self-interests can enhance their own wellbeing as individuals as well as the wellbeing of their ventures.

Discussion

This chapter offers a nuanced overview of the prosocial motivations and self-interests that social entrepreneurs pursue when starting, leading, and managing social ventures. It challenges the taken-for-granted assumption that social entrepreneurs are fueled only by prosocial motivations. Building on this nuanced view of social entrepreneurs' diverse motivation, the chapter examines how prosocial motivations and self-interests interact in conflicting and synergetic ways to influence the wellbeing of social entrepreneurs and of their ventures. This chapter has two main implications for social entrepreneurship research and offers suggestions for future research.

Implications

First, this chapter highlights the overlooked self-interests of social entrepreneurs in starting, leading, and managing social ventures, thus portraying them as multidimensional human beings. Dominant portrayals of social entrepreneurs (e.g., Bornstein, 2004) depict them as moral and heroic figures who accomplish the impossible in pursuit of their prosocial motivations. However, social entrepreneurs are multidimensional human beings with lives and responsibilities outside of their ventures and as such they have multiple self-interests. Their self-interests include not only diverse financial self-interests, but also professional development, dissatisfaction with prior work, authenticity, and addressing social issues that directly affect them and their loved ones. Indeed, by overlooking these self-interests, research overlooks a key antecedent of social entrepreneurship activity that can explain why individuals start and persist in an activity that is challenging and complex with high personal risks (Battilana & Lee, 2014; Renko, 2013). Focusing only on the prosocial motivations of social entrepreneurs not only overlooks key motivational factors, but it also contributes to a discourse that individuals can struggle to live up to. At the same time, self-interests to start, lead, and manage a new social venture are not inherently wrong or harmful. Social entrepreneurs demonstrate that benefitting oneself can take various forms (e.g., authenticity, financial gain, learning and professional development) and does not need to occur at the cost of hurting others.

Second, this chapter explores the wellbeing of social entrepreneurs, another area overlooked in social entrepreneurship research. While research examines how social entrepreneurship contributes to the wellbeing of individuals, communities, and environments and the challenges social ventures face in this process, the wellbeing of social entrepreneurs as the individuals engaged in this complex, uncertain, and demanding process is missing from current research. This omission of the wellbeing of social entrepreneurs suggests that either their wellbeing is taken for granted or alternatively considered inconsequential for social entrepreneurship. However, both of these assumptions are simplistic. The autobiographies of celebrated social entrepreneurs present multiple issues related to work-life imbalance, self-sacrifice, and prioritizing the social venture at the expense of personal health and burnout (Dempsey &

Sanders, 2010). At the same time, entrepreneurs' wellbeing is important for the entrepreneurship process, contributing to diverse organizational outcomes (Stephan, 2018). Thus, understanding what contributes to and hinders social entrepreneurs' wellbeing is an important task that can contribute to the performance of social ventures in achieving their social objectives and addressing grand societal challenges (George et al., 2016) with different scope and scale.

Directions for Future Research

The conceptual arguments presented in this chapter offer at least two main avenues for future research. First, future research can explore the outcomes of the interactions between social entrepreneurs' prosocial motivations and self-interests across levels of analysis. As an initial step, future empirical research can test the proposed relationships between the synergies and conflicts between social entrepreneurs' prosocial motivations and self-interests and individual and organizational wellbeing. This stream of research can be extended to examine how synergies and conflicts between social entrepreneurs' diverse motivations can influence other individual, team, and organizational outcomes. For example, such outcomes can include entrepreneurial performance and learning at the individual level; trust and performance at the team level, and innovation and collaboration at the organizational level. Recognizing that social ventures include not only social entrepreneurs, but also employees and volunteers, also calls for attention on: 1) how social entrepreneurs' conflicting and synergetic motivations influence the wellbeing of employees and volunteers; and 2) the effects of employees' and volunteers' conflicting and synergetic motivations for their own wellbeing and performance.

Second, future research can expand our understanding of social entrepreneurs' wellbeing. Given the limited attention so far on social entrepreneurs' wellbeing, yet its importance for social ventures (Stephan, 2018), it is essential to develop a nuanced understanding of what contributes to or hinders social entrepreneurs' wellbeing. Considering that social entrepreneurs are multidimensional human beings, future research can examine both work-specific (e.g., job satisfaction) and general wellbeing (e.g., life satisfaction) and how personal and work characteristics are associated with both across domains. Longitudinal studies are particularly pertinent to capture how the changing personal lives of social entrepreneurs influence their work-related wellbeing by creating new work-related stressors (e.g., financial pressures) as well as how social entrepreneurs' wellbeing varies across the different lifecycle stages of their ventures (e.g., from new to established organizations).

Conclusions

This chapter offers a nuanced overview of social entrepreneurs' diverse prosocial motivations and self-interests. It proposes that prosocial motivations and self-interests interact in conflicting and synergetic ways that hinder or enhance the wellbeing of social entrepreneurs and of their social ventures. In doing so, this chapter calls for more attention on social entrepreneurs as multidimensional human beings instead of heroic figures.

References

Allen, J. C., & Malin, S. (2008). Green entrepreneurship: A method for managing natural resources? *Society & Natural Resources, 21*(9), 828–844.

Almeida, P.I. L., Ahmetoglu, G., & Chamorro-Premuzic, T. (2014). Who wants to be an entrepreneur? The relationship between vocational interests and individual differences in entrepreneurship. *Journal of Career Assessment, 22*(1), 102–112.

Bargsted, M., Picon, M., Salazar, A., & Rojas, Y. (2013). Psychosocial characterization of social entrepreneurs: A comparative study. *Journal of Social Entrepreneurship, 4*(3), 331–346.

Battilana, J., & Dorado, S. (2010). Building sustainable hybrid organizations: The case of commercial microfinance organizations. *Academy of Management Journal, 53*(6), 1419–1440.

Battilana, J., & Lee, M. (2014). Advancing research on hybrid organizing – Insights from the study of social enterprises. *Academy of Management Annals, 8*(1), 397–441.

Battilana, J., Sengul, M., Pache, A. C., & Model, J. (2015). Harnessing productive tensions in hybrid organizations: The case of work integration social enterprises. *Academy of Management Journal, 58*(6), 1658–1685.

Baumeister, R. F., & Vohs, K. D. (2007). Self-regulation, ego depletion, and motivation. *Social and Personality Psychology Compass, 1*(1), 115–128.

Bornstein, D. (2004). *How to Change the World: Social Entrepreneurs and the Power of New Ideas*. New York, NY: Oxford University Press.

Braga, J. C., Proença, T., & Ferreira, M. R. (2014). Motivations for social entrepreneurship – Evidences from Portugal. *Tékhne, 12*(2014), 11–21.

Campin, S., Barraket, J., & Luke, B. (2013). micro-Business Community Responsibility in Australia: Approaches, Motivations and Barriers. *Journal of Business Ethics, 115*(3), 489–513.

Chen, C.-A. (2012). Explaining the difference of work attitudes between public and nonprofit managers: The views of rule constraints and motivation styles. *The American Review of Public Administration, 42*(4), 437–460.

Chen, C.-A. (2014). Nonprofit managers' motivational styles: A view beyond the intrinsic-extrinsic dichotomy. *Nonprofit and Voluntary Sector Quarterly, 43*(4), 737–758.

Chliova, M., Brinckmann, J., & Rosenbusch, N. (2015). Is microcredit a blessing for the poor? A meta-analysis examining development outcomes and contextual considerations. *Journal of Business Venturing, 30*(3), 467–487.

De Hoogh, A. H. B., Den Hartog, D. N., Koopman, P.L., Thierry, H., Van Den Berg, P.T., Van Der Weide, J. G., & Wilderom, C. P.M. (2005). Leader motives, charismatic leadership, and subordinates' work attitude in the profit and voluntary sector. *The Leadership Quarterly, 16*(1), 17–38.

Dempsey, S. E., & Sanders, M. L. (2010). Meaningful work? Nonprofit marketization and work/ life imbalance in popular autobiographies of social entrepreneurship.*Organization, 17*(4), 437–459.

Denison, D. R., Hooijberg, R., & Quinn, R. E. (1995). Paradox and performance: toward a theory of behavioral complexity in managerial leadership. *Organization Science, 6*(5), 524–540.

Department for Digital, Culture, Media & Sport & Department for Business, Energy, Industrial Strategy. (2017). Social Enterprise: Market Trends 2017. Retrieved from https://www.gov.uk/government/publications/social-enterprise-market-trends-2017.

Diaz, F., & Rodriguez, A. (2003). Locus of control, nAch and values of community entrepreneurs. *Social Behavior and Personality: An International Journal, 31*(8), 739–747.

Egri, C. P., & Herman, S. (2000). Leadership in the North American environmental sector: Values, leadership styles, and contexts of environmental leaders and their organizations. *Academy of Management Journal, 43*(4), 571–604.

Fauchart, E., & Gruber, M. (2011). Darwinians, communitarians, and missionaries: The role of founder identity in entrepreneurship.*Academy of Management Journal, 54*(5), 935–957.

George, G., Howard-Grenville, J., Joshi, A., & Tihanyi, L. (2016). Understanding and tackling societal grand challenges through management research. *Academy of Management Journal, 59*(6), 1880–1895.

Giridharadas, A., & Bradsher, K. (2006). Microloan pioneer and his bank win Nobel Peace Prize. *New York Times,* October, 13.

Goldman, B. M., & Kernis, M. H. (2002). The role of authenticity in healthy psychological functioning and subjective well-being. *Annals of the American Psychotherapy Association,* 5(6), 18–20.

Grant, A. M. (2008). Does intrinsic motivation fuel the prosocial fire? Motivational synergy in predicting persistence, performance, and productivity. *Journal of Applied Psychology, 93*(1), 48–58.

Greco, A., Morales Alonso, G., Vargas Perez, A. M., Pablo Lerchundi, I., & Petruzzelli, A. M. (2014). Social companies as an innovative and sustainable way of solving social problems. A case study from Spain. In G. Carlucci, D, & Spender, JC and Schiuma (Ed.). *IFKAD 2014: 9TH*

International forum on knowledge asset dynamics: knowledge and management models for sustainable growth (pp. 2516–2539). Matera, Italy: IKAM-INST KNOWLEDGE ASSET MANAGEMENT.

Hockerts, K. (2015). How hybrid organizations turn antagonistic assets into complementarities. *California Management Review, 57*(3), 83–106.

Hockerts, K. (2017). Determinants of social entrepreneurial intentions. *Entrepreneurship: Theory and Practice, 41*(1), 105–130.

Katre, A., & Salipante, P. (2012). Start-up social ventures: Blending fine-grained behaviors from two institutions for entrepreneurial success. *Entrepreneurship: Theory and Practice, 36*(5), 967–994.

Koe, W.-L., Omar, R., & Majid, I. A. (2014). Factors Associated with Propensity for Sustainable Entrepreneurship.In W. Chui, CTB, & Rashid (Ed.). *4th International Conference on Marketing and Retailing (INCOMAR 2013)* (Vol. 130, pp. 65–74). Amsterdam, NL: ELSEVIER SCIENCE BV.

Lazarus, R. S., & Folkman, S. (1984). *Stress, Appraisal and Coping.* New York, NY: Springer.

Mair, J., Battilana, J., & Cardenas, J. (2012). Organizing for society: A typology of social entrepreneuring models. *Journal of Business Ethics, 111*(3), 353–373.

Mair, J., & Martí, I. (2006). Social entrepreneurship research: A source of explanation, prediction, and delight. *Journal of World Business, 41*(1), 36–44.

Mair, J., & Schoen, O. (2007). Successful social entrepreneurial business models in the context of developing economies: An explorative study. *International Journal of Emerging Markets, 2*, 54–68.

Miller, T. L., Grimes, M. G., Mcmullen, J. S., & Vogus, T. J. (2012). Venturing for others with heart and head: How compassion encourages social entrepreneurship.*Academy of Management Review, 37*(4), 616–640.

Miron-Spektor, E., Gino, F., & Argote, L. (2011). Paradoxical frames and creative sparks: Enhancing individual creativity through conflict and integration. *Organizational Behavior and Human Decision Processes, 116*(2), 229–240.

Ometto, M. P., Gegenhuber, T., Winter, J., & Greenwood, R. (2018). From balancing missions to mission drift: The role of the institutional context, spaces, and compartmentalization in the scaling of social enterprises. *Business and Society*, Online First.

Pache, A.-C., & Santos, F. (2013). Inside the hybrid organzation: Selective coupling as a repsonse to competing institutional logics. *Academy of Management Journal, 56*(4), 972–1001.

Perrini, F., Vurro, C., & Costanzo, L. A. (2010). A process-based view of social entrepreneurship: From opportunity identification to scaling-up social change in the case of San Patrignano. *Entrepreneurship & Regional Development, 22*(6), 515–534.

Putnam, L. L., Fairhurst, G. T., & Banghart, S. (2016). Contradictions, dialectics, and paradoxes in organizations: A constitutive approach. *Academy of Management Annals, 10*(1), 65–171.

Renko, M. (2013). Early challenges of nascent social entrepreneurs. *Entrepreneurship: Theory and Practice, 37*(5), 1045–1069.

Ross, T., Mitchell, V. A., & May, A. J. (2012). Bottom-up grassroots innovation in transport: motivations, barriers and enablers. *Transportation Planning and Technology, 35*(4), 469–489.

Ruskin, J., Seymour, R. G., & Webster, C. M. (2016). Why create value for others? An exploration of social entrepreneurial motives. *Journal of Small Business Management, 54,* 1015-1037

Sastre-Castillo, M. A., Peris-Ortiz, M., & Danvila-Del Valle, I. (2015). What is different about the profile of the social entrepreneur? *Nonprofit Management and Leadership, 25*(4), 349–369.

Seiz, R. C., & Schwab, A. J. (1992). Value orientations of clinical social work practitioners. *Clinical Social Work Journal, 20*(3), 323–335.

Smith, R., Bell, R., & Watts, H. (2014). Personality trait differences between traditional and social entrepreneurs. *Social Enterprise Journal, 10*(3), 200–221.

Smith, W. K., Lewis, M. W., & Tushman, M. L. (2012). Organizational Sustainability: Organization Design and Senior Leadership to Enable Strategic Paradox. In K. Cameron, & G. Spreitzer (Eds.). *The Oxford Handbook of Positive Organizational Scholarship* (pp. 798-810). New York, NY: Oxford University Press.

Social Enterprise UK. (2017). *The Future of Business - State of Social Enterprise Survey 2017.* Retrieved from https://www.socialenterprise.org.uk/the-future-of-business-state-of-social-enterprise-survey-2017.

Stephan, U. (2018). Entrepreneurs' mental health and well-being: A review and research agenda. *Academy of Management Perspectives,* Online First.

Stephan, U., & Drencheva, A. (2017). The person in social entrepreneurship: A systematic review of research om the social entrepreneurial personality. In G.Ahmetoglu, T. Chamorro-Premuzic, B. Klinger, & T. Karcisky (Eds.). *The Wiley Handbook of Entrepreneurship* (pp. 205-229). Chichester: John Wiley.

Tigu, G., Iorgulescu, M.-C., Ravar, A. S., & Lile, R. (2015). A pilot profile of the social entrepreneur in the constantly changing Romanian economy. *Amfiteatru Economic, 17*(38), 25–43.

Tracey, P., & Jarvis, O. (2007). Toward a theory of social venture franchising. *Entrepreneurship: Theory and Practice, 31*(5), 667–685.

Van Praag, C. M., & Versloot, P.H. (2007). What is the value of entrepreneurship? A review of recent research. *Small Business Economics, 29*(4), 351–382.

Venkataraman, S. (1997). The distinctive domain of entrepreneurship research: An editor's perspective. In J. Katz & R. Brockhaus (Eds.). *Advances in Entrepreneurship, Firm Emergence, and Growth, Vol 3* (pp. 119–138).

Wilson, F., & Post, J. E. (2013). Business models for people, planet (& profits): Exploring the phenomena of social business, a market-based approach to social value creation. *Small Business Economics, 40*(3), 715–737.

Wong, L., & Tang, J. (2006). Dilemmas confronting social entrepreneurs: Care homes for elderly people in Chinese cities. *Pacific Affairs, 79*(4), 623-630.

World Health Organization. (2014). Mental health: A state of well-being. Retrieved from http://www.who.int/features/factfiles/mental_health/en/.

Wry, T., & York, J. (2017). An identity based approach to social enterprise. *Academy of Management Review, 42,* 437-460.

Yitshaki, R., & Kropp, F. (2016). Motivations and opportunity recognition of social entrepreneurs. *Journal of Small Business Management, 54*(2), 546–565.

Yunus, M. (1998). *Banker to the Poor: The Autobiography of Muhammad Yunus, Founder of the Grameen Bank.* London: Aurum.

Zahra, S. A., Gedajlovic, E., Neubaum, D. O., & Shulman, J. M. (2009). A typology of social entrepreneurs: Motives, search processes and ethical challenges. *Journal of Business Venturing, 24*(5), 519–532.

Chapter 3

Personalistic Economics: Caring, Justice, and Christian Charity

Edward J. O'Boyle,
Mayo Research Institute, USA

Introduction

Though different and distinct, the virtues of caring, justice, and Christian charity are alike in that all three do not fit within the conventional economics paradigm. Nevertheless, when acted upon each one contributes to the character of the person who engages in economic activity. When they are replaced by the vices of neglect, injustice, and hatred each one diminishes the character of the agent. Opportunity cost draws attention to the cost of what an economic agent cannot do or have when that person makes a decision. This cost applies even in those instances where the agent does not deliberately take it into account. Caring and charity are alike in the both require us to re-think opportunity cost. There is no opportunity cost associated with caring and charity because neither one involves agents transacting business in which *economic gain* for both parties is essential. Even when something material is involved, caring and charity are gifts in which nothing is foregone or expected by the caring or loving person. Caring and charity contribute to the character of the caring person and loving person through the concept we refer to as personalist capital which is one of the determinants of greater integral human development. Neglect and hatred diminish personalist capital, thereby exerting a negative impact on human development.

However, caring and charity are not identical in that caring is a *secular* virtue and charity, along with faith and hope, is a *theological* virtue. Taken by itself, justice is, "a very cold virtue," "the most terrible of the virtues." Strictly speaking, justice results in a condition wherein no one *owes* anything to anyone else. Schall describes this condition as an "isolated hell" (Schall, 2004, p.409, 412, 419). The remedy is found in the virtues of gratitude, benevolence, and charity.

> We get what is due —no more, no less. This indifference to the person to whom we are just or who is unjust to us is what I meant earlier in suggesting that gratitude, benevolence, and charity are needed in addition to justice. (Schall, 2004, p.419)

Heinrich Pesch (2002) insists that justice and love "belong together." Love is the "moral bond that holds society together" but presupposes the "observance of all of the obligations imposed by justice" (Pesch, 2002, p.36). Reflecting on Pesch's *Lehrbuch*, Mulcahy describes love and justice as the "twin bulwarks of human well-being." (Mulcahy, 1951, p.68). The virtue of forgiveness is another remedy for what is lacking in the virtue of justice. In economic affairs, forgiveness is the golden mean between, for instance, enabling irresponsible financial behavior and crushing the human spirit under an unbearable load of debt. Forgiveness must be given freely by the one who holds the debt claim. The physician who does not charge an impoverished patient for care that is rendered, and the landlord who allows a single mother who has lost her job and cannot pay the rent to remain in her apartment with her children, exemplify the true meaning of forgiveness. In every instance, forgiveness involves a need that otherwise would not be met.

Critics of conventional economics have been searching for ways to incorporate caring or generosity into their way of thinking about economic affairs. We argue herein that caring cannot be separated from justice or charity and that all three taken together require re-thinking economic agency and re-considering the philosophy of individualism upon which conventional economics is constructed. We begin with economic gain and then turn to justice because gain is linked to justice and justice without caring or Christian charity falls short of a fully functional economy.

An Introduction to Economic Gain

Before moving on to justice, it is instructive to address what happens in the exchange process. Every exchange involving economic agents who are well-informed and free to act entails a gain for the parties involved: what is gotten is more highly valued than what is given up. In this regard, it is essential to differentiate between exchange value and use value. Exchange value is what is given up for the good or service acquired through exchange. Use value is what is gotten, the usefulness of the good or service to the person who acquires it.

Under competitive market conditions, exchange value should not vary from one person to the next. The price paid for the same dog food in a supermarket is the same for everyone buying that brand of dog food. However, use value is not the same for everyone who buys that dog food because some persons are more deeply attached to their dogs and derive greater pleasure from feeding and caring for them than do others. While exchange value is determined by market conditions at the time and place of the exchange, use value is determined by the value systems of the uniquely different persons involved in the exchange. Exchange value is an objective piece of information. Use value, on the other hand, is a subjective human experience. For every one of the persons involved, use value (what is gotten) must be greater than exchange value (what is given up). Without that gain, the exchange cannot be carried out.

However, without a limit to the extent of that gain —in the form of profits, rent, and consumer surplus —and its origins, some persons in the exchange process are able to take more than their due while others are left with less. Some would take what rightfully belongs to others. Those gains clearly are ill-gotten. Conventional economics brushes aside the problem of exploitation and victimization with the invisible hand argument. Every economic agent in the pursuit of their self-interest serves the good of all through the invisible hand of the market. Introducing justice into economic affairs is unnecessary and threatens the value-free nature of conventional economic science. We reject the invisible hand on the grounds that its appeal to magic and rhetoric is no substitute for the call of justice to reason and substance, and accept value-laden economics as the price for aligning the study of economics more closely with economic reality.

Gain-seeking behavior is rooted in self-interest or self-love. Indeed self-love is both legitimate and necessary for conducting ordinary economic affairs. A problem arises from self-love in the service of evil ends and thus the need for a limit. Pesch explains that the limit originates in an awareness of and respect for the well-being of others and the personal virtue of moderation (Pesch, 2002).

John Paul II (1991) reinforces Pesch's argument about self-interest and emphasizes the importance of finding ways to reconcile self-interest and the interests of the state. Furthermore, the violent suppression of self-interest may lead to limitation of creativity and initiative (John Paul II, 1991). In what follows we will see more specifically that those limits are grounded in the duties that economic agents owe one another under commutative justice, distributive justice, and contributive justice.

Justice

Justice is "the perpetual and constant will to render to each one that which is his." (Dempsey, 1958, p.164, quoting Aristotle). In economic affairs, there are three principles of justice that apply: commutative, distributive, and contributive. There are three principles of justice because there are only three modes of human interaction in economic affairs: person to person, superior to subordinate, and member to group.

Commutative justice sets forth the duty of buyer and seller in the marketplace and worker and employer in the workplace. Both parties are to exchange things of equal value and impose equal burdens on one another. Distributive justice defines the duties of the superior to their subordinates whether that interaction takes place in the marketplace or the workplace. The superior is to share the benefits and burdens of the group in some equal fashion. Contributive justice sets down the duties of the member to the group in interactions occurring in the workplace or the marketplace. Insofar as a member benefits from membership in the group that person has a duty to support and maintain the group.

Social Justice

Social justice is not distinct and separate from commutative justice, distributive justice, or contributive justice. Rather, it embraces all three. In addressing social justice, we find the comments in Pius XI's 1937 encyclical *Divini Redemptoris* especially instructive.

Now it is of the very essence of social justice to demand from each individual all that is necessary for the common good.

John Paul II defines the common good as "the good of all and of each individual, because we are all really responsible for all" (John Paul II, 1987, § 38). At all times and in whatever community a person works or lives, what is required under social justice is all that is necessary for the common good. Dempsey, along with Pesch, asserts that social justice is grounded in contributive justice (Dempsey, 1958, p. 370, 372): anyone who benefits from being a member of a group has a duty to contribute to the common good. We agree with them, but more than contributive justice is necessary. Common needs are needs that are "common to *all* members of the community" (Dempsey, 1958, p.272-273; emphasis added). Accordingly, the common good involves provisioning those common needs. Thus, in addition to their duty to contribute all that is necessary for the common good human beings have a right to whatever goods are necessary to live in common.

In conformance with the principle of subsidiarity, the common good is served first by private goods and then by public goods as necessary. It is not served by the production of strictly personal goods, the goods that are specific to a given person.

Living in common means living in a network of intertwined communities including family, neighborhood, and church. Acknowledging that trust is one of the goods necessary to live in common, trust is maintained only through the faithful practice of commutative justice, distributive justice, and contributive justice taken together. Contributive justice alone will not do. Thus social justice requires the faithful practice of the three principles of economic justice because all three are based on different human social interactions: person to person, superior to subordinate, and member to group.

Limits on Gain-seeking Behavior

Limits on the amount of gain in the form of profits, consumer surplus, and economic rent are necessary to prevent one party from taking advantage of another and to assure that market exchange serves everyone fairly and effectively. Commutative justice limits ill-gotten or excessive gain because what is gotten and what is given up in the exchange are what has been freely and openly agreed to before the exchange takes place. For example, the ill-gotten gain for the employer who operates a sweatshop is the added profits from denying their workers what is due them. The ill-gotten gain for the employee who embezzles is money that rightfully belongs to the employer.

Distributive justice limits ill-gotten gain because the superior assures that what is gotten and what is given up are the same for everyone in the same or similar circumstances. To illustrate, the ill-gotten gain for the employer who pays some workers less than others for the same work is the added profits gotten through discrimination. The ill-gotten gain for the public official who has been bribed to award a contract for a substandard proposal is the money which that official has gotten dishonestly. Contributive justice limits excessive gain because each member gives up (contributes) what is necessary to maintain the group provided what is gotten by that member is the same or similar to what is gotten by the other members of the group. The ill-gotten gain for the inside trader comes at the expense of persons who sell shares that the inside trader knows are undervalued or buy shares that the insider knows are overvalued. The ill-gotten gain in industrial spying is the property that rightfully belongs to someone else. Justice alone, however, is insufficient to restore and maintain social order. We turn next to the virtue of caring.

Caring

Caring does not replace justice. Rather it rises above the demands of justice to render to another person that which is owed. The truly caring person is generous even to the extreme of not asking for or expecting anything in return. Even though there is an exchange between the caring person and the needy one, caring is not gain-seeking behavior. It is a gift rendered freely. It is, however, required of the caring professions as demonstrated in the swearing to the Hippocratic Oath upon graduation from medical school. Practitioners of the law who normally exhibit gain-seeking behavior at times express caring through their *pro bono* services.

Caring operates in product markets, resource markets, and financial markets *through* generous merchants and grateful customers, workers who are especially attentive to the quality of the tasks they are assigned, through resource holders for whom profitability and sustainability are everyday concerns, and through financial planners who live out their fiduciary obligation and investors who trust and are grateful to those planners for successfully managing their portfolios in financial markets too complex for the typical investor.

First responders often are called on to rescue persons trapped in a building on fire, are injured in a bomb explosion, or are victims of massive flooding. Professional first responders are paid for their services but in risking their own lives, they rise above the demands of justice. Other caring persons often respond as neighbors or private citizens, as in the 2017 flooding in Houston where rescue efforts were spearheaded by private owners of fishing and leisure boats from neighboring Louisiana. They are known as the Cajun Navy.

Clearing, the newborn baby requires care in order to survive. At that time caring can be very expensive if the baby has to be admitted to a newborn intensive care unit. Thereafter caring is imparted instructionally to children at a very early age by their parents who, for example, separate quarreling children and scold an older child for bullying a younger one. As children develop, this virtue is reinforced by the caring behavior of their parents, teachers, and friends. Child abuse originates with parents, siblings, and caretakers who see the child as bothersome or, worse yet, an object that provokes anger or an instrument for sexual pleasure. Frequently the teenage or adult abuser was abused as a child. Caring contributes to personalist capital through action that is virtuous and, along with human capital, social capital, and economic well-being, is one of the determinants of integral human development. The vice of neglect or callousness, which in effect rejects the virtue of caring, diminishes personalist capital and thereby undermines human development.

As mentioned above, caring has no opportunity cost because it involves persons who are not interacting for the purpose of economic gain. For sure, the service or material thing freely offered and graciously received has economic value. At the same time, the caring person appears to be giving up something of value without getting anything of value in return. But there is a real return for the caring person in the form of further human development. Caring persons experience greater respect from needy persons who in turn may tell others of the generosity of the persons who care. If the caring person is actively engaged in business, the firm acquires the real though intangible asset of goodwill. This asset is real as reflected on the balance sheet of such a business when it is sold. The interaction between the needy person and the caring person has a positive-sum outcome. Unlike other economic resources, the virtue of caring is not depleted through use, and in that sense is unlimited.

Functioning at third-level action the *person of action* stores up personalist capital when acting virtuously, and draws it down when he/she acts viciously. Third-level action has two effects: the objective effect of what is produced and the subject effect on the person who produces. To illustrate, two friends fish together regularly for two reasons: to catch fish and to enjoy one another's company (Grisez & Shaw, 1974). The *innocent person* has not yet begun to engage in action at the third-level and therefore has no stock of personalist capital. See schematic below. Emphasis on virtue in economic affairs is not a new idea. In his *Moral Sentiments* Smith repeatedly calls attention to the importance of sympathy, generosity, and benevolence. In addition, thrift and diligence are accepted in conventional economics though perhaps not with the same emphasis. In her lengthy discourse on water, mineral, and energy resources, Barbara Ward sees stewardship as the proper role of humankind. She emphasizes that at the level of the community the most important element in protecting the environment is the quality of the *caring* of its members (Ward, 1976, p.256).

John Paul II (1995b) sees an important role for women in many socio-economic matters including the environment, particularly in challenges of the future like the quality of time, migration or social services. The women's presence might be the force to shape the "civilization of love" (John Paul II, 1995b, § 4). Though he does not make this point, mothers perhaps more so than anyone else are noteworthy as caring human beings.

Caring and Christian Charity

In addition to justice, Christian charity is necessary to check abuses that derive from excessive gain-seeking behavior. To repeat, in a market economy transactions are driven by gain-seeking behavior. Without the prospect of some gain, economic agents are not motivated to complete a transaction. However, at times agents are exploited, deceived, mistaken and consequently are deprived of the gain that is their due. The virtues of justice and Christian charity are "twin bulwarks" (Mulcahy, p.68) that help protect humans from the abuses that originate in the excessive gain-seeking behavior of others. Commutative justice, distributive justice, and contributive justice, if faithfully executed, protect human wellbeing by curbing the destructive human attraction to ill-gotten gains.

Pesch (1998, p.177) asserts that "charity must complement justice so that one person will help the other, even when he is not compelled to do so by any kind of legal obligation." The same can be said for the secular virtue of generosity in combination with justice. With generosity, human beings are seen as living, breathing, existential actualities, as ends in themselves more so than means, as equals with certain inalienable rights that must not be violated. Christian charity rises above the negative character of Kant's second imperative that humans are not to be treated as mere instrumentalities. Every follower of Christ is required to actively affirm all human beings as persons (John Paul II, 1994, p.201). John Paul II refers to charity as the "distinguishing mark of Christ's disciples" and citing Psalm 8: 5-6 identifies every human being as being nearly divine. (John Paul II, 1987, § 40; 1995a, § 84; 1998a, §§ 7, 12). The Kantian imperative is a negative command, putting limits on what one person may do to another. No human being is ever to be treated as a means to an end. Christian charity, on the other hand, is an affirmative command requiring everyone to be treated as a human person with a sacred dignity that surpasses all human reckoning. Generosity and Christian charity along with justice eliminate the ill-will, disorder, and dishonesty that otherwise is common to a marketplace and workplace, replacing them with goodwill, solidarity, and authentic bargains. Neither virtue has value when it is hoarded. Both come alive and take on value only when given away. Uniquely both are never depleted by use. However, both are missing from the conventional economics way of thinking.

Caring and Christian charity can be represented in two scenarios. First, with both virtues action is undertaken on behalf of a *stranger*. A product or service is given freely to the needy stranger, but reciprocity is not expected or necessary. However, as already noted, the personal character of the caring or loving person is enhanced and effects economic affairs and human development through the acquisition of personalist capital. This scenario is best described in the parable of the Good Samaritan who came to the aid of a stranger who while traveling alone on a dangerous road was beaten, robbed, and left for dead. The parable teaches that anyone in need is a neighbor even when he has no one to blame for his troubles, and that need demands some active intervention. Christians must do more than feel sorry for the stranger in need. They must be like the Good Samaritan (Barclay, 1975/2001). Therefore, the goodness of the Samaritan contributes to their personalist capital.

Second, a product or service is given to someone who is a *family member, friend, neighbor, workmate* with no absolutely clear expectation that the recipient will reciprocate someday in the future. The person who freely shares the tomatoes from their garden with a neighbor who later may return the favor by sharing their homemade jelly.

Figure 3.1. **Acting virtuously or viciously and personalist capital: development of the person of action.**

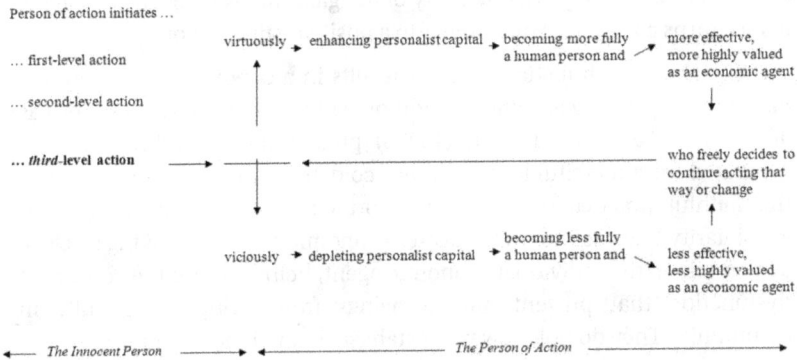

Person of action initiates ...

	virtuously → enhancing personalist capital →	becoming more fully a human person and	more effective, more highly valued as an economic agent
... first-level action			
... second-level action			
... *third*-level action			who freely decides to continue acting that way or change
		becoming less fully	
	viciously → depleting personalist capital →	a human person and →	less effective, less highly valued as an economic agent

The Innocent Person ← → ← The Person of Action →

Note. First-level action refers to reflexive or instinctive action that humans have in common with animals. Second-level action is purposeful or intentional. Third-level action produces a change (good or bad) in the person who engages in that action. With justice, caring, and Christian charity, acting virtuously means *justly, generously, lovingly.* In contrast, acting viciously means *unjustly, miserly, hatefully.*

The friend who offers assistance with moving furniture to another location may be invited to share a meal with the person who is moving. However, beware of the adult child of a dying parent who faithfully attends to the needs of that parent throughout the dying process. That child may appear to exhibit caring or Christian charity when in fact is actually motivated principally by a desire for favorable treatment in the dying parent's will. This scenario is best characterized as holier-than-thou.

At times caring and Christian charity become common practice as with a baby shower and contributions to a charitable organization as a fitting memorial in the name of a deceased workmate or friend. In all such cases, the personalist capital of the generous or loving giver is enriched with real-world economic effects. This scenario is depicted in O.Henry's short story "The Gift of the Magi" where newlyweds who are poor express their love for one another by their mutual sacrifices to provide the other with a gift at Christmas. He sells his watch to give her a comb for her long hair. She has her hair cut short and sold to give him a chain for his pocket watch.

Conclusions

We began by observing that exchange takes place only when there is an economic gain for the parties involved. For the most part, exchange has a positive-sum outcome. At times, however, exchange can have a zero-sum outcome and for that reason, gain has to be limited. Commutative justice, distributive justice, and contributive justice must be applied to remedy any outcome that derives from such practices as exploitation, deception, and mistakes that deprive one party of the gain that is their due. Applying justice turns a zero-sum outcome into a positive-sum outcome.

The problem with justice is that it results in a condition where no one *owes anything to anyone else*, a condition which Schall (2004) describes as an *isolated hell*. John Paul II (1998b) puts it this way: "... justice, if separated from merciful love, becomes cold and cutting." In other words, the faithful practice of those three principles of justice, along with subsidiarity that preferentially locates economic decision-making as close as possible to the individual economic agent, helps remove the sources of dysfunction that prevent human beings from living successfully in community. They do not, however, establish a functional community.

For a truly functional community and economy, the faithful practice of all three principles of economic justice *taken together* is required. As with a three-legged stool, all three legs are necessary to keep the stool from tipping over. We refer to that faithful practice of all three kinds of economic justice as *social justice*.

Caring is the deliberate reaching out of a generous person to assist a needy person. Without caring justice strictly speaking is cold and calculating. Caring in effect supplies the three cross members that stabilize a tall stool. Caring can be inserted into economic affairs only by an economic agent who is a social being. This, in turn, forces us to abandon the strict individuality and passivity of the conventional economic agent and the underlying philosophy of individualism. The economic agent in personalist economics is represented as a human being who at once is both an individual and social being who sometimes acts in accordance with their individual nature and at other times in accordance with their social nature. To paraphrase John Paul II, all human existence is co-existence. The underlying philosophy is personalism.

Advocates for including caring somehow would add this secular virtue to the conventional way of thinking about the economic agent and economic affairs. Their efforts fall short because (1) the exchange that is triggered by caring involves need fulfillment not want satisfaction, and (2) the economic gain applies only to the person in need. The caring person does not realize or even desire economic gain. Instead, the generous person has an enhancement of personalist capital because caring is a good habit that rises above the demands of justice. In sharp contrast, the person with resources who sneers at and walks past a person in need experiences an erosion of character and a depletion of personalist capital because callousness is a bad habit.

Personalist economics sees the economic agent as a *person of action* rather than one who is like the largely passive *homo economicus.* John Paul II argues that the basic difference between the individual and the person is that the individual is entirely separated from the divine whereas the person is nearly divine. The individuality, sociality, and near divinity of the *person of action* are beautifully rendered in Michelangelo's *Act of Creation* in the Sistine Chapel. Christian charity and caring are alike in that both are grounded in the equality of all human beings. Further, they are alike in that they have a role in economic affairs only when they are used. Unlike economic resources, neither one is depleted through use. Even so, they are considerably different. With generosity, human beings are seen as ends in themselves more so than means, as persons with inalienable rights that must not be violated. Christian charity goes beyond the passive Kantian imperative to not view humans as mere instrumentalities. Every follower of Christ is *duty bound* to actively affirm all human beings as persons. Charity is the distinguishing mark of Christ's disciples.

Opportunity cost does not apply to caring or Christian charity because both involve persons who are not interacting for the purpose of *mutual* gain. For sure, the service or material thing freely offered and graciously received has economic value. However, for the persons who receive those gifts nothing is foregone. At the same time, the person prompted by caring or Christian charity appears to be giving up something of value without getting anything of value in return. But there is a real return in the form of enhanced human development. If the caring person or the one who is expressing Christian charity are actively engaged in business, the firm acquires goodwill that is accounted for on the balance sheet of that business when it is sold. Christian charity and caring are alike in two ways. First, neither one is depleted through use, and in that sense, both are unlimited resources. Second, both virtues fairly acted upon in economic affairs strengthen the character of the economic agent. We refer to that human characteristic as personalist capital that helps determine integral human development. Vices such as injustice, favoritism, and callousness weaken the character of the economic agent, are accounted for in terms of diminished personalist capital, and are harmful to human development.

Caring and Christian charity may be represented in two scenarios. First, with both virtues action is undertaken on behalf of a *stranger* with no expectation of reciprocity. Second, a product or service is given to a *family member, friend, neighbor, workmate* motivated in part that the recipient may reciprocate in the future. In conventional micro-economics, human material well-being (utility and profits) is maximized. In macro-economics production is maximized. From a personalist perspective, micro-and macro-economics are unified around the final goal of maximizing integral human development through improvements in personalist capital, along with social capital, human capital, and material well-being. Thus, caring and Christian charity are essential to a functional economy. Caring and Christian charity alter the basic requirement for economic exchange to take place. For the self-interested *homo economicus* of conventional economics, a comparison is made as to whether what is gotten in the exchange is more highly valued than what is given up. In contrast, the person in need who accepts what has been offered by a generous or loving person gives up nothing of economic value. For the *person of action* who is prompted by generosity or love nothing of tangible value is gotten in the gift-giving process. However, caring and Christian charity enhance the personal character of the gifting human being and in personalist economics are taken into account as personalist capital that in turn contributes to integral human development.

In the end, the machine-like and passive *homo economicus* is a static concept because he or she is unable to develop more fully as a human being. Like a machine, *homo economicus* is emptied of any personal essence. The dynamic *person of action* is capable of change by acting virtuously in economic affairs and thereby becoming a more fully developed human. By acting viciously that person sets back human development. By personal choice, the *person of action* functions along a spectrum of two extremes: a person of integrity and a person of ill repute.

References

Barclay, W. (1975/2001). *The new daily study Bible. The Gospel of Luke.* Louisville: The Westminster Press.

Dempsey, B. W. (1958). *The Functional Economy: The Bases of Economic Organization.* Englewood Cliffs NJ: Prentice-Hall.

Divine, T. F. (1960). *Economic Principles and Social Policy,* unpublished but available at Raynor Memorial Libraries, Marquette University, Milwaukee WI.

Grisez, G. & Shaw, R. (1974). *Beyond the New Morality: The Responsibilities of Freedom.* Notre Dame: University of Notre Dame Press.

John Paul II, P. (1987). *Sollicitudo Rei Socialis.* Retrieved from http://w2.vatican.va/content/john-paul-ii/en/encyclicals/documents/hf_jp-ii_enc_30121987_sollicitudo-rei-socialis.html .

John Paul II, P. (1991). *Centesimus Annus.* Retrieved from http://w2.vatican.va/content/john-paul-ii/en/encyclicals/documents/hf_jp-ii_enc_01051991_centesimus-annus.html .

John Paul II, P. (1994). *Crossing the Threshold of Hope.* New York: Alfred A. Knopf.

John Paul II, P. (1995a). *Evangelium Vitae.* Retrieved from http://w2.vatican.va/content/john-paul-ii/en/encyclicals/documents/hf_jp-ii_enc_25031995_evangelium-vitae.html .

John Paul II, P. (1995b). *Letter of Pope John Paul II to Women.* Retrieved from https://w2.vatican.va/content/john-paul-ii/en/letters/1995/documents/hf_jp-ii_let_29061995_women.html .

John Paul II, P. (1998a). *Fides et Ratio.* Retrieved from http://w2.vatican.va/content/john-paul-ii/en/encyclicals/documents/hf_jp-ii_enc_14091998_fides-et-ratio.html.

John Paul II, P. (1998b). *From the Justice of Each Comes Peace for Al.* Retrieved from http://w2.vatican.va/content/john-paul-ii/en/messages/peace/documents/hf_jp-ii_mes_08121997_xxxi-world-day-for-peace.html .

Mulcahy, R. E. (1951). Economic Freedom in Pesch: His System Demands, But Restrains, Freedom, *Social Order.*

Pesch, H. (1998). *Heinrich Pesch on Solidarist Economics: Excerpts from the Lehrbuch der Nationalökonomie,* translated by Rupert J. Ederer. Lanham MD: University Press of America.

Pesch, H. (2002). *Lehrbuch der Nationalökonomie: Teaching Guide to Economics,*Volume 1/Book 1, translated by Rupert J. Ederer, Lewiston NY: The Edwin Mellen Press.

Pius XI (1937). *Atheistic Communism: (Divini Redemptoris): encyclical letter of Pope Pius XI.* New York: Paulist Press.

Schall, J. V. (2004). Justice: The Most Terrible of the Virtues, *Journal of Markets and Morality,* 7(2), 409-421.

Ward, B. (1976). *The Home of Man,* New York: W.W. Norton.

Part II:
Dimensions of Selflessness at Work Environment

Chapter 4

Dimensions of selflessness at work: A closer look at organizational altruism

Joanna M. Szulc,
Huddersfield Business School, University of Huddersfield, UK

Introduction

Helpful behaviors among employees have been a central issue in the study of organizations for centuries (Katz & Kahn, 1966) and their positive influence made it a particularly popular topic among Management scholars (e.g., Frenkel & Sanders, 2007; Podsakoff, Blume, Whiting, & Podsakoff, 2009). More specifically, changes in the nature of workplace relationships reflecting the growing mutual dependencies of employees (Grant & Parker, 2009) turned our attention to examining behaviors which are clearly other-oriented (e.g., Bolino & Grant, 2016; Grant & Patil, 2012; Li, Kirkman, & Porter, 2014) and moving away from the traditional theories assuming the principle of rational self-interest (Cropanzano, Anthony, Daniels, & Hall, 2017). Such other-oriented behaviors are not only characterized by higher levels of persistence (Bing & Burroughs, 2001; Deci & Ryan, 2000; Grant, 2008; Grant et al., 2007), but they also elicit more positive reactions among organizational members in comparison to egoistically driven behaviors (Halbesleben, Bowler, Bolino, & Turnley, 2010; Lemoine, Parsons, & Kansara, 2015). Thus, encouraging people to act selflessly in business has given organizations means to outcompete their rivals and to bring ensuing benefits to the company.

Despite their significance, our knowledge of individual selfless acts in the organizational context is still scant compared to the scholarly attention devoted to self-serving workplace behaviors (e.g., Bowler & Brass, 2006; Cropanzano et al., 2017; Hui, Lam, & Law, 2000). In this chapter, I will therefore focus on the concept of organizational altruism which, in a way, represents the idea of selflessness in business on the part of individuals. First of all, I will briefly discuss the meaning behind organizational altruism. Subsequently, acknowledging that someone sceptical may contest the existence of selfless acts in a competitive world of business, I will outline the empirical evidence demonstrating the existence of altruistic motives. Finally, building on management and social psychological research around the concept, I will theorize about varying dimensions of organizational altruism that are not limited solely to heroic acts of extraordinary self-sacrifice. In fact, each of us may have engaged in selfless or altruistic actions towards different organizational stakeholders to some extent. You may have saved your co-worker's life by rescuing them from the fire in the office and risking your own life at the same time. This is a rather extreme example though. More often you probably had a chance to pick up your colleague's post from the mailroom or give them a good word when they did not seem themselves and something was clearly bothering them. These relatively different examples may equally well represent selfless actions – or what I call – 'organizational altruism'. It is important that organizations are able to spot such behaviors and recognize them because altruists are amongst us (they just do not need to be dressed up as super-heroes).

The Meaning behind organizational Altruism

The concept of altruism goes back as far as the nineteenth century, when Auguste Comte, a French philosopher, first coined the term (1854). He associated altruism with a fundamental maxim to live for others (*vivre pour l'autrui*) which was based largely on his uncompromising belief in collectivism and a utopian view of the world where altruism would always triumph over egoism.

The topic of organizational altruism has quickly gained popularity among management scholars (Clarkson, 2014; Kanungo & Conger, 1993; Li et al., 2014; Loi, Ngo, Zhang, & Lau, 2011; Organ & Ryan, 1995; Wagner & Rush, 2000) who borrowed the term to be used in the organizational context. Although different labels are commonly used (such as workplace altruism, team altruism, organizational altruism, altruistic citizenship behavior or prosocial behavior), the common theme is that it is regularly contrasted with selfishness (Avolio & Locke, 2002), greed (Haynes, Josefy, & Hitt, 2015), or aggression (Cropanzano et al., 2017).

In order to demonstrate the essence of the meaning behind organizational altruism, I will build on the theory of prosocial behavior (Batson, 2011) which experimentally distinguishes between two underlying drivers of helping behaviors: egoistic and altruistic motivation. Whereas egoistic motivation is based on the desire to reduce one's own unpleasant emotional arousal or the perception that helping another will result in a reward, altruistic motivation is defined by the need to help another reduce their needs. In other words, the key to differentiating whether a given behavior is driven by egoistic or altruistic motivation is the ultimate reason for engaging in such acts.

Consistently, in broad terms, organizational altruism can be defined as benefiting an organizational stakeholder as an end in itself (Szulc, Clarkson, & Bown, 2016). This means that benefiting another constitutes the actor's anticipatory outcome rather than being instrumental means for reaching a selfish goal (see also: Lemmon & Wayne, 2015; Sosik, Jung, & Dinger, 2009). Such a way of looking at organizational altruism emphasises the importance of the underpinning motivation behind an individual's actions. Whereas motivations are particularly important in definitions of general altruism among strangers (Batson, 2011), most organizational scholars are interested in altruism as a general helping behavior. In other words, there is a tendency to take a behavioral perspective to studying the concept and to describe as altruistic any form of helping directed at others, no matter what the intentions behind it (Li et al., 2014). Efforts to equate organizational altruism with a range of prosocial behaviors are also problematic since prosocial motivation can be based on one or more of four different ultimate goals: altruism, egoism, principlism, and collectivism (Batson et al., 2008). The existing literature, however, implies that varying ultimate goals will result in different processes associated with a given behavior and, ultimately, different consequences (e.g., Bolino, Turnley, & Niehoff, 2004; Bowler, Halbesleben, & Paul, 2010).

Does organizational altruism exist in the business?

"Raising a question of the existence of altruism opens a Pandora's box of complex issues and conceptual traps." (Batson, 1991, p.2)

Observing today's increasingly competitive workplace environment, one might perhaps wonder if selfless behaviors are possible. Can people engage in altruistic acts with the ultimate goal of helping others rather than reaping benefits at a later point in time? Ultimately, it has been over two decades since Kanungo and Conger (1993, p.37) have argued that "the game of business is played in a competitive arena and hence few expect business people to be altruistic." What is more, while acts of *seemingly* altruistic behavior are not disputed, the claim that altruism does *not* exist has a long tradition in many areas of biological, economic, political and philosophical thought (Wilson, 2015, p.3). The arguments against the existence of altruism are that the "altruist" invariably has some self-serving motive in carrying out the "altruistic" act. This leaves organizational member embroiled and confused in complex considerations of their personal motives regarding any act of altruistic behavior.

While it may be the relative lack of conceptual clarity on organizational altruism in the field of Management that made it difficult to test its existence, we can build on the extensive research conducted by social psychologists who experimentally demonstrated that altruism exists even among strangers (for reviews see: Batson, 2011; Eisenberg & Miller, 1987). This assertion is grounded in the empathy-altruism hypothesis developed by Batson, Duncan, Ackerman, Buckley, and Birch (1981). It suggests that the feeling of empathy for the person in need evokes altruistic motivation in humans – thus, it contradicts the concept of our fundamentally egoistic nature. It further argues that we are capable of caring for the welfare of others without expecting any rewards. Some subsequent heated debates around the egoistic explanations for the seemingly altruistic motivation such as striving for rewards, avoiding punishment or reducing aversive arousal have triggered much empirical research in that area ultimately demonstrating that our ultimate goals can be empirically ascertained and proving that altruism does exist (for reviews see: Batson, 2011).

While altruistic motivation was demonstrated to exist, social psychologists compared it to a "fragile flower", which can be easily crushed by egoistic concerns (Batson, 1991, p.125-126) – thus suggesting that there are limits on the maintenance and expression of altruistic motivation. Factors inhibiting our altruistic desires at work are an interesting research question that still warrants more academic research. In order to get a detailed picture of such factors, we first need to understand the different ways in which organizational altruism can be exhibited. As mentioned in the introduction, organizational altruism does not involve only heroic, highly self-sacrificial acts. In fact, we observe it in everyday interactions with colleagues, customers, as well as superiors and subordinates. Consistently, by introducing the typology of organizational altruism in the following section, I will describe the many faces of the concept or, indeed, of selflessness at work.

Multiple Faces of Selflessness in business: Typology of organizational Altruism

From a practical standpoint, if practitioners are not aware of selfless acts on the part of their employees or, at least, a potential for such acts, they will likely fail to understand how they could play an important role in organizations and, ultimately, to capitalize on their power and associated advantages. Consistently, to comprehensively understand this important workplace behavior and outline its different dimensions, in this section I develop a typology of organizational altruism. The typology considers organizational altruism in terms of the beneficiaries of such behaviors, the degree of effort involved, associated costs to the actor, the focus of help, level of planning involved, the actor's initiative, the outcomes of such behaviors, and the durability of consequences of such acts. The introduced typology (see Figure 4.1.) points out to the complexity of organizational altruism and demonstrates that it is a multi-dimensional phenomenon. The subsequent sections describe each of its dimensions in depth.

Figure 4.1. Typology of organizational altruism.

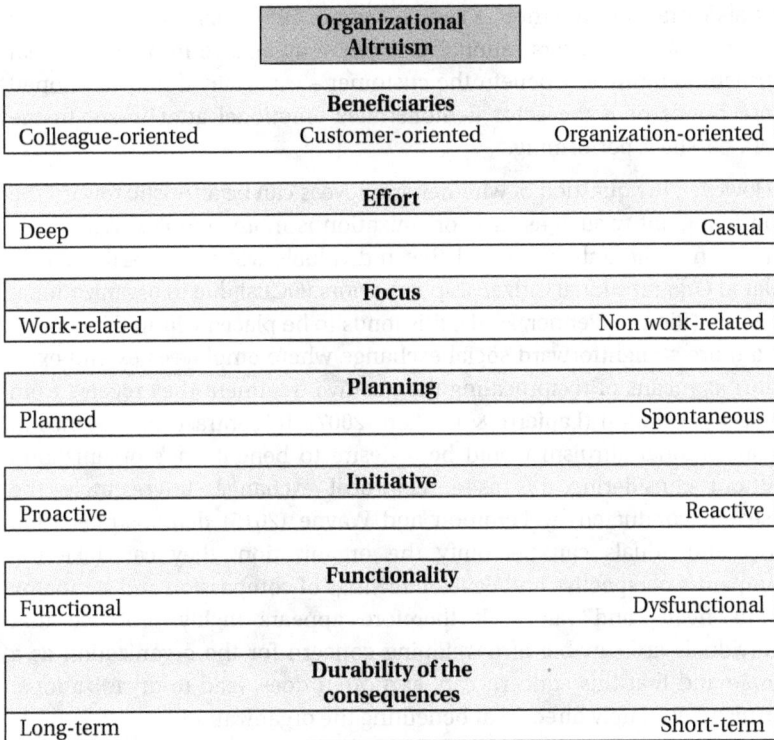

Organizational Altruism		

Beneficiaries		
Colleague-oriented	Customer-oriented	Organization-oriented

Effort	
Deep	Casual

Focus	
Work-related	Non work-related

Planning	
Planned	Spontaneous

Initiative	
Proactive	Reactive

Functionality	
Functional	Dysfunctional

Durability of the consequences	
Long-term	Short-term

Beneficiaries

The proposed typology considers three subtypes of organizational altruism based on different beneficiaries:

- Organizational altruism towards a colleague;
- Organizational altruism towards a customer;
- Organizational altruism towards the organization.

The overall tendency in the existing literature is to associate the beneficiaries of organizational altruism and related helping behaviors with specific persons (e.g., Carmeli, 2005; Farh, Podsakoff, & Organ, 1990; Glomb, Bhave, Miner, & Wall., 2011; Smith, Organ, & Near, 1983) who are helped particularly in "face-to-face situations" (Loi et al., 2011, p.672). Consistently, it is not surprising that one form of organizational altruism will be that aimed at benefiting an organizational colleague.

Given a significant amount of research demonstrating that individuals are capable of altruistic actions towards not only people they care about but also strangers (Bierhoff, Klein, & Kramp, 1991; Clary & Snyder, 1991; Oliner, 2002), it appears rational that one may engage in organizational altruism to ultimately benefit the customer – especially if they developed close bonds or if the actor demonstrates emotional attachment to the work he/she is performing.

However, the question of whether employees can be altruistic toward the non-living entity such as their organization is more complex. Whereas it has been commonly suggested that individuals will often participate in related Organizational Citizenship Behaviors (OCBs) due to organizational concern (Rioux & Penner, 2001), this tends to be placed within the context of a more straightforward social exchange where employees extend extra effort as means of reciprocating the positive treatment they receive from their organization (Lapierre & Hackett, 2007). In contrast, the essence of organizational altruism would be a desire to benefit one's organization without considering this as a reciprocal exchange. Interestingly, the research conducted by Lemmon and Wayne (2015) demonstrated that since individuals can personify the organization, they can take the company's perspective and develop feelings of compassion and sympathy to its needs and values. It therefore appears highly probable that individuals are capable of developing concern for the organization as a whole and that this concern can, and often does, lead to organizational altruism ultimately directed at benefiting the organization.

Effort

Based on the degree of effort involved, the proposed typology considers two subtypes of organizational altruism:

- Deep organizational altruism;
- Casual organizational altruism.

Relating to the self-sacrifice criterion, in the existing literature cost appears to be a particularly important aspect present in the economic and behavioral definitions of altruism that see it as "costly acts that confer economic benefits on other individuals" (Fehr & Fischbacher, 2003, p.785). Similarly, Grant and Berry (2011, p.77) emphasised the critical role of self-sacrifice criterion that characterizes organizational altruism and makes it different from prosocial workplace behaviors. This is also consistent with other scholars who consider organizational altruism as acts that incur a considerable cost as a result of one's actions (e.g., Furnham, Treglown, Hyde, & Trickey, 2016) and who evaluate it based on the extent to which it decreases the actor's immediate benefits (for further discussion see: Li et al., 2014).

However, such conceptualizations, rather than paying attention to individuals' motivation for engaging in a given behavior, instead look into the costs associated. The following example illustrates this point. Imagine two situations:

1. Marie brought Anna a coffee and had a small chat with her during lunch break before going back to her duties.
2. Marie volunteered to be a mentor for a group of new employees which would involve working overtime and taking up new responsibilities.

It may appear as if the second situation is "more altruistic" than the first. We judge it solely by the degree of effort, or cost to the actor involved. However, let us have a look at these two situations with more contextual information:

1. Marie found out today that Anna is going through a difficult time as her husband is waiting for an important surgery. She felt sorry for Anna and wanted her to cheer up. Marie brought Anna a coffee and had a small chat with her during lunch break before going back to her duties.
2. Marie is fed up of being in the same position and on the same salary grade for what seems like forever. She decided she needs to take on extra responsibilities to demonstrate she deserves a promotion. Marie volunteered to be a mentor for a group of new employees which would involve working overtime and taking up new responsibilities.

Having more contextual information now, it is clear that the first example, despite not incurring much cost to the actor, is an example of organizational altruism. While those who altruistically support others are usually prepared to sacrifice their own energy and time perhaps more than others (see also: Bergeron, Shipp, Rosen, & Furst, 2013; Bolino &

Turnley, 2005; Meglino & Korsgaard, 2004; Moon, Kamdar, Mayer, & Takeuchi, 2008), it is essential to note that organizational altruism lies on a continuum from acts which involve hardly any sacrifice to behaviors which require a significant cost to the actor.

Focus

Taking into consideration the focus of the actor, the proposed typology considers two subtypes of organizational altruism:

1. Work-related organizational altruism;
2. Non-work-related organizational altruism.

The existing conceptualizations of organizational altruism (whatever the label) characterize it as majorly concerned with work-related problems (see also: Guinot, Chiva, & Mallén, 2015; Heilman & Chen, 2005; Loi et al., 2011; Organ, 1988). Indeed, organizational altruism will often involve practical assistance with the resolution of work-related problems or dealing with organization-based issues. However, individuals also engage in behaviors that entail emotional support or solving problems of a more personal nature (Colbert, Bono, & Purvanova, 2016). These types of behaviors are often grounded in friendships and social support.

Consistently, organizational altruism refers to both work-related as well as non-work-related activities. Such work-related examples of organizational altruism may include helping others with the workload, covering for colleagues who cannot come to work, orienting new employees, developing the skills of others, or making sure that colleagues are not experiencing problems. Non-work-related activities, on the other hand, include mostly support with personal issues.

Planning

The proposed taxonomy further distinguishes between two subtypes of organizational altruism based on the level of planning involved in the action:

*   Planned organizational altruism;
*   Spontaneous organizational altruism.

Building on Clary and Snyder (1991), a distinction can be made between spontaneous and non-spontaneous altruistic acts. The former ones are triggered by highly salient situation cues which affect an individual's decision to help for a relatively limited period of time. Important situational influences on spontaneous organizational altruism include the presence of others, the pressure of time and exposure to helpful models. On the other hand, non-spontaneous organizational altruism should be defined in terms of circumstances in which potential helpers have time to decide whether and how to engage in an altruistic act (for instance, volunteering on a regular basis). Contrary to situational factors that define spontaneous organizational altruism, non-spontaneous acts are, at least to an extent, influenced by one's dispositional characteristics (Clary & Snyder, 1991; Batson, 2011).

The distinction between intuitive and rational modes of information processing which lie at the heart of dual-processing theory (Kahneman & Frederick, 2002) might facilitate our understanding of spontaneous and non-spontaneous dimensions of organizational altruism. In general, the theory distinguishes between unconscious, automatic and rapid System 1 thinking and conscious, slow and deliberative System 2 thinking. Although the research combining the theory with workplace help is only fledgling (see: Kinnunen & Windmann, 2013; Rand, Greene, & Nowak, 2012), empirically investigating whether and how these processing modes influence organizational altruism could yield interesting results and further contribute to the existing literature.

Initiative

The proposed typology of organizational altruism further distinguishes between:

- Proactive organizational altruism;
- Reactive organizational altruism.

I suggest that whereas proactive organizational altruism is initiated by the actor, reactive form is passive and occurs as a consequence of being asked for support. This perspective somewhat deviates from the assumptions made by Spitzmuller and Van Dyne (2013) in their influential work on helping behaviors, where they made an argument that while reactive help is often associated with altruistic motives, proactive help would be predominantly based on fulfilling personal needs such as reputational benefits, self-development, well-being, or favorable self-evaluations. Contrary to this, social psychological research on altruism (for reviews see: Batson, 2011) demonstrated that once individuals perceive somebody else to be in need and they are concerned with their welfare, they are usually prepared to altruistically help that person in order to alleviate their need and not to gain benefits for oneself.

Further attention should also be drawn to scholars increasingly often emphasizing the importance of proactive behaviors as critical determinants of organizational success (e.g., Bergeron, Ostroff, Schroeder, & Block, 2014; Crant, 2000; Grant, Parker, & Collins, 2009; Parker & Collins, 2010; Parker, Williams, & Turner, 2006; Rank, Carsten, Unger, & Spector, 2007). While I am not debating their significance, reactive behaviors are as important as those behaviors where one actively seeks opportunities for improving things and therefore their potential impact on organizations should not be underestimated.

Outcomes

Based on the potential intended and unintended outcomes of organizational altruism, its two further subtypes are identified:

- Functional organizational altruism;
- Dysfunctional organizational altruism.

The profound benefits of organizational altruism are self-evident. Other-oriented intentions associated with organizational altruism are regularly found to promote both individual performance outcomes (Grant, 2008; Grant & Berry, 2011; Grant & Sumanth, 2009) as well as overall team effectiveness (Hu & Liden, 2015).

However, sometimes altruistic actions aimed at promoting the welfare of others instead lead to unanticipated negative consequences. Importantly, the potential hurtful aspects of organizational altruism have received only limited attention in the scientific enquiry. Following Oakley, Knafo, Madhavan, and Wilson (2012, p.8), I argue that if science is truly to serve as an ultimately altruistic enterprise, then science must examine not only the good but also the harm that can arise from feelings of altruism and empathetic care for others.

Most research on potential negative effects of altruism in general concerns the notion of parochial altruism – a concept introduced by Choi and Bowles (2007). It combines parochialism (hostility towards out-group members) with altruism (benefiting in-group members at an enormous cost to oneself). Examples of parochially altruistic behaviors can be found where emotion bonds between group members become strong enough to motivate an extreme form of self-sacrificial act in service to one's in-group against perceived out-group. Although such extreme examples may not be common at workplace, Sober (2002) argues that our actions can be altruistically motivated but at the same time morally wrong. Put simply, "being nice to someone can involve being nasty to third parties" (Sober,

2002; p.26). This is well illustrated by Clarkson (2014) who talks about the possibility of dysfunctional altruistic behaviors at different and potentially conflicting levels of organizational identity. In other words, the varying relations between different groups of which we are members may create possibilities for conflicting interest. Take an example of an academic who is a member of a Business School faculty, but who also strongly identifies with academics who are members of a particular research center. It is hypothesized that at times, such an individual might engage in actions which are altruistic for other members of their research center, but in the same time detrimental to the overall faculty he or she is part of. As a consequence, and consistently with the suggestions of Clarkson (2014), research is now required to specify if, and at what level altruistic behaviors can become dysfunctional.

Moving the field forward, Oakley et al. (2012) introduced the concept of pathological altruism. It is defined as behavior in which attempts to promote the welfare of another result in objectively foreseeable and unreasonable harm to either the self, the target of altruism, or to others beyond the target. Pathological altruism constitutes a new way of framing and understanding altruism which has not been researched yet, but which may open new and potentially useful lines of inquiry and move the field toward a mature and scientifically informed understanding of altruism.

Durability of the consequences

Another way to distinguish between different forms of organizational altruism is to look at the durability of the consequences of such acts. Consistently, the proposed typology considers the following subtypes of organizational altruism:

- Long-term organizational altruism;
- Short-term organizational altruism.

Imagine an employee is asked to help a new colleague with inputting data into the system that they are not familiar with yet. In such a situation, an altruist may simply help a person by inputting the data into the system on his or her own. In the long-term, however, although incurring more costs in terms of time and effort, an altruist would make sure that the recipient of help understands how to operate the system and will be able to use it on his or her own in the future (see also: Schroeder, Penner, Dovidio, & Piliavin, 1995).

Short-term versus long-term organizational altruism might have its foundations in the psychology of intertemporal discounting even though these two disciplines have not, to my knowledge, been combined in the literature before. Individuals tend to assign different values to the costs and benefits of their actions at different points in time. The research on intertemporal choice suggests that the value of present costs and benefits is always superior to their value in the future (Soman et al., 2005). Put in the context of organizational altruism, the value of a new employee knowing how to operate the system in the future appears smaller to us than the value of the same employee having the information put into the system by us in the present so that they can continue with their tasks.

Building from the marketing field, here we might further refer to the concept of "vices" and "virtues" (Wertenbroch, 1998). "Vices" are actions offering positive consequences in the short term, but negative consequences/increased costs in the longer term. Conversely, "virtues" are actions offering positive consequences in the long term, but negative consequences or higher costs in the short term. According to Soman et al. (2005, p.352), humans are "myopic" and therefore they tend to overemphasize short-term benefits relative to long-term benefits. We also often experience conflict between short- and long-term consequences of options and therefore end up imposing self-controls in order not to over-consume vices and under-consume virtues (O'Donoghue & Rabin, 1999; Soman et al., 2005).

Importantly, we should remain careful when defining short-term helping behavior as organizational altruism as such actions often tend to be superficial and perfunctory (Bolino, 1999; Bolino et al., 2004; Bowler et al., 2010). On the contrary, helpers sensitive to the long-term consequences are likely to be characterized by a deeper commitment and are therefore more likely to be deeply altruistic (Sibicky, Schroeder, & Dovidio, 1995).

Discussion

We are more regularly observing organizations moving away from corporate greed into the direction of building corporate philanthropy into their business plans. Being committed to charitable giving or aligning business with a good cause is what sets an organization apart from the competition. However, equally significant, are the selfless actions on the part of individuals within organizations. In this chapter, a focus has been placed on organizational altruism – where one benefits an organizational stakeholder as an end in itself. This special type of workplace behavior is concerned with acting for the well-being of others without regard to one's self-interest and appears particularly likely to bring ensuing benefits for individuals and organizations.

Table 4.1. Dimensions of organizational altruism

Beneficiaries		
Dimension	**Colleague-oriented organizational altruism**	**Customer-oriented organizational altruism**	**Organization-oriented organizational altruism**
Characteristics	Organizational altruism towards a colleague	Organizational altruism towards a customer	Organizational altruism towards an organization
Example	John helps Adam with lifting heavy boxes from one room to another because he is concerned about his problems with a back.	John goes out of his way to help his students learn the topic well because he wants them to do well in final exams to get to the university they are dreaming about.	John volunteers to represent his organization during a national conference.

Effort		
Dimension	**Deep organizational altruism**	**Casual organizational altruism**
Characteristics	Serious, formal, and substantial organizational altruism	Informal, trivial, low cost organizational altruism
Example	John becomes a mentor for Adam, a new employee. He will guide him in the first 12 months at his new position. This would involve weekly meetings, teaching him how to use the systems, and being a first point of contact for any queries.	John takes Adam's printing job and leaves at his desk.

Focus		
Dimension	**Work-related organizational altruism**	**Non work-related organizational altruism**
Characteristics	Organizational altruism concerned with work-related problems	Organizational altruism concerned with personal problems unrelated to work
Example	John helps Adam with a report.	John offers Adam emotional support because he is suffering from increased levels of stress.

Planning		
Dimension	**Planned organizational altruism**	**Spontaneous organizational altruism**
Characteristics	Well-thought out and carefully considered organizational altruism	Unplanned, instinctive, or emergency organizational altruism

Example	John sees that Adam is struggling with the use of a new system. After considering different ways in which he can help him, he sets up a meeting with him, brings his notes about the tips on using the system and some further printouts available from the web.	As John walks along Adam's desk, he notices that Adam inputs the data into the system in the wrong way. He points out to his mistake and shows him how to input the data in the correct way.
Initiative		
Dimension	**Proactive organizational altruism**	**Reactive organizational altruism**
Characteristics	Organizational altruism initiated by the actor	Passive organizational altruism occurring after having been asked for help
Example	John notices that Adam is not coping with his workload so he offers to take over some of his tasks.	John is approached by Adam to take over some of his tasks as he is not coping with his workload. John agrees to take over some of Adam's duties.
Functionality		
Dimension	**Functional organizational altruism**	**Dysfunctional organizational altruism**
Characteristics	Organizational altruism positive in consequences	Organizational altruism negative in consequences
Example	John helps Adam with some of his tasks which relieves some pressure from Adam.	John consistently helps Adam with the use of the new system without giving Adam a chance to learn how to operate it himself.
Durability of the consequences		
Dimension	**Long-term organizational altruism**	**Short-term organizational altruism**
Characteristics	Organizational altruism with long-lasting consequences	Organizational altruism with consequences limited to a short period of time
Example	John teaches Adam how to use the new system so that in the future Adam can use it himself.	John inputs the data into the system for Adam who is not familiar with its use.

Interestingly, the typology of organizational altruism introduced in this chapter suggests that it is not a term reserved for only highly sacrificial acts that require employees to act like heroes or martyrs. Rather, selflessness in business may have many faces and it is essential that practitioners are able to recognize when such acts take place. For instance, they may take a form of simple acts of kindness like a good word to a colleague in distress or picking up someone's printing on your way to the office. Similarly, they may be simply a response to someone asking for help and have short-term consequences. However, they may also be more carefully planned acts that require significant amount of effort. They may consider personal problems as well as work-related issues. They may be targeted at our colleagues, customers, or an organization in general. Finally, while most often they will bring a range of benefits for organizations and their members, there may be a threshold at which organizational altruism will be no longer a positive behavior. Thus, it is important that organizations are aware of the potential for such acts and – their many faces – to allow their employees to advance the common good without becoming martyrs or putting other people or groups at a disadvantaged position. I summarize the suggested multiple dimensions of organizational altruism with their characteristics, and I provide further examples from a workplace context to illustrate these in Table 4.1.

One thing a reader should definitely take away from the introduced typology is that no matter what dimension – who the beneficiary is, how much effort, cost, planning involved, what the focus or the consequences are, it is benefiting other(s) as an end in itself that makes an act altruistic. Whereas a tendency is to portray organizational altruism on a continuum from more self-serving to more purely altruistic actions (see, e.g., Li et al., 2014), this seems to contradict the initial idea behind altruism as introduced by Comte. Consistently, I suggest that organizational altruism should consist only of those purely altruistic actions. These, however, can be portrayed on a range of continua (as illustrated in Figure 4.1. before) involving different degrees of effort, planning, initiative, functionality, durability, and different types of beneficiaries and focus, as explained in previous sections.

The Future of altruistic Research

Despite the growing interest in organizational altruism and scholars having acknowledged the importance of distinguishing between altruistic versus self-serving workplace behaviors (Avolio & Locke, 2002; Bowler et al., 2010; Kim, Van Dyne, Kamdar, & Johnson, 2013; Lai, Lam, & Lam, 2013; Lemmon & Wayne, 2015; Rioux & Penner, 2001; Snell & Wong, 2007; Sosik et al., 2009), still more organizational theory and research is needed in this area.

First, as an object of research, organizational altruism encompasses different perceptions and varying definitions (e.g., Clarkson, 2014; Haynes et al., 2015; Li et al., 2014; Loi et al., 2011; Organ & Ryan, 1995; Wagner & Rush, 2000). A lack of clear distinction between them has resulted in the illusion of agreement and amalgamating acts that substantially differ in nature. This, in turn, is problematic because without an appropriate level of specification we are not able to fully understand the concept. Consequently, more empirical evidence is needed on individuals' experiences of organizational altruism. This information should enable scholars to gain a comprehensive understanding of the specific meaning behind organizational altruism. The introduced typology is the first step in this direction. However, more research is needed – especially – focusing on the complexity of considerations of personal motives regarding altruistic and seemingly altruistic behaviors.

Secondly, while there is abundance of studies on antecedents of more general organizational citizenship behaviors (for a review, see: Organ, Podsakoff, & MacKenzie, 2006), they do not distinguish between the underlying motivations behind such acts. Given that extensive research conducted by social psychologists clearly demonstrated that the actual motivations behind one's actions will dictate when and where help can be expected (e.g., Batson, 1991; Clary & Snyder, 1991; 1998; Kanungo & Conger, 1993), there is a pressing need understand the specific mechanisms that initiate and govern organizational altruism which is uniquely motivated by concern for others.

What is more, although the general picture in the literature is that any act of help should result predominantly in positive consequences for employees and organizations (Podsakoff et al., 2009), an emerging stream of work has begun to recognize the potential negative consequences of such behaviors (e.g., Bergeron et al., 2014). Consequently, it appears essential that any exploration of organizational altruism also critically assesses the impact that it has on organizations and their members.

The scarcity of research on organizational altruism is regrettable because it is the sort of evidence that would raise scholarly and practitioners' awareness of this specific phenomenon and would enable organizations to understand how it can be effectively managed to the advantage of key organizational stakeholders. Characteristics of organizational altruism, the processes associated with it, and the consequences of such behaviors are, of course, very much an open empirical question that the future research will hopefully set out to explore.

References

Avolio, B. J., & Locke, E. E. (2002). Theoretical letters. Contrasting different philosophies of leader motivation: Altruism versus egoism. *The Leadership Quarterly, 13*, 169-191.

Batson, C. D. (1991). *The altruism question: towards a social-psychological answer.* New Jersey: Hove and London.

Batson, C. D. (2011). *Altruism in Humans.* New York: Oxford University Press.

Batson, C. D., Duncan, B. D., Ackerman, P., Buckley, T., & Birch, K. (1981). Is empathic emotion a source of altruistic motivation? *Journal of Personality and Social Psychology, 40,* 290-302.

Bergeron, D., Ostroff, C., Schroeder, T. D., & Block, C. (2014). The Dual effects of organizational citizenship behavior: Relationships to research productivity and career outcomes in academe. *Human Performance, 27,* 99-128.

Bergeron, D., Shipp, A. J., Rosen, B., & Furst, S. (2013). Organizational Citizenship Behavior and Career Outcomes: The Cost of Being a "Good Citizen." *Journal of Management, 39*(4), 958-984.

Bierhoff, H. W., Klein, R., & Kramp, P.(1991). Evidence for the Altruistic Personality from Data on Accident Research. *Journal of Personality, 59*(2), 263-280.

Bing, M. N., & Burroughs, S. M. (2001). The predictive and interactive effects of equity sensitivity in teamwork-oriented organizations. *Journal of Organizational Behavior, 22,* 271-290.

Bolino, M. C. (1999). Citizenship and impression management: Good soldiers or good actors? *Academy of Management Review, 24*(1), 82-98.

Bolino, M. C., & Grant, A. M. (2016). The Bright Side of Being Prosocial at Work, and the Dark Side, Too: A Review and Agenda for Research on Other-Oriented Motives, Behavior, and Impact in Organizations. *Academy of Management Annals, 10*(1), 599-670.

Bolino, M. C., & Turnley, W. H. (2005). The personal costs of citizenship behavior: the relationship between individual initiative and role overload, job stress, and work-family conflict. *Journal of Applied Psychology, 90*(4), 740-748.

Bolino, M. C., Turnley, W. H., & Niehoff, B. P.(2004). The other side of the story: Reexamining prevailing assumptions about organizational citizenship behavior. *Human Resource Management Review, 14,* 229–246.

Bowler, W. M., & Brass, D. J. (2006). Relational correlates of interpersonal citizenship behavior: A social network perspective. *Journal of Applied Psychology, 91,* 70-82.

Bowler, W. M., Halbesleben, J. B., & Paul, J. R. (2010). If you're close with the leader, you must be a brownnose: The role of leader–member relationships in follower, leader, and coworker attributions of organizational citizenship behavior motives. *Human Resource Management Review, 20*(4), 309-316.

Carmeli, A. (2005). Perceived External Prestige, Affective Commitment, and Citizenship Behaviors. *Organization Studies, 26*(3), 443-464. doi: 10.1177/0170840605050875

Choi, J.-K., & Bowles, S. (2007). The coevolution of parochial altruism and war. *Science, 318*(5850), 636-640.

Clarkson, G. P. (2014). Twenty-First Century Employment Relationships: The Case for an Altruistic Model. *Human Resource Management, 53*(2), 253-269.

Clary, E. G., & Snyder, M. (1991). A Functional Analysis of Altruism and Prosocial Behavior: The Case of Volunteerism. In M. S. Clark (Ed.). *Prosocial Behavior* (Vol. 12, pp. 119-148). Newbury Park: Sage.

Clary, E. G., Snyder, M., Ridge, R. D., Copeland, J., Stukas, A. A., Haugen, J., & Miene, P. (1998). Understanding and assessing the motivations of volunteers: a functional approach. *J Pers Soc Psychol, 74*(6), 1516-1530.

Colbert, A. E., Bono, J. E., & Purvanova, R. K. (2016). Flourishing via workplace relationships: Moving beyond instrumental support. *Academy of Management Journal, 59*(4), 1199-1223.

Comte, A. (1854). *Système de politique positive, ou traité de sociologie instituant la religion de l'Humanité Paris* (Vol. 4). Paris: Carilian-Goeury.

Crant, J. M. (2000). Proactive behavior in organizations. *Journal of Management, 26*, 435-462.

Cropanzano, R., Anthony, E. L., Daniels, S. R., & Hall, A. (2017). Social Exchange Theory: A Critical Review with Theoretical Remedies. *Academy of Management Annals, 11*(1), 1-38.

Deci, E. L., & Ryan, R. M. (2000). The "what" and "why" of goal pursuits: Human needs and the self-determination of behavior. *Psychological Inquiry, 4*, 227-268.

Eisenberg, N., & Miller, P.A. (1987). The relation of empathy to prosocial and related behaviors. *Psychol Bull, 101*(1), 91-9119.

Farh, J. L., Podsakoff, P.M., & Organ, D. W. (1990). Accounting for Organizational Citizenship Behavior: Leader Fairness and Task Scope versus Job Satisfaction. *Journal of Management, 16*(4), 705-721.

Fehr, E., & Fischbacher, U. (2003). The nature of human altruism. *Nature, 425*(6960), 785-791.

Frenkel, S. J., & Sanders, K. (2007). Explaining Variations in Co-worker Assistance in Organizations. *Organization Studies, 28*(6), 797-823. doi: 10.1177/0170840607073079

Furnham, A., Treglown, L., Hyde, G., & Trickey, G. (2016). The Bright and Dark Side of Altruism: Demographic, Personality Traits, and Disorders Associated with Altruism. *Journal of Business Ethics, 134*(3), 359-368.

Glomb, T., Bhave, D. P., Miner, A. G., & Wall., M. (2011). Doing good, feeling good: examining the role of organizational citizenship behaviors in changing mood. *Personnel Psychology, 64*, 191-223.

Grant, A. M. (2008). Does Intrinsic Motivation Fuel the Prosocial Fire? Motivational Synergy in Predicting Persistence, Performance, and Productivity. *Journal of Applied Psychology, 93*(1), 48-58.

Grant, A. M., & Berry, J. W. (2011). The necessity of others is the mother of invention: Intrinsic and prosocial motivations, perspective taking, and creativity. *academy of Management Journal, 54*(1), 73-96.

Grant, A. M., Campbell, E. M., Chen, G., Cottone, K., Lapedis, D., & Lee, K. (2007). Impact and the art of motivation maintenance: The effects of contact with beneficiaries on persistence behavior. *Organizational Behavior and Human Decision Processes, 103*, 53-67.

Grant, A. M., & Parker, S. (2009). Redesigning work design theories: The Rise of relational and proactive perspectives. *The Academy of Management Annals, 31*(1), 317-375.

Grant, A. M., Parker, S., & Collins, C. (2009). Getting credit for proactive behavior: supervisor reactions depend onwhat you value and how do you feel. *Personnel Psychology, 62,* 31-55.

Grant, A. M., & Patil, S. V. (2012). Challenging the norm of self-interest: Minority influence and transitions to helping norms in work units. *Academy of Management Review, 37*(4), 547-568.

Grant, A. M., & Sumanth, J. J. (2009). Mission Possible? The Performance of Prosocially Motivated Employees Depends on Manager Trustworthiness. *Journal of Applied Psychology, 94*(4), 927-944.

Guinot, J., Chiva, R., & Mallén, F. (2015). The effects of altruism and relationship conflict on organizational learning. *International Journal of Conflict Management, 26*(1), 85-112.

Halbesleben, J. B., Bowler, W. M., Bolino, M. C., & Turnley, W. H. (2010). Organizational concern, prosocial values, or impression management? How supervisors attribute motives to organizational citizenship behavior. *Journal of Applied Psychology, 40,* 1450-1489.

Haynes, K. T., Josefy, M., & Hitt, M. A. (2015). Tipping Point: Managers' Self-Interest, Greed, and Altruism. *Journal of Leadership & Organizational Studies, 22*(3), 265-279.

Heilman, M. E., & Chen, J. J. (2005). Same behavior, different consequences: reactions to men's and women's altruistic citizenship behavior. *J Appl Psychol, 90*(3), 431-441. doi: 10.1037/0021-9010.90.3.431

Hu, J., & Liden, R. C. (2015). Making a difference in the teamwork: linking team prosocial motivation to team processes and effectiveness. *academy of Management Journal, 57*(4), 1102-1127.

Hui, C., Lam, S., & Law, K. (2000). Instrumental values of organizational citizenship behavior for promotion: A field quasi-experiment. *Journal of Applied Psychology, 85,* 822-828.

Kahneman, D., & Frederick, S. (2002). Representativeness revisited: Attribute substitution in intuitive judgment. In T. Gilovich, D. Griffin & D. Kahneman (Eds.). *Heuristics and biases: The psychology of intuitive judgment* New York: Cambridge University Press.

Kanungo, R. N., & Conger, J. A. (1993). Promoting altruism as a corporate goal. *Academy of Management Perspectives, 7*(3), 37-48.

Katz, D., & Kahn, R. L. (1966). *The social psychology of organizations.* New York: Wiley.

Kim, Y. J., Van Dyne, L., Kamdar, D., & Johnson, R. E. (2013). Why and when do motives matter? An integrative model of motives, role cognitions, and social support as predictors of OCB. *Organizational Behavior and Human Decision Processes, 121,* 231-245.

Kinnunen, S. P., & Windmann, S. (2013). Dual-processing altruism. *Frontiers in Psychology, 4*(193), 1-9.

Korsgaard, M. A., Meglino, B. M., & Lester, S. W. (1997). Beyond helping: Do other-oriented values have broader implications in organizations? *Journal of Applied Psychology, 82,* 160-177.

Lai, J. Y., Lam, L. W., & Lam, S. S. (2013). Organizational citizenship behavior in work groups: A team cultural perspective. *Journal of Organizational Behavior, 34,* 1039-1056.

Lapierre, L. M., & Hackett, R. D. (2007). Trait conscientiousness, leader-member exchange, job satisfaction and organizational citizenship behavior: A test of an integrative model. *Journal of Occupational and Organizational Psychology, 80,* 539-554.

Lemmon, G., & Wayne, S. J. (2015). Underlying Motives of Organizational Citizenship Behavior: Comparing Egoistic and Altruistic Motivations. *Journal of Leadership & Organizational Studies, 22*(2), 129-148.

Lemoine, G. J., Parsons, C. K., & Kansara, S. (2015). Above and beyond, again and again: Self-regulation in the aftermath of organizational citizenship behaviors. *Journal of Applied Psychology, 100*(1), 40-55.

Li, N., Kirkman, B., & Porter, C. (2014). Toward a model of work team altruism. *Academy of Management Review, published ahead of print March 25, 2014.*

Loi, R., Ngo, H.-Y., Zhang, L., & Lau, V. P. (2011). The interaction between leader-member exchange and perceived job security in predicting employee altruism and work performance. *Journal of Occupational and Organizational Psychology, 84*(4), 669-685. doi: 10.1348/096317910x510468

Meglino, B. M., & Korsgaard, M. A. (2004). Considering Rational Self-Interest as a Disposition: Organizational Implications of Other Orientation. *Journal of Applied Psychology, 89*(6), 946-959.

Moon, H., Kamdar, D., Mayer, D. M., & Takeuchi, R. (2008). Me or we? The role of personality and justice as other-centered antecedents to innovative citizenship behaviors within organizations. *Journal of Applied Psychology, 93,* 84-94.

O'Donoghue, T., & Rabin, M. (1999). Doing It Now or Doing It Later. *The American Economic Review, 89*(1), 103-121.

Oakley, B., Knafo, A., Madhavan, G., & Wilson, D. S. (2012). *Pathological Altruism.* USA: Oxford University Press.

Oliner, S. (2002). Extraordinary acts of ordinary people: Faces of heroism and altruism. In P.S., U. L., S. J. & H. W. (Eds.). *Altruism and altruistic love: Science, philosophy and religion in dialogue.* (pp. 123–139). New York: Oxford University Press.

Organ, D. W. (1988). *Organizational citizenship behavior: The good soldier syndrome.* Lexington: Lexington Books.

Organ, D. W., Podsakoff, P.M., & MacKenzie, S. B. (2006). *Organizational citizenship behavior: Its nature, antecedents and consequences.* Thousand Oaks: Sage.

Organ, D. W., & Ryan, M. (1995). A meta-analytic review of attitudinal and dispositional predictors of organizational citizenship behavior. *Personnel Psychology, 48,* 775-802.

Parker, S., & Collins, C. G. (2010). Taking Stock: Integrating and Differentiating Multiple Proactive Behaviors. *Journal of Management, 36*(3), 633-662.

Parker, S., Williams, H. M., & Turner, N. (2006). Modeling the Antecedents of Proactive Behavior at Work. *Journal of Applied Psychology, 91*(3), 636-652.

Podsakoff, N. P., Blume, B. D., Whiting, S. W., & Podsakoff, P.M. (2009). Individual- and organizational-level consequences of organizational citizenship behaviors: A meta-analysis. *Journal of Applied Psychology, 94,* 122-141.

Rand, D. G., Greene, J. D., & Nowak, M. A. (2012). Spontaneous giving and calculated greed. *Nature, 489,* 427-430.

Rank, J., Carsten, J. M., Unger, J. M., & Spector, P.E. (2007). Proactive customer service performance: Relationships with individual, task, and leadership variables. *Human Performance, 20,* 363-390.

Rioux, S. M., & Penner, L. A. (2001). The causes of organizational citizenship behavior: A motivational analysis. *Journal of Applied Psychology, 86*(6), 1306-1314.

Schroeder, D. A., Penner, L. A., Dovidio, J. F., & Piliavin, J. A. (1995). *The Psychology of Helping and Altruism.* New York: McGraw-Hill.

Sibicky, M. E., Schroeder, D. A., & Dovidio, J. F. (1995). Empathy and helping: Considering the consequences of intervention. *Basic and Applied Social Psychology, 16,* 435-453.

Smith, C. A., Organ, D. W., & Near, J. P. (1983). Organizational citizenship behavior: Its nature and antecedents. *Journal of Applied Psychology, 68,* 655–663.

Snell, R. S., & Wong, Y. L. (2007). Differentiating Good Soldiers from Good Actors. *Journal of Management Studies, 44*(6), 883-909.

Sober, E. (2002). The ABCs of altruism. In S. G. Post, L. G. Underwood, J. P.Schloss & W. B. Hurlbut (Eds.). *Altruism & Altruistic love : science, philosophy, & religion in dialogue* (pp. 17-28). Oxford: Oxford Univeristy Press.

Soman, D., Ainslie, G., Frederick, C., Li, X., Lynch, J., Moreau, P., Zauberman, G. (2005). The Psychology of Intertemporal Discounting: Why are Distant Events Valued Differently from Proximal Ones? *Marketing Letters, 16*(3), 347-360.

Sosik, J. J., Jung, D., & Dinger, S. L. (2009). Values in Authentic Action Examining the Roots and Rewards of Altruistic Leadership. *Group & Organization Management, 34*(4), 395-431.

Spitzmuller, M., & Van Dyne, L. (2013). Proactive and reactive helping: Contrasting the positive consequences of different forms of helping. *Journal of Organizational Behavior, 34*(4), 560-580. doi: 10.1002/job.1848

Szulc, J. M., Clarkson, G. P., & Bown, N. J. (2016). *Organizational Altruism: A Conceptual Review and Call for Parsimony.* Paper presented at the European Academy of Management Paris.

Wagner, S. L., & Rush, M. C. (2000). Altruistic organizational citizenship behavior: Context, disposition, and age. *The Journal of Social Psychology, 140*(3), 379-391.

Wertenbroch, K. (1998). Consumption Self-Control by Rationing Purchase Quantities of Virtue and Vice. *Marketing Science, 17*(4), 317-337.

Wilson, D. S. (2015). *Does Altruism Exist? Culture, Genes, and the Welfare of Others.* London: Yale University Press.

Chapter 5

Quantum Leadership:

Toward ethical Selflessness

Michael A. Piel,
IceBridge Research Institute, USA

Karen Putnam,
School of Advanced Studies, University of Phoenix, USA

Karen K. Johnson,
School of Advanced Studies, University of Phoenix, USA

Introduction

Ethical selflessness in business opens doors to many opportunities to support others first with no expectation of a return. Despite the waves of possibilities that exist to turn away from selfishness to selflessness, many organizations around the world, both governmental (Rodrigues, 2015) and private (Sahu, 2017), suffer from ineffective leadership which has been infected by some variant of corruption, perhaps because leaders fail to recognize the power of ethical selflessness, utilizing the constructs of quantum leadership.

Corruption in organizations has been around for as long as there have been organizations (Slager, 2017). Whether the corruption phenomenon is a humble result of the nature of humanity, that vast discussion is beyond the scope of this chapter. While eliminating every instance of organizational corruption may not be possible, leaders can still make a real and lasting difference in turning the organizational trajectory away from corroding corruption toward a more ethical behavior pattern (Hauser, 2018; Nelson, 2016). That pattern could include ethical selflessness through quantum leadership.

While the multifaceted concept of corruption can be viewed from numerous perspectives (Dion, 2017; Gjalt, 2007), to effectively combat instances of corruption no matter what lens one uses, leaders must promote a viable alternative which provides an equal or better financial, social, and moral value to their organization's individual stakeholders (Fedran, Dobovšek, Ažman, & Bren, 2018; Xie, Qi & Zhu, 2018). Ethical selflessness through quantum leadership is one immunogenic mechanism which has the potential to transform organizational cultures and mitigate the corruption infection (Wódka, 2017). Quantum leadership opens individuals and organizations to the powerful potential of ethical selflessness.

After briefly introducing the concepts and principles of quantum leadership, this chapter leads the reader to exploring the frameworks of corruption and avoiding it through ethical selflessness practiced by quantum leaders. In examining several representative ethical theories (Fieser, 2001), the selflessness construct is described in detail within the context of quantum leadership principles and practices. Further unveiling this leadership dynamic through a range of various philosophical and literary perspectives, the reader can ultimately decide whether to adopt, disregard, or intermit judgment on implementing this leadership approach within their organizations.

The power of selflessness transcends the impotence of selfishness. We stalwartly endorse that any organizational stakeholders currently plagued by corruption would benefit from the ethical selflessness actualized in exercising quantum leadership. The ethical wave of possibilities is unlimited for those organizations and individuals who embrace quantum leadership.

Quantum Leadership

Quantum leadership has been introduced to the world as a new way of seeing the universe as well as understanding ourselves through the constructs of quantum mechanics (Piel, Johnson, & Putnam, 2017). Such diverse fields as computing (Jakubczyk, Majchrowski, & Tralle, 2017), sociology (Kahil & Zaazou, 2016), neuropsychology (Downes, 2016), biology (Arndt, Juffmann, & Vedral, 2009; Koch, 2017), medicine (Stagnaro, 2011), anthropology (Russel, 2013), and archeology (Marshell & Alberti, 2014) have already begun to secure the benefits of this stimulating and exhilarant perspective. Fundamental to applying this paradigm to leadership, four key concepts of quantum mechanics serve as the groundwork: quantum duality, quantum superposition, quantum entanglement, and quantum observation (Piel & Johnson, 2015).

Quantum Duality

First of the quantum concepts is wave-particle duality. A photon has a fascinating attribute of being both a wave and a particle; depending on how the photon is observed determines which behavior is witnessed (Rab et al., 2017).

A similar duality applies to leadership in a variety of ways. The duality of quantum leadership is, for example, reflected in the "leader-follower/follower-leader" dynamic (Piel & Johnson, 2015). As with a photon potentially being either a wave or a particle, persons, participating as leaders and/or followers, are equally engaged in this duality (Piel, Johnson, & Putnam, 2017). Leaders are potentially followers while followers are potentially leaders. Observation actualizes which of these characteristics becomes a reality in this dynamic.

Quantum Superposition

Particles can exist in many physical states. Quantum particles exist in all possible states all at the self-same time (Olijnyk, 2018). This simultaneity dynamic is referred to as quantum superposition. This superposition phenomenon appears to occur at the macroscopic level (Izumi et al., 2018).

From a quantum perspective, the working world that leaders encounter exists in a plethora of possible states. Which of these possible worlds becomes actualized depends on which state is observed. Being able to see all these potential possibilities is a hallmark of quantum leadership. A quantum leader understands that this level of visibility to what is possible only arises in an environment which acknowledges the interconnectedness and interdependency of the followers. Quantum leaders use this wider lens to see the world.

Quantum Entanglement

Quantum entanglement is the attribute of two non-local particles acting as if interconnected with each other (Amorim, 2018; Choi, Deng, Laurat, & Kimble, 2008). Einstein referred to this astonishing intertwining as *spooky-action* at a distance (Novak, 2017; Rios, 2016). Changing one particle instantaneously changes another distant particle, regardless of the distance between them (Wasak, Smerzi, & Chwedeńczuk, 2018). Multiple researchers (Dimić & Dakić, 2018; Kaufman et al., 2015; Zarkeshian et al., 2017) have shown through varying mechanisms and experiments the reality of non-local quantum entanglement.

In an ever increasingly complex landscape punctuated by the unexpected and seemingly impossible, no one person has a complete lens for understanding the whole evolving path.

For a quantum leader, awareness of this fundamental environment promotes a self-deepening sensitivity to the reality of entanglement and the necessity for engagement of the other. The other becomes the stimulus for together seeing and opening new possibilities. The quantum leader is aware of and appreciates the importance of selflessness in this collaborative entanglement.

Quantum Observation

The Heisenberg uncertainty principle postulates that one can know either where a particle is or how fast the particle is moving, but not both speed and location at the same time (Benítez Rodrìguez & Arévalo Aguilar, 2018). One must conclude that our knowledge of particles is fundamentally limited. To exacerbate this restraining conundrum, in the quantum world particles exist only as mere possibilities (Brumfiel, 2012). *Schrödinger's cat* metaphor, regarding whether a cat in a box is dead or alive, highlights the phenomenon that actuality occurs only through and in observation (Raghavan, 2018).

To account for the experiences of our world, physicists refer to the concept of decoherence (Tanona, 2013). Decoherence refers to the concept that everything in the universe is interconnected and entangled (Benítez Rodrìguez & Arévalo Aguilar, 2018; Raghavan, 2018). While environmental decoherence is still debated among researchers, in decoherence one observation alone would be sufficient to actualize all experiential reality.

Duality, superposition, and entanglement are coordinately consolidated through observation. Quantum leaders are keenly mindful that our shared reality is created not by oneself but through and with others (Piel & Johnson, 2015). Of all possible worlds that can exist, the one world that exists is the shared world created through the collaboration with others.

Collapsing the Wave Function

Quantum leadership behavior collapses the wave function of possibilities. These possibilities cover the complete range of all organizational activities. Although one can frame these behaviors in the context of several leadership attributes (see Figure 5.1), quantum leadership is foremost and primarily a philosophical perspective influencing every encounter, activity, and decision.

Figure 5.1. Quantum Leadership.

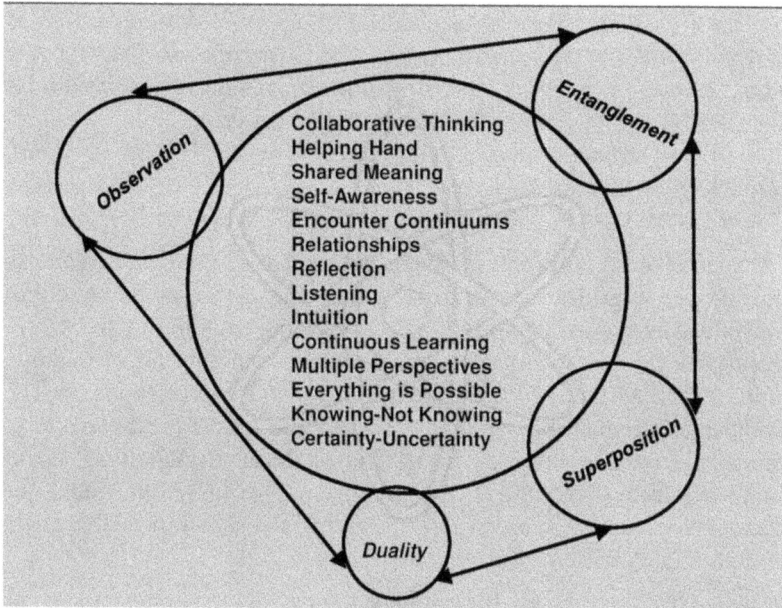

In every listed behavioral characteristic and attribute of quantum leaders there exists one central underlying and defining constituent. That grounding factor is the significance of the other in the overall dynamic. Quantum leadership is not actually about the leader at all. Since the other is what makes a leader a quantum leader, selflessness of the leader is at the heart of quantum leadership. As such, quantum leadership is a way of being, a philosophical perspective founded on the importance of the other in all organizational encounters. One is a leader not because of what they do, but rather one is a leader precisely because of what one becomes in being with others.

Quantum leadership itself becomes a reality when leaders selflessly encounter followers and followers selflessly encounter leaders. In that in-between space of authentic encountering relationships (Buber, 1937/1970), the magic and wonder of leadership emerges to collapse the wave function of possibilities. Business leaders who study and adopt the theory of quantum leadership, with ethical selflessness at its core, may find that corruption becomes less likely in their organizations.

Corruption

Corruption has many faces, causes, and effects and is equally unconstrained and unimpeded by any specific professions or occupations (Li, Gong, & Xiao, 2016). As a result, defining the corruption phenomenon is considerably complex (Dion, 2010; Dixit, 2018; Hauser, 2018). Nevertheless, due to the negative impacts on numerous human activity domains, combating corruption, however, defined, is an incontrovertible necessity (Guo & Li, 2015).

Organizational corruption can be categorized as emerging from sources outside the organization or from within the organization by either individuals or groups (Voliotis, 2017). The overall costs to the public and businesses from this contagion is widespread and substantial (Huong, Tran, Tuan, & Lim, 2018; Schlenther, 2017; Tjen, & Evans, 2017). Companies around the world are fighting back with anti-corruption campaigns totaling upwards to billions of dollars (USD) (COE, 2014; Sampson, 2010; UNDP, 2017). The negative impact on an individual's or business's reputation is even more staggering and significant (UN Global Compact, 2015; Wisler, 2018).

Dion (2017) explored the understanding of the phenomena of corruption at three historical periods from an effects-based and a cause-based perspective. Each historical period drifted to one or the other perspective based on a variety of factors. According to Dion (2017), our current historical time drifts to a cause-based view. Deciding what is the cause of corruption is as difficult as deciding what to do about the effects. Irrespective of which perspective is espoused, establishing a common understanding of corruption is decisive to its elimination and mitigation. In the realm of organizational related corruption, leaders and followers may not be harmonized in their perspectives or understanding of the corruption challenge (Dion, 2017). Li, Gong, & Xiao (2016) stated that alongside combating corruption, those authentic efforts must equally be effective.

To be effective in combating the symptoms of corruption, one must be focused on eliminating the root cause of corruption. Dion (2010) provided a conceptual architecture framing corruption as consisting of five distinct levels: principles, moral behaviors, people, organizations, and states. Whether corruption at any of these levels is done for reasons of organizational or personal gain, there is strong evidence to consider selfishness as one of the primary root causes of each.

While a leader's selfishness can damagingly infect an entire organization, a leader can mitigate the infection by authentically communicating gratitude (Ritzenhöfer, Spörrle, & Welpe, 2017). Xu, Su, Han, Fang, Xu, & Gan (2016) framed selfishness in a twofold manner: weak, and extreme. In either framing, cooperative participation, critical to organizational survival, was negatively obstructed. Paradoxically, Bravetti & Padilla (2018) research showed that individual competition benefits by selfishness and that selfishness itself promotes individual cooperation. However, one can reasonably and logically argue that selfishness initiated individual cooperation does not equal selfless initiated cooperative participation.

Corruption can be regarded as a leadership challenge (Kong & Volkema, 2016). Intrinsically, the leader-follower dynamic takes center stage when attempting to both understand and then effectively combat organizational corruption. Kong and Volkema (2016) provided strong evidence in their research study that self-serving leadership increases corruption. As an unethical behavior, self-serving leadership degrades organizations (Peng, Wang, & Chen, 2018). To eliminate or mitigate organizational corruption, leaders should avoid adopting self-serving leadership perspectives.

Corruption is a surprisingly human unique behavior which has an infectious magnitude. Whether considering individuals, or groups, or organizations, the dynamics of corruption at the nethermost and rudimentary level can be framed in the context of selfishness. In some form or another, the lowest denominator of any form of corruption is selfishness, which is the opposite of the selflessness practiced by the quantum leader.

Selflessness

In discussing selflessness, one is catapulted, or perhaps more precisely, constrained by a framework delineated by one's own individual understanding of the constructs of self and consciousness. Consciousness is the lynchpin in how one interprets self (Chalmers, 1996; Van Gulick, 2014). Unfortunately, since these concepts are philosophically rich, we limit ourselves in this chapter to merely accepting that selflessness is a concept with very wide-ranging dimensions and therefore use a precise and rather restricted definition.

Selflessness is a perspective and state of being that is outward looking. In selflessness, concern for the other is the imperative and principle concern (Sharp, 1994; Wrenn, 1990). When the other becomes more important to one than oneself, the self becomes more one with itself; the one instantly transcends oneself. In looking outwards, one becomes connected with others, and in so doing one's own self-transcendence unfolds exponentially magnified. Self-actualization is the process by which one moves from self-centeredness (selfishness) to selflessness (D'Souza & Gurin, 2016). Self-actualization progresses toward an enduring state of self-transcendence (Maslow, 1973; Maslow, 2014).

Self-awareness, as a component of self-consciousnesses, is a type of cognition. Morgan (2018) promoted a perspective which expands cognition beyond the confines behind our glasses encompassing the totality of the body envelope and environment. In this type of conceptual expansion, self-transcendence takes on a wider dimension. The concept of selflessness must be considered in an equally expanded scope.

Since selflessness is outward looking, self-awareness and self-consciousness as the foundations of selflessness should also have their borders extended outwards. Self-awareness must depend to an even higher degree on awareness of the other and their environment. Self-consciousness depends to an even higher degree on an awareness of the consciousness of the other and their environment. Self-awareness becomes an awareness of the other. In effect, the other defines one's own realization of selflessness. Without the other, there is no ethical selflessness.

Ethics

According to Aristotle, ethics is about human behavior and good conduct while being with others (Burger, 2008). Since selflessness and its foundations are about the other, grounding selfless activities on a strong ethical position is critical to being successful in authentically being selfless. From a leadership perspective, in combating variant forms of selfishness originated or instigated corruption, promoting a selflessness value and culture becomes an overall organizational success factor. Both leader and follower behaviors are of concern to leaders wishing to act ethically (O'Keefe, Messervey, & Squires, 2018).

There is something about being human which pushes to the surface of our daily lives the pressure to consider the ethical dimension of our activities and decisions (Hartman, 2005). Over the centuries various civilizations have addressed this urge and codified numerous responses (Fieser, 2001). Philosophers consider the study of ethics from three distinct categories: metaethics focuses on meaning; normative ethics focuses on right and wrong; and applied ethics focuses on answering specific ethical questions (Beebe & Sackris, 2016). Any evaluation of the relationships between ethical selflessness and quantum leadership should emerge from a shared contextual understanding unfolding from a few representatives of these well-established theoretical categorizations. In this spirit, five common ethical perspectives are offered: cultural relativism, moral objectivism, virtue theory, natural law theory, and utilitarianism.

Cultural Relativism

In adopting the cultural relativism perspective, one accepts that society determines what is ethical behavior (Brandt, 1967; Fieser, 2001). While there are variants to this perspective, each relativistic outlook frames good conduct with others in accordance with a set of socially accepted behaviors (Tännsjö, 2007). Correct moral behavior varies according to the specific location, time, and environmental situation (McDonald, 2010). These socially accepted ethical behaviors are not grounded in any type of objective reality but rather in an everchanging social perspective (Häyry, 2005). Demuijnck (2015) highlighted how cultural relativism seems to be the default ethical posture that most people generally accept.

Determining if a hypothetical action X is ethical in cultural relativism is exclusively determined by the social conventions in force at the time and place of the action (Hartman, 2005). Whether action X is an instance of corruption is correspondingly determined by that same social convention. What is ethical in one society or culture may be unethical in another society or culture (McDonald, 2010).

If societal beliefs determine ethical behavior, and if the "other" determines societal beliefs, then ethical behavior is determined by the other. The quantum leadership perspective essentially transcends any limiting social and cultural relativism. In understanding the entanglement, superposition, and duality of the other, the quantum leader in promoting ethical selflessness responds to any hypothetical action X from a philosophical perspective of other-centeredness

Moral Objectivism

In adopting the moral objectivism perspective, one would accept that an objective foundation determines what is ethical behavior (Harrison, 1976; Fieser, 2001). The Greek philosopher Plato held that moral values are eternal non-physical forms residing in the real world of ideas and one should pursue and adapt to these values (Häyry, 2005). What is ethical is based on objective unalterable facts and applicable to all regardless of culture (Beebe & Sackris, 2016; Theriault, Waytz, Heiphetz, & Young, 2017). While management researchers have cautiously avoided the concept of an absolute right or wrong, a belief in moral objectivity shows itself during normal existential experiences where one value is regarded over another (Tae & Donaldson, 2018). From a moral objectivist posture, any ethical disagreements between two individuals yield only one correct answer (Björnsson, 2012). It follows, like Fisher, Knobe, Strickland, & Keil (2017) demonstrated, that social interaction is itself a variable of one's perception of truth.

Within the moral objectivism opinion, moral obligation extends beyond oneself to include others (Rodríguez, 2017). Determining if a hypothetical action X is ethical in moral objectivism is exclusively determined by some immutable objective reality. Quantum leaders are well positioned for the moral objectivism obligation towards others by considering the other's beliefs with equal weight as their own. By promoting selflessness in others, quantum leaders, appreciating superposition and entanglement, can bridge any dividing differences of perceptions of objective reality between the contributors, whether from followers or leader.

Virtue Theory

In adopting the virtue theory perspective, one would accept that ethical behavior is the resulting by-product of the development of virtue (Fieser, 2001). Socrates, Plato, and later Aristotle in the Nicomachean Ethics and the Eudemian Ethics initially described virtue theory (Hursthouse & Pettigrove, 2016). Virtue is a complex philosophical construct with varying definitions and differing categorizations. Most of the evolving virtue theories include a prescriptive set of virtues necessary for moral development (Hughes, 2015).

Virtues promote individual actions which are essentially positive and other-centered (Kotzee, Ignatowicz, & Thomas, 2017; Lail, Macgregor, Marcum & Stuebs, 2017). Cordell (2017) and Arjoon, Turriago-Hoyos, & Thoene (2018) suggested that virtue be considered also in the context of a social group rather than solely as an individual trait.

Determining if a hypothetical action X is ethical in virtue theory is exclusively determined by the virtuousness that is actualized between the leader and the follower. Since the quantum leader is in an interacting and encountering relationship with followers, the virtues of the followers influence the leader as much as the leader's virtues influence the followers. Quantum leaders, understanding duality, appreciate and promote the development of virtue both in themselves and within their followers. This encounter promotes a further self-replicating self-expanding selflessness between leader and followers.

Natural Law Theory

In adopting the natural law theory perspective, one would accept that ethical behavior is an action that is natural (Fieser, 2001). Regrettably, determining what is natural or unnatural is a complicated undergoing resulting in with varying and often opposing opinions (Danto, 1965). Because of this inherent complexity, natural law theory has morphed into various forms (Wollheim, 1965). The Greek Stoics formulated the perspective on how to live naturally (Pigliucci, 2015). Aristotle, Cicero, Aquinas, St. Thomas, Hume, and other thinkers have contributed to the evolving concepts of natural law theory (Seagrave, 2009). In every instance of numerous natural law theories, a common concern remains that of the individual's natural predispositions and how those distinct inclinations influence others.

Determining if a hypothetical action X is ethical in natural law theory is exclusively determined by whether that action is considered natural. Quantum leaders, from a perspective of duality and superposition, are deeply sensitive and aware of the interrelationship and interconnectedness of leader and follower predispositions regarding what is natural. Consequently, in modeling selflessness and promoting selflessness in others, quantum leaders create selflessness as being natural. It is this naturalness which serves as the basis for ethical behavior.

Utilitarianism

In adopting the utilitarianism perspective, one would accept that ethical behavior is that behavior which does the greatest good for the greatest number of people (Graham, 2017; Fieser, 2001; Smart, 1967). Epicurus, Jeremy Bentham, and John Stuart Mill among others have each provided differing perspectives on the nature, context, and practice of utilitarian behavior (Lindebaum & Raftopoulou, 2017). As a coherent normative ethics theory, utilitarianism has evolved considerably over time and has diverged into multiple tremendously influential models. Most significant in these various perspectives is the idea that maximizing good involves the good of both oneself and of the other (Driver, 2014).

Determining if a hypothetical action X is ethical in utilitarianism is exclusively determined by whether that action is encouraging the greatest good for oneself and for others. Quantum leaders, sensitive to the entanglement between leaders and followers, as well as between each follower, understand that promoting selflessness creates a collective backdrop for encouraging a shared understanding of the greatest good for the greatest number of receivers.

Philosophy

Leadership styles, behaviors, habits, beliefs, values, and predilections are predominantly grounded in one's evolving philosophical perspective. To understand and appreciate another's outlook on leadership is not without significant challenge. Subsequently, by framing the quantum leadership perspective through several philosophical filters, one is opened to the possibilities of seeing this innovative approach as exercised by quantum leaders. Five philosophical filters are presented, as rudimentary lenses, in which to view quantum leadership and ethical selflessness: phenomenological, hermeneutic, existential, ontological, and epistemological.

Phenomenological Filter

Phenomenology is the study of the structures of consciousness and subjective experience (Schmitt, 1967; Smith, 2013). Reflecting on conscious experience is an insightful and rewarding but byzantine endeavor. Husserl, Hegel, Kant, and many other philosophers present substantial variances in their framing of phenomenology (Rockmore, 2017). The phenomenological filter is not an isolated lens but rather one component of a larger integrated set of lenses. Husserl, Heidegger, Sartre, Merleau-Ponty, Derrida, and other philosophers envisioned phenomenology in the context of their overall philosophical system (Cromwell, 2012). Common in all variants of phenomenology is the *phenomenological epochē*. In this conscious bracketing of *noumena* (things in themselves), one focuses on the personal experience of the *phenomena* which is what appears to the subject, rather than an emphasis on the essence of the specific object itself (Curran & Kearney, 2012).

By means of a phenomenological filter, the quantum leadership experience appears as an encounter event between the leader and a follower. Owing to the superposition and entanglement features, the meaning of the subjective experience of this quantum leadership encounter is intercalated with the subjective experience of the follower. This same dynamic equally applies to the follower's experience. Using this same filter, the selflessness experience unfolds as a reflecting mirror between the leader and follower. Each participant's consciousness of selflessness in this quantum dynamic increases the intensity and probability of further selflessness experiences. A closer look at each of the filters is in order.

Hermeneutic Filter

Hermeneutic as the methodology and the art of interpretation is an omnipresent and universal activity influencing all experiences (Mantzavinos, 2016). The concept of the hermeneutic circle refers to the circular flow of influencing interpretations between items; X influences Y while Y simultaneously influences X (Mackinlay, 2017). One language fragment is only fully understood in the context of all the other interconnected and interrelated parts (Davidson, 2001; Sarup, 1993). In this continuously ongoing hermeneutic circle, an everchanging interpretation, and as a result ever-evolving understanding, is never terminal (Cunningham, 2017; Malpas, 2016). While two individuals can read the same text, the understanding of each reader remains utterly unique (Saramifar, 2017). In this Aesopian hermeneutic circle, the past influences the future as much as the future influences the past.

By means of a hermeneutic filter, the interpretation and meaning of a communication for quantum leadership resides in the circular *in-between* space of the interminable dialogue of the leader and follower. Due to quantum duality, the result of quantum leadership communication remains both the interpretation of the follower as well as the interpretation of the leader. Both these possible interpretations fuse into the actual embryonic meaning emerging in the in-between space. Using this same filter, the meaning of selflessness continually evolves over time being fed by the merged interpretations of both the leader and follower. As awareness of selflessness upsurges, actual instances of selflessness increase.

Existential Filter

Existentialism is a branch of continental philosophy focusing on authentic human existence rather than on objective essences (Crowell, 2015; Luper, 2000). Covering the vast expanse of human activities, encounters, and interactions, existential philosophies introspectively resist being unequivocally categorized (MacIntyre, 1967a). Nevertheless, a common emphasis among the existentialists is in discovering the meaning of various individual experiences (Heimbach, 2017). Heidegger, Buber, Marcel, and other philosophers considered human existence as co-existence with others (Piel, Johnson, & Putnam, 2017). Relational quantum mechanics states that all physical systems are interrelated (Laudisa & Rovelli, 2008). Individual experiences are existentially interconnected with others. To find meaning one must engage with, and ultimately learn from, others.

By means of an existential filter, quantum leadership recognizes the importance and significance of authentic co-existence. Due to duality, entanglement, and superposition, authentic co-existence is never experienced alone. All experiences of leadership experiences occur co-simultaneously with accompanying followers' experiences. A quantum leader cannot truly lead without the engagement of others. In engaging with others, quantum leaders learn from the experiences of others and together create shared meaning. Using this same filter, the selflessness experience is only possible in co-existence. Since all experiences are interconnected in a co-existence web, the selflessness of a quantum leader both facilitates and encourages the selflessness experiences of the followers.

Ontological Filter

Ontology is the study of being, on what exists; not surprisingly, determining what questions to ask about being is itself a question given the wide variety of philosophic conceptions on this topic (Hofweber, 2017; MacIntyre, 1967b). The question of *what is being* has roots in the earliest civilizations and has continued throughout human history. A recent philosophical trajectory has been toward social ontology, the study of social entities emerging from societal encounters (Epstein, 2018). Heidegger considers human existence as *Dasein*, that is, being-in-the-world (Paul, 2017). In our world, we are always with others (Bechtol, 2018). In being with others, *Dasein* is concerned about the being of others (Murchadha, 2018).

By means of an ontological filter, quantum leadership manifests itself as a concern of others. Understanding that the world is the backdrop for all social activities, quantum leaders understand that the entire world is entangled, superposed, and dual in nature. As such, concern for others is a concern for all others and all possible others. Quantum leaders, in caring for others, promote caring for others in others. Using this same filter, the quantum leader's selflessness is rooted in the ontological concern for all others. Selflessness becomes a mode of being for the quantum leader. In caring for others, others become promoters of selflessness and caring for others.

Epistemological Filter

Epistemology is the study of knowledge and encompasses a wide range of areas including definitions, structures, and parameters (Hamlyn, 1965; Steup, 2005). While epistemologists diverge in their focus and conclusions, they are intensely interested in being able to firmly confirm the truth of our knowledge. Verifying the validity of what is known has become an increasing concern today being challenged by the increasing phenomena of fake news and alternative facts (Baird & Calvard, 2018). Knowledge itself, what one knows or does not know, is very often framed, and/or slanted, through various cultural and social paradigms (Naude, 2017). While all knowledge arises from within our shared place and time, one's understanding of that knowledge remains distinctively as per individual self-knowledge.

Using an epistemological filter, quantum leaders understand and acknowledge that what is known is the result of all that has come before. Each individual contribution to the body of knowledge brings with it a set of assumptions, opinions, cultural biases, and perhaps even some mistakes. With understanding and knowledge being entangled and superposed, quantum leaders appreciate, seek out, and consider each individual knowledge contribution as being a valuable addition to the whole. Using this same filter, quantum leaders enrich the understanding of selflessness by acknowledging the selflessness of others. In so doing the acknowledgment and amplified awareness of selflessness actualizes the potential for increases in selflessness occurrences. Literature is an incredible province for facilitating an individual's experiencing of another's perspective.

Literature

The power of literature as pabulum to enhance the understanding of various aspects of leadership is unique and valuable (Badaracco, 2006; Bisoux, 2018). The self-knowledge of leaders and followers can benefit from this inimitable potential. Any perspectives on selflessness, ethics, leadership, or corruption would benefit through addressing the transdisciplinary nature of these interdependent and interconnected constructs. While the world of literature is rich in potential examples to explore, the following instances covering a part of those human experiences serve solely as intriguing initial illustrations to inspire the imagination and create innovative connections to quantum leadership. Readers may want to explore others but these few were selected to provide the backdrop of how quantum leadership, even though the concept itself might not have been known to the author, was demonstrated by the characters discussed here.

Magic Mountain

In the novel *The Magic Mountain* (Mann, 1952/1969), Hans Castorp surprisingly finds himself faced with an unexpected delay in his return to his comfortable engineering lifestyle. Starting as a two-week visit to his sickly cousin recovering at a sanatorium in the high Alps, his holiday visit turns into an intellectually challenging and potentially indefinite stay. During his time in the sanatorium, Hans Castorp slowly adjusts to life in the high Alps. Sharing experiences and perspectives with the various staff and patients at the sanatorium while getting to know them, Hans Castrop starts to see in different ways. When patients were challenged by their health circumstances, Hans Castorp selflessly spent time authentically visiting them.

From a quantum leadership perspective, Hans Castorp showed several key qualities of quantum leadership; continuous learning, considering multiple perspectives, providing a help-hand, and listening. In these several attributes, Hans demonstrates a sophisticated degree of selflessness. Quantum leaders value these same attributes and encourage the same in their followers.

The Cambrian Rod

In the science-fiction novel *The Cambrian Rod* (Jayvee, 2016), a group of university professors decide to make a difference in the world by tackling several of the recent United Nations sustainable development goals for peace, poverty, pollution, and hunger. In their endeavor, each professor finds themselves faced with a myriad of ethical decisions. Given their discovery of a powerful ancient tool, the team reinforces each other's selflessness and through collaborative dialogue eventually decide to continue addressing and pursuing the United Nations goals. The ancient artifact's potential could have been used for limitless personal and self-centered needs and wants, but through the leadership of each professor working selflessly together, a higher ethical collective attitude was realized.

From a quantum leadership perspective, each of the six professors demonstrated several of the qualities associated with quantum leadership. In analyzing the problems and results of their efforts in addressing the UN goals, they showed a perspective that everything is possible. Aware of both the known and unknown, the professors' collaborative thinking consistently created selflessly shared meaning about their proposed resolutions. Quantum leaders demonstrate these same qualities.

Moby-Dick

In the novel *Moby-Dick* (Melville, 1851/1993), Captain Ahab, having previously lost a leg to the white whale Moby Dick, sails this ship Pequod seeking to destroy Moby Dick. His crew even after enduring several calamities at sea still fail to persuade Captain Ahab to change course and abandon his self-centered mission of odium. Ishmael, the story's narrator, highlights the differences between Ahab and Ishmael particularly in how they perceive the world around them. Ishmael is exceptionally open-minded in contrast to the inexorable single-mindedness of the obdurate and hermetic Captain Ahab. The impact of how one sees the world and how that perception impacts others is dreadfully evident in the crews' eventual destruction, save Ishmael, onboard their whaling ship Pequod.

From a quantum leadership perspective, Captain Ahab demonstrated the exact opposite of the qualities required and associated with quantum leadership. Sometimes seeing what something is not, provides surprising insight into what something is. In the case of Captain Ahab, it is easy to frame his behavior as an overly selfish pursuit. Quantum leaders avoid this behavior exhibited by Captain Ahab.

Little Gidding

In the fourth section of the poem *Four Quartets*, the *Little Gidding* (Eliot, 1943/1971), the temporal energy of the quartet provides insight for leaders and followers. The poem frames experience as a circular adventure of unfolding understanding. Only in the context of the end is the beginning truly understood.

From a quantum leadership perspective, intuition and reflection are significant components of effective relationships. Cognizant that understanding is never complete and always evolving, quantum leaders seek out the intuition of others while promoting reflection. In this selfless atmosphere of giving others' understanding equal weight to their own, quantum leaders can see both the end and beginning more clearly.

Siddhartha

In the novel *Siddhartha* (Hesse, 1951/1976), Siddhartha leaves his family in a personal quest for enlightenment. Along his chosen path he meets a beautiful woman, marries her, has a child, and later finds himself personally tormented in being sidetracked from his original self-knowledge pursuit. Siddhartha once again leaves his family in search of illumination by re-engaging in a humbler lifestyle by a river. Siddhartha does eventually reach his enlightenment objective.

From a quantum leadership perspective, quantum leaders value and emulate Siddhartha's traits of self-awareness and reflection. While self-knowledge and self-awareness is an individual pursuit, attainment of these quests occurs paradoxically in the context of and with others. Quantum leaders appreciate that the decisions and actions they make are valuable to others only to the extent that they emerge from an awareness and knowledge of selflessness.

Conclusions

Selflessness is a powerful attribute that has the power to change our world. Quantum leadership is both a way of being and a way of becoming. In modeling, valuing, and promoting selflessness, quantum leaders create a shared world that values the ideas, experiences, expectations, contributions, diversity, knowledge, and cultures of others. Quantum leaders collapse the wave function of selflessness. In so doing a common vision, a shared knowledge, a humane harmony, and a compelling narrative unfolds. In selflessness, corruption's infection is vaccinated.

References

Amorim, C. (2018). Indistinguishability as nonlocality constraint. *Scientific Reports (Nature Publisher Group), 8*, 1-12.

Arjoon, S., Turriago-Hoyos, A., & Thoene, U. (2018). Virtuousness and the common good as a conceptual framework for harmonizing the goals of the individual, organizations, and the economy. *Journal of Business Ethics, 147*(1), 143-163.

Arndt, M., & Juffmann, T., & Vedral, V. (2009). Quantum physics meets biology. *HFSP Journal, 3*(6), 386-400.

Badaracco, Jr., J. L. (2006). *Questions of character: Illuminating the heart of leadership through literature.* Boston: Harvard Business School.

Baird, C., & Calvard, T. S. (2018). Epistemic vices in organizations: Knowledge, truth, and unethical conduct. *Journal of Business Ethics, 1*, 1-14.

Bechtol, H. B. (2018). Event, death, and poetry: The death of the other in Derrida's "Rams." *Philosophy Today, 62*(1), 253-268.

Beebe, J. R., & Sackris, D. (2016). Moral objectivism across the lifespan. *Philosophical Psychology, 29*(6), 912-929.

Benítez Rodrìguez, E. & Arévalo Aguilar, L. M. (2018). Disturbance-disturbance uncertainty relation: The statistical distinguishability of quantum states determines disturbance. *Scientific Reports (Nature Publisher Group), 8*, 1-10.

Bisoux, T. (2018). Educating artful leaders: Founded on the idea that leadership and the arts are interconnected, the Bled School infuses creativity throughout its culture and programs. *Bized, 17*(3), 45-46.

Björnsson, G. (2012). Do 'Objectivist' Features of Moral Discourse and Thinking Support Moral Objectivism? *Journal of Ethics, 16*(4), 367-393.

Brandt, R. B. (1967). Ethical relativism. In P.Edwards (Ed.). *The Encyclopedia of Philosophy.* (Vol. 3, pp. 75-78). London: Collier Macmillan.

Bravetti, A., & Padilla, P. (2018). An optimal strategy to solve the Prisoner's dilemma. *Scientific Reports (Nature Publisher Group), 8,* 1-6.

Brumfiel, G. (2012). Physics Nobel for quantum optics. *Nature, 490*(7419), 152.

Buber, M. (1937/1970). *I and thou* (W. Kaufmann, Trans.). New York, NY: Charles Scribner's Sons.

Burger, R. (2008). *Aristotle's Dialogue with Socrates: on the Nicomachean Ethics.* Chicago: The University of Chicago Press.

Chalmers, D. (1996). *The Conscious mind.* Oxford: Oxford University Press.

Choi, K. S., Deng, H., Laurat, J., & Kimble, H. J. (2008). Mapping photonic entanglement into and out of a quantum memory. *Nature, 452*(7183), 67-71.

Cordell, S. (2017). Group virtues: No great leap forward with collectivism. *Res Publica, 23*(1), 43-59.

Council of Europe (COE). (2017). Project on controlling corruption through law enforcement and prevention (CLEP). *Action against economic crime and corruption.* Retrieved from https://www.coe.int/en/web/corruption/projects/clep

Crowell, S. (2012). The last best hope. *Continental Philosophy Review, 45*(2), 311-324.

Crowell, S. (2015). Existentialism. In E.N. Zalta (Ed.). *The Stanford Encyclopedia of Philosophy* (Winter 2017 ed.). Retrieved from https://plato.stanford.edu/archives/win2017/entries/existentialism/

Cunningham, J. (2017). Unsound method: Gadamer's hermeneutics and Heart of Darkness. *Papers on Language and Literature, 53*(1), 32-54,98.

Curran, K., & Kearney, J. (2012). Introduction. *Criticism, 54*(3), 353-364.

D'Souza, J., & Gurin, M. (2016). The universal significance of Maslow's concept of self-actualization. *The Humanistic Psychologist, 44*(2), 210-214.

Danto, A. C. (1967). Naturalism. In P.Edwards (Ed.). *The Encyclopedia of Philosophy.* (Vol. 5, pp. 448-450). London: Collier Macmillan.

Davidson, D. (2001). *Inquiries into truth and interpretation* (2nd ed.). Oxford; Oxford Press.

Demuijnck, G. (2015). Universal values and virtues in management versus cross-cultural moral relativism: An educational strategy to clear the ground for business ethics. *Journal of Business Ethics, 128*(4), 817-835.

Dion, M. (2010). What is corruption corrupting? A philosophical viewpoint. *Journal of Money Laundering Control, 13*(1), 45-54.

Dion, M. (2017). Philosophical connections between the classical and the modern notion of corruption: From the Enlightenment to post-modernity. *Journal of Financial Crime, 24*(1), 82-100.

Dimić, A., & Dakić, B. (2018). Single-copy entanglement detection. *NPJ Quantum Information, 4,* 1-8.

Dixit, A. (2018). Anti-corruption institutions: Some history and theory. In K. Basu, & T. Cordella (Eds.). *Institutions, Governance, and the Control of Corruption.* International Economic Association Series: Palgrave Macmillan, Cham

Downes, P. (2016). Concentric and diametric spatial structures of relation: Exploring a neutral bridge language between quantum physics and neuropsychology. *NeuroQuantology, 14*(3), 619-629.

Driver, J., (2014). The History of Utilitarianism. In E.N. Zalta (Ed.). *The Stanford Encyclopedia of Philosophy* (Winter 2014 ed.). Retrieved from https://plato.stanford.edu/archives/win2014/entries/utilitarianism-history/

Eliot, T. S. (1943/1971). *The Complete Poems and Plays.* New York: Hartcourt.

Epstein, B. (2018). Social Ontology, In E.N. Zalta (Ed.). *The Stanford Encyclopedia of Philosophy* (Summer 2018 ed.). Retrieved from https://plato.stanford.edu/entries/social-ontology/

Fisher, M., Knobe, J., Strickland, B., & Keil, F. C. (2017). The influence of social interaction on intuitions of objectivity and subjectivity. *Cognitive Science, 41*(4), 1119-11134.

Fedran, J., Dobovšek, B., Ažman, B., & Bren, M. (2018). Integrity plan: A useful measure for curbing corruption at national and local level. *Lex Localis, 16*(1), 167-191.

Fieser, J. (2001). *Moral philosophy through the ages.* London: Mayfield.

Gjalt, D. G. (2007). Causes of corruption: Towards a contextual theory of corruption. *Public Administration Quarterly, 31*(1), 39-86.

Graham, D. W. (2017). Socrates as a deontologist. *The Review of Metaphysics, 71*(1), 25-43.

Guo, Y., & Li, S. (2015). Anti-corruption measures in china: Suggestions for reforms. *Asian Education and Development Studies, 4*(1), 7-23.

Hamlyn, D. W. (1967). Epistemology. In P.Edwards (Ed.). *The Encyclopedia of Philosophy.* (Vol. 3, pp. 8-38). London: Collier Macmillan.

Harrison, J. (1967). Ethical objectivism. In P.Edwards (Ed.). *The Encyclopedia of Philosophy.* (Vol. 3, pp. 71-74). London: Collier Macmillan.

Hartman, L. P. (2005). *Perspectives in business ethics* (3rd ed.). New York: McGraw-Hill.

Hauser, C. (2018). Fighting against corruption: Does anti-corruption training make any difference?. *Journal of Business Ethics, 1*(1), 1-19.

Häyry, M. (2005). A defense of ethical relativism. *Cambridge Quarterly of Healthcare Ethics, 14*(1), 7-12.

Heimbach, D. (2017). The trinitarian nature of biblical bioethics: A theological corrective to Frame's philosophical paradigm. *Ethics & Medicine, 33*(3), 171.

Hesse, H. (1951/1976). *Siddhartha.* (H. Rosner, Trans.). New York: Bantam Books.

Hofweber, T. (2017). Logic and Ontology. In E.N. Zalta (Ed.). *The Stanford Encyclopedia of Philosophy* (Summer 2018 ed.). Retrieved from https://plato.stanford.edu/entries/logic-ontology/

Hughes, J. J. (2015). Moral enhancement requires multiple virtues. *Cambridge Quarterly of Healthcare Ethics, 24*(1), 86-95.

Huong, V. V., Tran, T. Q., Tuan, V. N., & Lim, S. (2018). Corruption, types of corruption and firm financial performance: New evidence from a transitional economy. *Journal of Business Ethics, 148*(4), 847-858.

Hursthouse, R., & Pettigrove, G. (2016). Virtue Ethics. In E.N. Zalta (Ed.). *The Stanford Encyclopedia of Philosophy* (Winter 2016 ed.). Retrieved from https://plato.stanford.edu/archives/win2016/entries/ethics-virtue/

Izumi, S., Takeoka, M., Wakui, K., Fujiwara, M., Ema, K., & Sasaki, M. (2018). Projective measurement onto arbitrary superposition of weak coherent state bases. *Scientific Reports (Nature Publisher Group)*, 8, 1-8.

Jakubczyk, P., Majchrowski, K., & Tralle, I. (2017). Quantum entanglement in double quantum systems and Jaynes-Cummings model. *Nanoscale Research Letters, 12*(1), 1-9.

Jayvee, K. Y. (2016). *The Cambrian rod.* Columbus, OH: Gatekeeper Press.

Kahil, M. E., & Zaazou, Z. A. (2016). Applying quantum physics principles in contemporary organizations. *Hyperion International Journal of Econophysics & New Economy, 9*(2), 151-171.

Kaufman, A. M., Lester, B. J., Foss-Feig, M., Wall, M. L., Rey, A. M., & Regal, C. A. (2015). Entangling two transportable neutral atoms via local spin exchange. *Nature, 527*(7577), 208-211C.

Koch, H. J. (2017). Quantum biology: Unit membrane reduces entropy due to wave particle duality. *NeuroQuantology, 15*(1).

Kong, D. T., & Volkema, R. (2016). Cultural endorsement of broad leadership prototypes and wealth as predictors of corruption. *Social Indicators Research, 127*(1), 139-152.

Kotzee, B., Ignatowicz, A., & Thomas, H. (2017). Virtue in medical practice: An exploratory study. *HEC Forum, 29*(1), 1-19.

Lail, B., Macgregor, J., Marcum, J., & Stuebs, M. (2017). Virtuous professionalism in accountants to avoid fraud and to restore financial reporting. *Journal of Business Ethics, 140*(4), 687-704.

Laudisa, F., & Rovelli, C. (2008). Relational Quantum Mechanics. In E.N. Zalta (Ed.). The Stanford Encyclopedia of Philosophy (Summer 2013 ed.). Retrieved from https://plato.stanford.edu/archives/sum2013/entries/qm-relational/

Li, H., Gong, T., & Xiao, H. (2016). The perception of anti-corruption efficacy in China: An empirical analysis. *Social Indicators Research, 125*(3), 885-903.

Lindebaum, D., & Raftopoulou, E. (2017). What would John Stuart Mill say? A utilitarian perspective on contemporary neuroscience debates in leadership. *Journal of Business Ethics, 144*(4), 813-822.

Luper, S. (2000). *Existing: An introduction to existential thought.* London: Mayfield Publishing.

MacIntyre, A. (1967a). Existentialism. In P.Edwards (Ed.). *The Encyclopedia of Philosophy*. (Vol. 3, pp. 147-154). London: Collier Macmillan.

MacIntyre, A. (1967b). Ontology. In P.Edwards (Ed.). *The Encyclopedia of Philosophy*. (Vol. 5, pp. 542-543). London: Collier Macmillan.

Mackinlay, S. (2017). Hermeneutic perspectives on ontology, after metaphysics has been overcome: From Levinas to Merleau-Ponty. *Sophia, 56*(1), 115-124.

Malpas, J. (2016). Hans-Georg Gadamer. In E.N. Zalta (Ed.). *The Stanford Encyclopedia of Philosophy* (Winter 2016 ed.). Retrieved from https://plato.stanford.edu/archives/win2016/entries/gadamer/

Mann, T. (1952/1969). *The Magic Mountain*. (H. T. Lowe-Porter, Trans,). New York: Random House.

Mantzavinos, C. (2016). Hermeneutics. In E.N. Zalta (Ed.). *The Stanford Encyclopedia of Philosophy* (Winter 2016 ed.). Retrieved from https://plato.stanford.edu/archives/win2016/entries/hermeneutics/

Marshall, Y., & Alberti, B. (2014). A matter of difference: Karen Barad, ontology, and archaeological bodies. *Cambridge Archaeological Journal, 24*(1), 19-36.

Maslow, A. H. (1973). *The farther reaches of human nature*. Chapel Hill, NC: Maurice Bassett.

Maslow, A. H. (2014). *Toward a psychology of being*. Floyd, VA: Sublime Books

McDonald, G. (2010). Ethical relativism vs absolutism: Research implications. *European Business Review, 22*(4), 446-464.

Melville, H. (1851/1993). *Moby Dick*. London: Wordsworth Editions Limited.

Morgan, D. L. (2018). Skinner, Gibson, and embodied robots: Challenging the orthodoxy of the impoverished stimulus. *Journal of Theoretical and Philosophical Psychology*. Advance online publication. http://dx.doi.org/10.1037/teo0000083

Murchadha, F. Ó. (2018). The passion of grace: Love, beauty, and the theological re-turn. *Philosophy Today, 62*(1), 119-136.

Naude, P. (2017). Decolonising knowledge: Can Ubuntu ethics save us from coloniality? *Journal of Business Ethics, 1*, 1-15.

Nelson, J.S. (2016). The corruption norm. *Journal of Management Inquiry, 26*(3), 280-286.

Novak, B. (2017). Quantum ontology: A guide to the metaphysics of quantum mechanics. The *Review of Metaphysics, 70*(4), 785-786.

O'Keefe, D. F., Messervey, D., & Squires, E. C. (2018). Promoting ethical and prosocial behavior: The combined effect of ethical leadership and coworker ethicality. *Ethics & Behavior, 28*(3), 235-260.

Olijnyk, N. V. (2018). Examination of China's performance and thematic evolution in quantum cryptography research using quantitative and computational techniques. *PLoS One, 13*(1).

Paul, K. B. (2017). The import of Heidegger's philosophy into environmental ethics: A review. *Ethics and the Environment, 22*(2), 78-98.

Peng, J., Wang, Z., & Chen, X. (2018). Does self-serving leadership hinder team creativity? A moderated dual-path model. *Journal of Business Ethics, (1)1*, 1-15.

Piel, M. A., & Johnson, K. K. (2015). Quantum leadership: Collapsing the wave function. In Sowcik, M., & et al. (Eds.). *Leadership 2050* (pp. 207-223). Bingley, UK: Emerald.

Piel, M. A., Johnson, K. K., & Putnam, K. (2017). Quantum person: Collapsing the wave function. *Appraisal: The Journal of the British Personalist Forum, 11*(2), 42-46. ISSN 1358-3336.

Pigliucci, M. (2015). Dying (every day) with dignity: lessons from Stoicism. *The Human Prospect, 5*(1), 11-26.

Rab, A. S., Polino, E., Zhong-Xiao, M., Nguyen Ba, A., Yun-Jie, X., Spagnolo, N., & Sciarrino, F. (2017). Entanglement of photons in their dual wave-particle nature. *Nature Communications, 8*, 1-7.

Raghavan, D., (2018). Schrödinger's cat: PSA screening is alive and dead. *HEM/ONC Today, 19*(6), 11.

Rios, J. J. (2016). Speculation on shaktipat as "spooky action at a distance." *NeuroQuantology, 14*(2).

Ritzenhöfer, L., Brosi, P., Spörrle, M., & Welpe, I. M. (2017). Satisfied with the job, but not with the boss: Leaders' expressions of gratitude and pride differentially signal leader selfishness, resulting in differing levels of followers' satisfaction. *Journal of Business Ethics, (1)1*, 1-18.

Rockmore, T. (2017). Hegel and Husserl: Two phenomenological reactions to Kant. *Hegel Bulletin, 38*(1), 67-84.

Rodrigues, U.R. (2015). The price of corruption. *Journal of Law & Politics, 31*(1), 45-101.

Rodríguez, C. (2017). A quantitative examination of the relationship of work experience to attitudes of business ethics in graduate students. *Journal of Leadership, Accountability, and Ethics, 14*(3), 64-75.

Russell, H. A., (2013). Quantum anthropology: Reimaging the human person as body/spirit. *Theological Studies, 74*(4), 934-959.

Sahu, V. (2017). Corruption: 'culture' in the dock. *Journal of Human Values, 23*(1), 21-26.

Sampson, S. (2010). The anti-corruption industry: from movement to institution. *Global Crime*, 11, 261-278.

Saramifar, Y. (2017). The shadows of knowability: Reading between opaque narrative and transparent text. *Cogent Arts & Humanities, 4*(1), 1-9.

Sarup, M. (1993). *An introductory guide to post-structuralism and postmodernism* (2nd ed.). Harlow, England: Pearson Education.

Schlenther, B. (2017). The impact of corruption on tax revenues, tax compliance and economic development: Prevailing trends and mitigation actions in Africa. *EJournal of Tax Research, 15*(2), 217-242.

Schmitt, R. (1967). Phenomenology. In P.Edwards (Ed.). *The Encyclopedia of Philosophy.* (Vol. 6, pp. 135-151). London: Collier Macmillan.

Seagrave, S. A. (2009). Cicero, Aquinas, and contemporary issues in natural law theory. The Review of Metaphysics, 62(3), 491-523.

Sharp, W. G., Sr. (1994). Selflessness: The golden rule of leadership. *Marine Corps Gazette, 78*(11), 34-35.

Slager, R. (2017). The discursive construction of corruption risk. *Journal of Management Inquiry, 26*(4), 366-382.

Smart, J. J. C. (1967). Utilitarianism. In P.Edwards (Ed.). *The Encyclopedia of Philosophy.* (Vol. 8, pp. 206-212). London: Collier Macmillan.

Smith, D. W. (2013). Phenomenology. In E.N. Zalta (Ed.). *The Stanford Encyclopedia of Philosophy* (Summer 2018 ed.). Retrieved from https://plato.stanford.edu/archives/sum2018/entries/phenomenology/

Stagnaro, S. (2011). Quantum biophysical semeiotics. *NeuroQuantology, 9(3),* 459-467.

Steup, M. (2005). Epistemology. In E.N. Zalta (Ed.). The *Stanford Encyclopedia of Philosophy* (Summer 2018 ed.). Retrieved from https://plato.stanford.edu/archives/sum2018/entries/epistemology/

Tae, W. K., & Donaldson, T. (2018). Rethinking right: Moral epistemology in management research. *Journal of Business Ethics, 148*(1), 5-20.

Tanona, S. (2013). Decoherence and the Copenhagen cut. *Synthese, 190*(16), 3625-3649.

Tännsjö, T. (2007). Moral relativism. *Philosophical Studies, 135*(2), 123-143.

Theriault, J., Waytz, A., Heiphetz, L., & Young, L. (2017). Examining overlap in behavioral and neural representations of morals, facts, and preferences. *Journal of Experimental Psychology: General, 146*(11), 1586-1605.

Tjen, C., & Evans, C. (2017). Causes and consequences of corruption in tax administration: An Indonesian case study. *EJournal of Tax Research, 15*(2), 243-261.

UN Global Compact. (2015). A practical guide for collective action against corruption. Retrieved from https://www.unglobalcompact.org/library/1781

United Nations Development Programme. (2014). *UNDP global anti-corruption initiative (GAIN) 2014-2017* Retrieved from http://www.undp.org/content/dam/undp/library/Democratic%20Governance/Anti-corruption/globalanticorruption_final_web2.pdf

Van Gulick, R. (2014). Consciousness. In E.N. Zalta (Ed.). The *Stanford Encyclopedia of Philosophy* (Spring 2018 ed.). Retrieved from https://plato.stanford.edu/archives/spr2018/entries/consciousness/

Voliotis, S. (2017). Establishing the normative standards that determine deviance in organizational corruption: Is corruption within organizations antisocial or unethical? *Journal of Business Ethics, 140*(1), 147-160.

Wasak, T., Smerzi, A., & Chwedeńczuk, J. (2018). Role of particle entanglement in the violation of bell inequalities. *Scientific Reports (Nature Publisher Group), 8,* 1-6.

Wisler, J. C. (2018). U.S. CEOs of SBUs in luxury goods organizations: A mixed methods comparison of ethical decision-making profiles. *Journal of Business Ethics, 149*(2), 443-518.

Wollheim, R. (1967). Natural law. In P.Edwards (Ed.). *The Encyclopedia of Philosophy.* (Vol. 5, pp. 450-453). London: Collier Macmillan.

Wódka, M. (2017). Social and economic significance of moral capital. *Annales.Ethics in Economic Life, 20*(4), 65-75.

Wrenn, C. G. (1990). From counselor toward becoming a person: Some suggestions. *Journal of Counseling & Development, 68*(5), 586.

Xie, X., Qi, G., & Zhu, K. X. (2018). Corruption and new product innovation: Examining firms' ethical dilemmas in transition economies. *Journal of Business Ethics,1*(1), 1-19.

Xu, Q., Su, Z., Han, B., Fang, D., Xu, Z., & Gan, X. (2016). Analytical model with a novel selfishness division of mobile nodes to participate cooperation. *Peer-to-Peer Networking and Applications, 9*(4), 712-720.

Zarkeshian, P., Deshmukh, C., Sinclair, N, Goyal, S. K., Aguilar, G. H., et al. (2017). Entanglement between more than two hundred macroscopic atomic ensembles in a solid. *Nature Communications, 8,* 1-10.

Chapter 6

Type of Obligation to the Company and the Loyalty of an Employee

Renata Rosmus,
Department of Psychology, Katowice School of Economics, Poland

Introduction

Research and discussions of employee loyalty embrace two separate perspectives. The first pertains to ethical problems, e.g., the assessment of loyal behavior or validity regarding the expectancy of loyalty in business. The second is of a pragmatic character and deals with the utility of loyalty for individuals' functioning as members of organizations. This perspective encompasses studies regarding the effectiveness of loyalty-shaping programs. Studies concerning determinants of loyal behavior discussed in the present paper verge upon these two perspectives. The analysis encompassed views of respondents regarding the sense of a moral obligation to being loyal manifested in the agreement for the hitherto employment contract to be renegotiated, salary decreased, but working hours quota increased. In addition, factors fostering loyalty in case the company finds itself in a crisis were examined. The present study was inspired by an actual case where the company's management requested employees to accept unfavorable conditions as an expression of employee loyalty. The fact that few staff members declined is noteworthy.

Loyalty is characterized by compliance with legal regulations, actions taken by national authorities or rulers. In direct relationships, it denotes faithfulness between people sharing mutual trust and honesty in interpersonal relations. Van Vugt and Hart (2004) define loyalty as a multi-element construct consisting of emotions, cognition and behavior. Loyal people experience strong positive emotions (joy, satisfaction, empathy) and the feeling of emotional bond with other group members. In cognitive terms, it may be manifested in the trust in competences of group members and optimism in the assessment of the future of the group. In behavioral terms, it may be exhibited in the inclination towards group protection, even at the risk of a personal loss. Despite several definitions of employee loyalty being available, authors agree that loyal behavior is based upon values, norms and social trust. The following constitute the most frequently mentioned terms associated with loyalty: involvement, responsibility, honesty, reliability, decency, solidarity, zeal, devotion, proceeding in accordance with contracts and legal regulations.

Definitions differ in the intensity of expectations associated with the behaviors of a loyal individual. Beginning simply with reliable and honest work, e.g., Myjak (2011) who understands loyalty as employees' reliability and honesty—performing their duties in the best possible way and with best possible outcomes. Other definitions emphasize the emotional aspect—values, feelings, faithfulness. In such a context, loyalty may be defined as a value that manifests in the attitude/ behavior and conceptualized as "(perceived) probability of employees' continuing their, lesser or greater, emotional engagement in the organization, which, despite a temporary loss of image on the labor market, cherishes lasting and positive emotions, due to a particular employee or other employees obtaining values themselves, or high cost associated with changing employers" (Lipka et al., 2012, p.20). Finally, the scope encompasses the expansion of loyal behavior to cover the surrounding environment. Niehoff, Moorman, Blakely, and Fuller (2013) emphasize the significance of promotion of the organization and protection of its image. According to the authors, loyalty denotes active behavior constituting a demonstration of pride and support for the organization. It can be manifested in, e.g. protecting the company against criticism, highlighting the organization's positive aspects, restraint with regard to publically complaining about the company (Niehoff, Moorman, Blakely, & Fuller, 2013, p.22). As a consequence, loyalty may be understood as a specific attitude composed of three elements—emotional, cognitive and behavioral. The definition does not make a redundant differentiation between "attitude" and "behavior" where the former is usually understood as an emotional and cognitive disposition, whereas the latter is not considered as its constituting element, but a manifestation of the attitude. Vandekerckhove and Commers (2004) define loyalty in a similar manner. They propose four determinants of loyalty:

1. Loyalty is an attitude towards a particular object;
2. Loyalty possesses a direct external manifestation;
3. Loyalty constitutes an acquired attitude;
4. Loyalty is bilateral.

These criteria are featured in several definitions of loyalty offered by various authors. Ladd, Gordon, Beauvais and Morgan (1982) mention the following as constituting elements of loyalty: responsibility for the relationship, intention of making an effort for the sake of the relationship, and belief in the idea of the relationship. One can be loyal to somebody or something, but faithful towards oneself. Loyalty requires a particular activity resulting from one entering into the relationship with the object, constituting a response to its presence and a basis for communication. As a consequence, we are interested in a loyal behavior rather than loyal views and beliefs. This is especially valid because a loyal norm may be enforced even when a loyal individual feels forced to act contrary to their own beliefs and interests. We learn and acquire loyal attitudes just like we do with other social competences. It stems from life experiences of an individual. Similarly, Ladd, Gordon, Beauvais and Morgan (1982) consider loyalty as an acquired behavior, and indicate loyalty towards a relationship among components of attachment, whose style and form are determined by the character of relations with supervisors or caretakers (Ladd et al., 1982). When examining loyalty as an intervening variable between attachment and a positive attitude towards the organization, and behavior focusing upon the organization or upon individual objectives, Tan and Aryee (2002) verified premises pertaining to the impact of attachment and loyalty upon the growth of pro-organizational behavior. In addition, the relationship between various forms of organizational behavior resulting from the type of employment (on the basis of devotion, investment, being non-resident, associated, allied, free agent, employed, and based upon satisfaction) and an affective and lasting attachment was verified as well (Sinclair, Tucker, Cullen, & Wright, 2005). As far as the bilateral attitude criterion is concerned, two approaches ought to be considered. Separate categories may be applied, and, a premise may be made that only absolute loyalty or disloyalty exist. Faithfulness and truthfulness are defined in a similar manner. One cannot be partly faithful or truthful. However, if a premise is made that loyalty is an attitude, then, like any attitude, it may undergo valuation on the continuum of valence, cohesion, and strength. An employee may be more or less loyal, may manifest more or less positive, stronger or weaker emotions towards their company, express diversified views regarding the organization's positive character. In relation to the behavioral component of the attitude, an employee may manifest a higher or lower interest in their behavior serving the benefit of the company. However, loyalty is always associated with the behavior of a privileged character. Therefore, it constitutes an attitude of a positive bias. Due to the fact that loyalty towards a company requires making a reference to its several aspects, which, to various degrees, may stimulate employees' acceptance, when assessing loyalty, its cohesion, unequivocal character and ambivalence ought to be evaluated as well.

Loyalty constitutes a relatively permanent but not necessarily unequivocal behavior. A loyal person may be loyal regarding some aspects of the organization's operations, and may not be loyal towards others. When a premise is made that loyalty requires absolute devotion, then it becomes equivalent to blind obedience. However, objectives pursued by the organization may not always lead to its general "good." On the other hand, loyal behavior is characterized by targeting the good of the attitude's object. A loyal person can be trusted to act with the good in mind. Two forms of trust may be distinguished — one based upon identification, and one based upon exchange. Loyalty ought to be considered in similar terms — via the continuum beginning with the absolute loyalty which is based most frequently upon identification, to conditional one — dependent upon a rational assessment of profits and losses. Loyal behavior gains significance when the balance is endangered or is negative. When explaining the term loyalty, Hirschman (1995) indicates conditions loyal behavior kicks in, and observes that loyal behavior denotes being loyal "despite." These conditions encompass the following: the feeling of dissatisfaction with continuing the relationship, recognition of the opportunity for changing own condition by discontinuing the relationship, and becoming aware of the internalized values and norms which, when pursued, raise guilty conscience. Hirschman (1995) defines employee loyalty as postponing the moment of separation despite dissatisfaction and guilty conscience. Loyalty is manifested in specific behavior located in between acting to the benefit of the relationship via remaining in it but expressing internal criticism (offered solely in the presence of the organization's management or other members), to discontinuing the relationship. Loyal behavior is directed towards improving the condition of the company as a result of employment continuance and internal criticism, which offer feedback on threats and faulty operation of the company. Studies by Olson-Buchaman and Boswell (2002) verified the significance of internal criticism. When examining loyal behavior, they observed that, as far as organizational attachment is concerned, employees prefer informal criticism, solving conflicts face to face and avoidance of pointing fingers at the guilty. A loyal employee has the courage to counteract irregularities and abnormities, and to express unpopular views and opinions. On the other hand, external criticism constitutes an example of disloyal behavior, which is discussed by other researchers, e.g., Niehoff et al. (2001).

The question regarding the validity of expecting morality from business activity remains without a straightforward answer. The "unitarian" approach considers business as an integral element of the society which ought to conform with the same moral principles as other social relations. The separatist approach excludes the ability to assess ethics in business because it only conforms with extra-moral market principles. The integrative approach admits that business is governed by separate principles. However, the operation of business entities undergoes a moral assessment. The entities are expected to comply with ethical principles (Pratley, 1998). Jeurissen (1995, after: Pratley, 1998) perceives difficulties in determining ethics in business in the duality of market operations, its social and functional sphere. The social sphere is subject to ethical principles which regulate the way social needs, such as security, support, recognition and development, are satisfied in. In the functional sphere (production, distribution, administration, and procedures ensuring rational organization), immoral behavior, e.g., dubious contracts, unethical competition, manipulation, is justified by profitability. Haber (1996) links the frequency ethical principles are broken in with the type of entrepreneurship: evolutionary, ethical, and spontaneous. As far as evolutionary entrepreneurship is concerned, it revolves around investments. The bond and cultural norms such as reliability, honesty, and loyalty, regulate the correctness of change. In case of ethical entrepreneurship, exemplified by public trust organizations, the state is responsible for conditions favorable to the ethical entrepreneurship model. Spontaneous entrepreneurship is associated with risk, creativity, unconventionality and unpredictability. It does not yield to control, thus unethical behaviors emerge here more frequently (Haber, 1996). Duska (2003) is a representative of a more radical approach. She argues that loyalty is something alien in business, due to the fact that it requires devotion and sacrifice without expecting rewards, and because business relations are not selfless. Profit-focus justifies disloyal behavior towards employees, e.g., increase of the working hours quota, reduction of costs by decreased salaries, increase in the scope of work without feeling obliged towards those who contributed significant effort in developing the institution and thus wore themselves out. According to Duska, reciprocity is limited in business — entrepreneurs do not always reciprocate loyalty of their employees. Duska does not consider companies as entities driven by morality, but views them as instruments for obtaining benefits. Therefore, she believes that loyalty towards the organization which is not morality-driven is pointless. According to Duska, the observation that a company strives to obtain profits owing to but also at the expense of employees is not surprising. Neither is the fact that, when striving to secure their profits, employees may limit their contribution. However, it is difficult to acknowledge the fact that a company ought to be considered as an instrument applied in order to obtain profits, but one devoid of objectivity. The Polish Civil Code, article 55 emphasizes that: "a company constitutes an organized collection of material and non-material resources applied in order to conduct business activity" (Rucińska, Świerkot, & Tatar, 2016). The resources are utilized by people who mold the company and set its dynamics, objectives, and achieve these. It is owners and employers, instead of abstract terms such as company, organization, enterprise, which constitute a moral entity whose decisions undergo ethical evaluation. Therefore, viewing companies as moral entities able to take responsibility, not only in family-run companies but in modern business as well, is possible, and even necessary. The fact was acknowledged by companies' interest in loyalty-based strategies, i.e., means of attracting and utilizing employees' and clients' loyalty. These strategies are effective only when they stimulate the trust of clients and their belief in the fact that they boost clients' satisfaction. From the business perspective, the strategy is successful if it translates into profits, i.e., when it estimates that consumers' or employees' (internal clients) contribution is lower than profits offered by loyalty. Undeniably, an asymmetric exchange is not always unfair. Everything boils down to the contribution, costs-benefits ratio, risk factors, etc. However, manipulating sympathy, pursuit of emotional attachment, fostering gratitude by offering presents in order to secure a disproportionate purchase, are disloyal towards the client (Valenzuela, Mulki, & Jaramillo, 2010) or employee.

In light of the above, a question regarding eligible requests in the name of loyalty and one about the extent the loyal individual feels obliged in relation to the company, still stands. The establishment of an answer to the question constitutes the objective of the current study.

Methods

Research Problem and Objectives

Based upon the review of the literature pertaining to loyalty, a premise can be made that loyalty as an attitude may assume various values in relation to the emotional bond with the object of the attitude, to the strength allowing alternative attitudes to be eliminated and fostering the stability of loyalty, to the cohesion of the emotional bond, views regarding the object of the attitude and loyal behavior, which is of a privileged character. The study focuses upon determinants of loyalty in light of the fact that lower-quality working conditions and lower salaries, along with the increased quota of working hours are accepted. The feeling of employees' moral obligation towards the company whose management justified the unfavorable change by calling upon employee loyalty, was also examined. Loyal behavior is determined by features such as prosocial attitude, reliability, feeling of responsibility, and identification with the group (Newson, Buhrmester, & Whitehouse, 2016). In addition, the features encompass altruism, trust, openness, faithfulness, and low inclination towards manipulation. The belief in the fact that an individual will eventually achieve their objectives constitutes a vital determinant of loyalty (Fullagar, 1986). The achievement of objectives is facilitated by, e.g. internal locus of control, coherence, conscientiousness, high self-esteem, as well as temperament-related characteristics such as persistence, resistance to distractors, activity. It turns out that even entrepreneurial people, those pursuing a one-sided exchange and accepting the application of manipulative strategies, behave loyally towards their companies as far as affiliative attachment is concerned (Rosmus, 2012). The situational context ought to be considered when establishing reasons behind the decision regarding loyal behavior being made and when assessing its value (effectiveness, morality). For example, alternatives to the decision. In conditions favorable to the person making the decision, positive alternatives are numerous. In unfavorable conditions, loyal behavior may be the best alternative. Loyal decisions may be motivated by consequences of a general punishment for acting against obligations, calculation of personal costs vs. benefits, recognition of the value of loyalty-stimulating object, the character of the public good, social norms, subjective norms, conformism, organizational attachment style, etc. In general, factors constituting the basis of the feeling of an individual's obligation may exert an impact upon views regarding the character and extent of duty and obligation towards the object of the attitude, upon beliefs regarding moral justification of particular requirements associated with the extent and form of loyal behavior, and finally, upon the decision on the behavior and its implementation being made, as well as the intensity and stability of loyal behavior. The following may be indicated with regard to the type of the obligation: 1. loyalty based upon an emotional bond, 2. loyalty based upon the principle of a fair exchange, 3. loyalty based upon values, 4. loyalty based upon social norms, 5. loyalty based upon trust that the object of loyalty favors the good of the loyal individual, 6. loyalty based upon identity-related identification, 7. loyalty based upon the fear of punishment, 8. loyalty as a tactic in manipulative strategies.

The objective of the present study is to establish the relationship between factors determining the decision on being loyal towards the institution in a difficult situation and the probability of the decision being made and a moral obligation to being loyal. Independent variables include external and internal determinants of the decision regarding being loyal towards the company. As far as internal determinants are concerned, Machiavellianism, a characteristic feature of personality which was broadly discussed in the literature, was taken into consideration. The external determinants of the decision, which constitute the factor enabling research groups to be established, encompass favorable and unfavorable labor market features, and context-dependent factors which justify the obligation towards being loyal. The following were indicated among the context-dependent factors which facilitate loyalty towards the company: emotional attachment, loyalty contracts, social norms, principle of reciprocity, values followed, respect for the company, habits and unwillingness for a change, risk avoidance, loyalty norms being internalized, conformism. The decision regarding being loyal towards the company constitutes the dependent variable. The decision is analyzed with regard to the extent of the moral obligation to accepting a reduced salary and an increased quota of working hours, and the probability of these conditions being accepted.

Research questions:

1. Does a relationship between the level of Machiavellianism and the locus of control and the perception of the moral obligation to being loyal and acceptance of the offered conditions exist?
2. Does a relationship between the type of factors facilitating loyalty and perception of the moral obligation to being loyal and acceptance of the offered conditions exist?

Hypotheses regarding the existence of the relationship between the isolated variables were made.

H.1. There exists a relationship between the level of Machiavellianism and perception of the moral obligation to being loyal and acceptance of the offered conditions, in the context of factors justifying loyal behavior in both favorable and unfavorable situations.

H.2. There exists a relationship between the level of the internal locus of control and moral obligation to being loyal and acceptance of the offered conditions, in the context of factors justifying loyal behavior, both in favorable and unfavorable situations.

Statistical and Research Tools

The study employed the Mach IV, the Delta Questionnaire, and the Questionnaire on Determinants of Loyalty. The Mach IV is composed of 20 statements respondents express their views on by means of a 7-point scale.

The Mach IV encompasses statements pertaining to three aspects: Tactics, Views, and Morality. The alpha coefficient amounted to 0.70 (Pilch, 2008).

The Drwal's Delta measures the general locus of control, i.e., the belief that one has influence upon and control over their lives, or the belief that these are determined by external circumstances. The reliability of the scale was tested by making a comparison with results of the Rotter scale. Correlation coefficients (phi) between individual questions in the scale and the I-E scale (Internal-External Control Scale) were calculated on the basis of the analysis of questions. The coefficients amounted to between 0.42 and 0.84, the split-half index 0.68, internal reliability 0.69, and absolute test-retest reliability from 0.38 to 0.79 (Drwal, 1995).

The Questionnaire on Determinants of Loyalty contains an instruction inviting respondents to relate to the role of an employee who must make a decision regarding the acceptance of unfavorable working conditions. The questionnaire contains descriptions of situations where the decision is made regarding new and unfavorable working conditions (reduced salary, increased quota of working hours), examples of 10 types of factors stimulating loyal obligation, and scales for assessing the extent of the moral obligation which stimulates remaining in the company, and the extent of agreement to the offered conditions. Respondents were requested to evaluate separately each factor which may contribute to the emergence of loyal behavior, e.g., due to emotional attachment to the company, due to unwillingness to take risk, or norms and values followed. The questionnaire was developed in two variations of employment opportunities on the labor market: favorable vs. unfavorable market situation.

Due to the fact that the distribution of results did not conform with the normal distribution, except the one regarding results for the Machiavellianism variable, the study applied statistical analysis, measures of the strength of the relationship between variables, the Mann–Whitney U test, and Spearman's rank correlation coefficient.

The Sample and Research Procedure

The study encompassed 125 participants: 34 men and 91 women, aged 18-51. The sample consisted of full-time and extramural students of the Medical University of Silesia and Katowice School of Economics. The study was conducted in the two institutions in October 2016. In the first stage of the study, respondents evaluated the level of the moral obligation to being loyal and the probability of them accepting unfavorable working conditions. The assessment encompassed 10 types of factors determining the obligation towards the organization. Respondents evaluated their perception of the moral obligation to being loyal and the probability of them accepting the proposed conditions separately for each determinant which may stimulate the loyal behavior. In total, 20 assessments were made — evaluation of the moral obligation and the probability of the loyal decision being made for each of the determinants. The study was conducted in two groups — one received background information regarding favorable labor market conditions (74 respondents) and the other regarding unfavorable conditions (50 respondents).

Results

I. Verification of H1 regarding the existence of a relationship between the level of Machiavellianism, perception of the moral obligation to being loyal, and the decision on accepting the offered conditions, in the context of factors stimulating loyal behavior in favorable and unfavorable situations. In case of Machiavellianism, the relationship between the general Machiavellianism level and dependent variables, as well one between dependent variables and aspects of Machiavellianism (constituting elements of the variable) — Tactics, Views Upon Human Nature, and Morality, were considered.

   1.   Machiavellianism vs. the conviction regarding the moral obligation to being loyal towards the company and the decision on being loyal in unfavorable and favorable situations.

Results outlined in Table 6.1 indicate the diversity of relations between the level of Machiavellianism and the perception of the moral obligation and the decision on being loyal in relation to the type of labor market situation. In an unfavorable situation, people manifesting stronger Machiavellian features pursue moral values and respect for the company more seldom. Instead, they are driven by conformism more frequently. In a favorable situation, all significant relationships become negative in value. The stronger the Machiavellianism, the less significant the official declaration of loyalty towards the company, existing social norms, perception of loyalty as a determinant of an appropriate interaction, and conformism are. The significance of conformism increases in case of unfavorable conditions, and declines when attractive alternatives to being loyal emerge. An analogous relationship occurs between Machiavellianism and conformism as far as the probability of accepting the unfavorable working conditions is concerned. In an unfavorable situation, the relationship is positive whereas, in case of favorable conditions, it is negative. The remaining significant relationships between Machiavellianism and the decision regarding being loyal are negative. In the favorable situation, it is the relationship between Machiavellianism and respect for the company. In the unfavorable situation, it is one between Machiavellianism and the perception of social norms, principle of reciprocity, risk avoidance, and appropriate interaction as a determinant of interaction.

Table 6.1 *Tactics vs. belief on moral obligation towards the company and the decision on loyal behavior in advantageous and disadvantageous situation*

Tactics	Unfavorable situation $n = 74$		Favorable situation $n = 50$	
	r_s	p	r_s	p
MORAL OBLIGATION				
Values	-0.31	0.004	-0.12	0.206
Respect	-0.28	0.007	-0.13	0.178
appropriate interaction	-0.23	0.025	-0.32	0.012
Conformism	0.12	0.154	-0.33	0.009
DECISION ON BEING LOYAL				
Social norms	-0.10	0.195	-0.28	0.025
Values	-0.15	0.100	-0.27	0.031
Respect	-0.26	0.012	-0.18	0.010
Risk avoidance	-0.12	0.156	-0.24	0.050
Appropriate interaction	-0.09	0.225	-0.38	0.003
Conformism	0.20	0.044	-0.17	0.116

In the context of factors determining loyal behavior, research results acknowledge the existence of a significant relationship between the general level of Machiavellianism, the perception of the moral obligation to being loyal, and the decision regarding moral behavior.

2. Views upon Human Nature vs. perception of the moral obligation towards the company and the decision regarding being loyal in favorable and unfavorable situations.

In unfavorable conditions, there exists a significant positive relationship between pessimistic views upon human nature and the perception of moral obligation to being loyal and conformism (Table 6.2). In case of the favorable situation, the relationship is negative. The decision on being loyal is positively correlated with conformism in the unfavorable situation. The correlation is negative for respect. In the positive situation, significant relationships are negative. The higher the score in the perception of human nature, the more seldom respondents are driven by the principle of reciprocity, appropriate interaction and conformism.

Table 6.2. *Views on human nature vs. belief on moral obligation towards the company and the decision on loyal behavior in advantageous and disadvantageous situation*

Views on human nature	Unfavorable situation $n = 74$		Favorable situation $n = 50$	
	r_s	p	r_s	p
MORAL OBLIGATION				
Declaration	-0.12	0.144	-0.35	0.0058
Conformism	0.33	0.002	-0.33	0.0088
DECISION ON BEING LOYAL				
Principle of reciprocity	-0.10	0.196	-0.28	0.025
Respect	-0.21	0.037	-0.16	0.140
Appropriate interaction	0.01	0.482	-0.36	0.005
Conformism	0.25	0.017	-0.25	0.040

3. Morality vs. the perception of the moral obligation towards the company and the decision on being loyal in favorable and unfavorable situations.

Table 6.3. *Morality vs. belief on moral obligation towards the company and the decision on loyal behavior in advantageous and disadvantageous situation*

Morality	Unfavorable situation $n = 74$		Favorable situation $n = 50$	
	r_s	p	r_s	p
MORAL OBLIGATION				
Attachement	0.20	0.046	-0.09	0.267
Principle of reciprocity	0.25	0.015	-0.15	0.150
Values	-0.09	0.236	-0.29	0.021
Appropriate interaction	0.11	0.180	-0.33	0.010
DECISION ON BEING LOYAL				
Attachement	0.21	0.036	-0.16	0.131
Social norms	0.22	0.029	-0.19	0.093
Principle of reciprocity	0.24	0.021	-0.11	0.227
Appropriate interaction	0.06	0.308	-0.28	0.023

II. Verification of hypothesis H2 regarding the existence of a relationship between the level of internal locus of control, perception of the moral obligation to being loyal and accepting offered conditions in the context of factors determining loyal behavior.

    1.   Locus of control vs. moral obligation towards the company and the decision on being loyal in favorable and unfavorable situations.

Table 6.4. *Locus of control vs. belief on moral obligation towards the company and the decision on loyal behavior in advantageous and disadvantageous situation*

Locus of control	Unfavorable situation n = 74		Favorable situation n = 50	
	r_s	p	r_s	p
MORAL OBLIGATION				
Declaration	-0.24	0.018	0.06	0.336
values	-0.25	0.016	0.01	0.466
Attachement	0.06	0.309	0.35	0.006
appropriate interaction	-0.11	0.164	-0.26	0.036
DECISION ON BEING LOYAL				
Social norms	-0.21	0.034	0.01	0.470
Principle of reciprocity	-0.26	0.014	-0.07	0.309
Values	-0.24	0.019	0.01	0.475
attachement	0.07	0.263	0.27	0.028

The relationship between the internal locus of control and the moral obligation to being loyal and the decision on being loyal, i.e., acceptance of the unfavorable working conditions, pertains to the diversity of relations between these variables and context-dependent factors in the favorable and unfavorable situation for finding employment opportunities (Table 6.4). The locus of control vs. perception of the moral obligation — in the unfavorable situation, there exists a negative relationship between loyalty and values. In the favorable situation, a positive relationship with the attachment emerged. In addition, similar to the unfavorable situation, a negative relationship between loyalty and interaction was observed. Results pertaining to the decision on being loyal in the unfavorable situation indicate a reverse relationship between the internal locus of control and social norms, principle of reciprocity, and values followed, and in the favorable situation a positive relationship with the attachment. The lower the internal locus of control, the greater the loyalty based upon declarations, values, social norms and principle of reciprocity in the unfavorable situation. On the other hand, in the favorable situation, the stronger the internal locus of control, the higher the significance of the attachment was observed. As far as loyal behavior is concerned, regardless of the prevalent conditions, people with a stronger internal locus of control are less driven by loyalty-based declarations regarding the acceptance of worse working conditions and by the feeling of the moral obligation.

Conclusions

Due to the complexity of the issue, it is difficult to isolate a narrow spectrum of factors determining the decision on being loyal. This is valid for both situational factors and personality traits. The obligation to being loyal has various grounds, which has been acknowledged in numerous studies.

The present chapter offers the following conclusions pertaining to the relationship between personality features, situational factors and the feeling of the moral obligation to being loyal and the decision on being loyal:

1. The significance of situational factors emerges in the assessment of the moral obligation and decisions of the Machiavellian. There exists a relationship between the level of Machiavellianism and perception of the moral obligation to being loyal and the decision regarding being loyal. People of various levels of Machiavellianism behave in a different way in the favorable and unfavorable situation. A relationship was also observed between context-dependent factors, such as emotional attachment, values, principle of reciprocity, or embracing loyalty as the basis of suitable interpersonal relations vs. Machiavellianism.

2. The relationship between Machiavellianism and the perception of the moral obligation and the decision on being loyal is manifested in a significant situational diversity of views and decisions. In the favorable situation, the Machiavellian predominantly included social factors stimulating loyalty. On the other hand, in the unfavorable situation, these bore little significance. This is especially valid as far as Morality is concerned.

3. The relationship between the internal locus of control and the moral obligation and the decision on being loyal suggests that the weaker the internal locus of control, the greater the loyalty based upon declarations, values, social norms, and the

principle of reciprocity in the unfavorable market situation. In the favorable situation, the attachment gains significance — the stronger the internal locus of control, the more significance is attributed to the attachment as far as the moral obligation to being loyal and the decision on being loyal are concerned.

References

Drwal, R. Ł. (1995). *Adaptacja kwestionariuszy osobowości.*[Adaptation of personality questionnaires.] Warsaw: PWN.

Duska, R. F. (2003). The gathering storm. *Journal of Financial Service Professionals, 57*(3), 28-30.

Fullagar, C. (1986). A factor analytic study on the validity of a Union Commitment Scale. *Journal of Applied Psychology, 71*(1), 129-136.

Haber, L. H. (1996). Działania przedsiębiorcze w biznesie. [Entrepreneurial activity in business.] *Przedsiębiorczość i Rynek, 1.*

Hirschman, A. O. (1995). *Lojalność, krytyka, rozstanie. Reakcja na kryzys państwa, organizacji i przedsiębiorstwa.* [Loyalty, critics, parting. Reaction to the crisis of the nation, organization, and enterprise.] Warsaw: Znak.

Ladd, R. T., Gordon, M. E., Beauvais, L. L., & Morgan, R. L. (1982). Union commitment: Replication and extension. *Journal of Applied Psychology, 67,* 640-644.

Lipka, A., Winnicka-Wejs, A., & Acedański, J. (2012). *Lojalność pracownicza. Od diagnozy typów lojalności pracowników po zarządzaniu relacjami z pracownikami.* [The employee loyalty. From diagnosis of loyalty types to relations management.] Warsaw: Difin.

Myjak, T. (2011). *Wpływ formy zatrudnienia na zachowania organizacyjne.*[The impact of the employement form on organizational behavior.] Toruń: Marszałek.

Newson, M., Burhrmester, M., & Whitehouse, H. (2016). Explaining lifelong loyalty: The role of identity fusion and self-shaping group events. *PloS One, 11*(8), e 0160427 doi.10.171/journal. pone. 0160427.

Niehoff, B. P., Moorman, R. H., Blakely, G., & Fuller, J. (2001). The influence of empowerment and job enrichment on employee loyalty in a downsizing environment. *Group and Organization Management, 26*(1), 93-113.

Olson-Buchaman, J. B., & Boswell, W. R. (2002). The role of employee loyalty and formality in voicing discontent. *Journal of Applied Psychology, 87*(6), 1167-1174.

Pilch, I. (2008). *Osobowość makiawelisty i jego relacje z ludźmi.* [The personality and interspersonal relationships of a Machiavellian]. Katowice: Silesian University Publishing.

Pratley, P.(1998). *Etyka w biznesie.* [Business Ethics]. Warsaw: Gebethner.

Rosmus, R. (2012). Lojalność osób przedsiębiorczych. Postawa czy taktyka? [The loyalty of entrepreneurial persons. An attitude or tactic?] In Z. Ratajczak (Ed.). *Przedsiębiorczość. Źródła i uwarunkowania psychologiczne*. [Entrepreneurship.Its sources and psychological conditioning.] Warsaw: Difin.

Rucińska, A., Świerkot, M., & Tatar, K. (2016). *Kodeks postępowanie cywilnego. The Code of Civil Procedure*. Warsaw: C.H. Beck.

Sinclair, R. R., Tucker, J. S., Cullen, J. C., & Wright, C. (2005). Performance. Differences among four organizational commitment profiles. *Journal of Applied Psychology, 90*(6), 1260-1287.

Tan, H. H., & Aryee, S. (2002). Antecedents and outcomes of union loyalty: A constructive replication and an Extension. *Journal of Applied Psychology, 87*(4), 715-722.

Valenzuela, L. M., Mulki, J. P., & Jaramillo, J. F. (2010). Impact of customer orientation, inducements and ethics on loyalty to the firm: Customers' perspective. *Journal of Business Ethics, 93*, 277-291.

Vandekerckhove, W., & Commers, M. S. R. (2004). Whistle blowing and rational loyalty. *Journal of Business Ethics, 53*, 225-233.

Van Vugt, M., & Hart, C. M. (2004). Social identity as social glue: The origins of group loyalty. *Journal of Personality and Social Psychology, 86*(4), 585-598.

Part III:
Dimensions of Selflessness and Gender

Chapter 7

Selfless Women in Capitalism?

Luka Boršić,
Rochester Institute of Technology (RIT), Croatia
Institute of Philosophy, Croatia

Ivana Skuhala Karasman,
Rochester Institute of Technology (RIT), Croatia
Institute of Philosophy, Croatia

Introduction

In his text "Why Women Vanish As They Move Up The Career Ladder", Bob Sherwin (2014a) lists three groups of explanations of why women are not present in senior management positions. He lists them under "statements women themselves would make": 1. "I don't want the role"; 2. "I can't succeed in the role"; and 3. "I can't have the role." Under each of these categories, Sherwin discusses different practical, psychological, discriminatory, etc. reasons that women *choose* not to advance (our italics, Sherwin, 2014a). The data Sherwin presented are even more confusing since, as he showed in an earlier text, he believed that women are, in broad terms, more successful leaders in business than men (Sherwin, 2014b). However, Sherwin, in his popular texts, instead of touching upon a deeper problem underlying this question, remained on a more pragmatic level of everyday business situations.

Our chapter aims to do exactly that – to go deeper. However, it will be, but a modest theoretical contribution to answering the vexing question of why in societies, which are presently considered the most advanced from economical, legal, and cultural perspectives – in the so-called "Western World" – in business women still occupy between one quarter and one third of senior management positions even though, in the West, around 45% of employees are women. In the European Union, 25.3 % of the senior management positions are occupied by women as of 2017 (compared to 10.4 % in 2007) (Eurostat, 2018). In Canada, there are 28.9 % women occupying senior management occupations in 2017 (Statistics Canada, 2018). In the United States, there are 26.5 % women among the senior-level officials and managers in the S&P 500 Companies as of 2018 (Catalyst, 2018). In Australia the situation is better: there are 34.9 % women occupying positions of senior managers in 2017 (The Workplace Gender Equality Agency, 2018).

There are many answers from various theoretical horizons that can be offered to the question of "why women vanish as they move up the career ladder", just to list them all would be a text on its own. However, instead of discussing or refuting any particular position, our goal is to offer an additional explanation of this problem from a perspective that at once seems so trivially obvious and yet surprisingly neglected in academic and popular literature.

Our position, in short, can be summarized in the form of the following syllogism:

1.   Women are selfless.
2.   Capitalism is based on selfishness.
3.   Therefore, capitalism is not a suitable "habitat" for women.[1]

A following corollary can be derived from the conclusion: since capitalism is not a suitable "habitat" for women, women's advancement within capitalist hierarchy is more difficult. Of course, this does not preclude that there are different other factors, unrelated to the specific nature of capitalism, that have a negative impact on women's climbing the corporate ladder: some of the psychological ones are listed in the above-mentioned Sherwin's text, a lot of feminists – and some Marxist – literature is dedicated to analyzing the sociological aspect of our predominantly patriarchic society for unequal positions of men and women, etc. However, the difference between our approach and the others is that ours is "essentialist": our claim is that capitalism *in its essence* is at least partially incompatible with "being woman." Career advancement, usually tied with the financial advancement, is one of the constitutive elements of capitalism as a system. If the system itself is not tailored to them, women are less likely to advance within it.

Obviously, both premises as well as the conclusion, are controversial, and the rest of the text will be dedicated to elucidating these controversies.

---

[1] Of course, this is not a syllogism in the formal sense of logic, it could be subsumed under a natural language deductive argument (on "natural language deductivism" see: Groarke, 1999). However, as the majority (or all, Walton & Gordon, 2015) of informal argument, this one could be formalized.

Premise 1: Women are selfless.

Sometime around fourth century BC, a bitter attack on an Athenian citizen, a certain Stephanus, was launched by his rival, Apollodorus, in form of suing Neaera. She, claimed Apollodorus, being herself an alien, was living as a wife with Stephanus. The Athenian law of the time said that such a woman should upon conviction be sold as a slave, and that the man living with her should be fined one thousand drachmae. In the juridical oration, i.e., Apollodorus's indictment, preserved in Demosthenic corpus (and most likely not being composed by Demosthenes himself) Apollodorus explains the role of women in Greek society in the following words:

> Mistresses we keep for the sake of pleasure, concubines for the daily care of our bodies, but wives to bear us legitimate children and to be faithful guardians of our households. (Demosthenes, 1939, p.445–447, translation slightly modified.)

This classical and unfortunate tripartition of women into "mistresses", "concubines" and "wives" is not limited just to classical antiquity. There is a plethora of feminist literature showing that in recent times, such as the nineteenth century, the tripartition of women into "lovers", "prostitutes" and "wives" as three most common roles for women was taken for granted – it is no wonder that Herodotus' quote was so popular in the nineteenth century. These roles have a common denominator: it is *care for others*. Either in an emotional, erotic/intellectual (as ancient Greek *hetairai* or Japanese *geishas*) and sexual manner, or for the family, women are there to care for others. As the historian Linda Kerber has already established, this division of men who engage in public, political, and business sphere, and women who realize themselves through caring for others within households is as old as the Western civilization and has in a large part defined what the virtue of a good woman is: good woman is the one who is successful in caring for others (Kerber, 1986, p.306).

That caring is "women's work" – of course not any more in the antiquated tripartition mentioned above – is also reflected in most recent analysis issued by the European Parliament's Committee on Women's Rights and Gender Equality and commissioned, supervised and published by the Policy Department for Citizen's Rights and Constitutional Affairs (Davaki, 2016). The report shows that when paid working hours are united with unpaid work hours and time spent in commuting, women work on average longer than men (64 hours vs 53 hours). It is noteworthy that men spend on average only 9 hours dedicated to caring activities, while women – 26 hours. So, even today, unfortunately in many aspects of our society, caring is thought to be one of the principal women's work. The tight bond between caring and womanhood is especially prominent in more traditionalist milieus. For instance, in the Apostolic Exhortation *Familiaris consortio* by the Pope John Paul II (1981), after establishing the equal dignity and responsibility of men and women in chapter 22, in the following chapter the Exhortation claims:

> While it must be recognized that women have the same right as men to perform various public functions, society must be structured in such a way that wives and mothers are not in practice compelled to work outside the home, and that their families can live and prosper in a dignified way even when they themselves devote their full time to their own family. Furthermore, the mentality which honors women more for their work outside the home than for their work within the family must be overcome. (John Paul II, 1981, ch 23.)

Nevertheless, it is underlined that a recognition of familiar and maternal role must be given by society to enhance and appreciate the development of a woman and femininity. According to the Exhortation, women are equal to men in respect to rights and dignity, but their natural habitat is home and family, they are supposed to *devote their full time* to others. Society, that is men, should see to that women should not be obliged (we read: encouraged or even indirectly disallowed) to work "outside the home." Moreover, such societies which support or even encourage women to work "outside the home" must be overcome, says the Exhortation. It is quite unclear what "overcoming" in this context would mean.

Parallel invectives can be found in our time also outside official Catholic teaching. For instance, some decades ago, in 1973, there was the first edition of the book entitled *The Total Woman* by Marabel Morgan. It is a simple self-help book for a woman to be happy as a married wife. Morgan's position is summarized in three pieces of advice she explicitly gives to wives: 1. be nice to your husband, compliment him, tell him he's great; 2. stop nagging at him and trying to change him; 3. understand and try to fulfill his sexual needs. Similarly and more recently, in 2011, Costanza Miriano published a book entitled *Sposati e sii sottomessa* (in English translated as *Marry Him and Be Submissive*) in which Miriano goes a step further than Morgan (whom Miriano does not mention in her book): there is no happiness for a woman outside marriage, in which woman has to take care of her husband and children. According to Miriano (2011), submissiveness is the only successful path to women's happiness.

As one would expect, both books received strong reactions from both extremes. There would be nothing special about these books – even flat-earthers publish some books – were it not for their being global best sellers: Morgan's book was sold in more than 10 million copies as of 2008 (Donaldson, 2008) and Miriano's book has been translated into six languages so far and is in on its best way to global popularity.

In a brilliant phenomenological analysis of the elusive concept of care, Julia Wood (1994) argues that care is not a simple concept. It rather depends on other psychological characteristics like: responsiveness, sensitivity to others, acceptance, and patience.

> To be responsive, sensitive, accepting, and patient with others depends fundamentally on being able and willing to let go of, at least temporarily, preoccupation with oneself and one's own concerns. This letting go, of course, is the basis of the pervasive association of selflessness with caring (...), (Wood, 1994, p.107).

Care depends on the ability to neglect one own's desires, needs, etc., in short, being/becoming selfless. In consequence, the concept of selflessness is more fundamental, or to use biological parlance, more rudimentary, than care, which appears to be a mixture of various qualities – Wood lists the four of them.

Before focusing on the notion of selflessness, a demarcation line should be drawn. We are not entering the discussion of the general position of selflessness, or its opposite, as a principal motivation for human behavior. Namely, in philosophical discussions, the question of predominance of selflessness (and its connate concepts like altruism, self-sacrifice, sympathy, etc.) vs. selfishness (and its connate concepts of egoism) is one of the most controversial, that occupies diametrical positions in different value systems. Some would argue that selflessness is the fundamental factor that motivates (or should motivate) human behavior (e.g., Kant, 1785; Nagel, 1970). On the other hand, there is a long tradition of those who claim that we cannot escape, but being egoistic and always act out of self-interest with the satisfaction of our own desires (e.g., Rand, 1964). Though such fundamental questions are related to our problem, it is not directly relevant since we are discussing women's selflessness regardless of broader moral consequences. For us, the most relevant fact is that in large portions of even contemporary societies good woman is the one who is perceived as selfless.

What is selflessness? The most deterministic views come from evolutionary biology, that is "biological altruism." Here the biological notion of selflessness or selfishness diverges from the philosophical or even everyday notions. In common parlance, an important requirement for an action to be called selfish or selfless is that it was done with the conscious intention of being concentrated on oneself or helping others. However, in the biological sense, there is no such requirement. E.g., there is evidence of "altruistic behavior" among creatures what are not conscious in our meaning of the word (e.g., insects, bats, birds, etc., Lozada, D'Adamo, & Fuentes, 2011). Similarly, we have interesting pieces of evidence coming from neuroscience. Moll et al. (2006) showed that the mesolimbic reward system would be engaged by donations in the same way as when monetary rewards are obtained. These findings indirectly support an "essentialist" interpretation. Essentialism entails "the attribution of a fixed essence to women. Women's essence is assumed to be given and universal and is usually, though not necessarily, identified with women's biology and "natural' characteristics" (Grosz, 1994, p.47). So for an essentialist, women's inclinations towards selflessness and care would be a part of their biological constitution. This is supported by some most recent findings showing that female and male brains display different reaction to selfless and selfish behavior, with women's brain showing a stronger reward signal for selfless behavior than men's (Soutschek et al., 2017).

On the other hand, Miller (1976) and Gilligan (1982) strongly emphasize the psychological factors as the crucial motivation. Miller thus writes:

> Women's great desire for affiliation is both a fundamental strength (...) and at the same time the inevitable source of many of women's current problems. (...) When women act on the basis of this underlying psychological motive [for affiliation], they are usually led into subservience. (Miller,1976, p.82.)

Similar to biological or physiological/neurological determinism, psychological determinism would suggest that, if we are psychologically determined, then in some way our control over our behavior is limited. Our behavior is determined by our nature which would absorb those social factors that become internalized into an individual so that they become a part of her very nature. In our specific case social factors – e.g., that selflessness is imposed on women by family, society, etc. – should be taken into consideration attentively since they present the basis of the still dominant distinction between sex and gender going back to Simone de Beauvoir's *Le deuxième sexe* (1949) and her famous dictum that "one is not born, but rather becomes, a woman." However many contemporary feminists are taking a critical stance toward the crude distinction between sex as biologically given fact, and gender as a social construct, still majority of present-day gender philosophers have not entirely given up the view that gender is about social factors and that it is distinct from biological sex – in whatever way (Mikkola, 2017).

One of the *crux* of grasping the notion of selflessness is that it includes two different connotations. On the one hand, on the grammatical level, the word implies "the loss of the self", with all its catastrophic consequences, like invisibility, subservient passivity, etc. In the case of feminist theories, it is a negative counterpart to the masculinized view of selfhood, its negative corollary. On the other hand, the term is tightly bound with the concept of altruism, promoting the good of the others at the expense of oneself, a self-sacrifice for the sake of others. Thusly understood, selflessness is a universally admirable and desirable characteristic for which both men and women are praised. Those who see selflessness as a basis of morality would argue that it is hard to see how someone could be claimed to be moral if he or she is not willing to sacrifice themselves, their time, comfort, sometimes even well-being or health for the sake of others.

A *caveat* should be put here. By no means, we want to suggest that *all* women are selfless by nature or by society's formation with the implication that selfish woman would be an aberration from the normal. We don't even enter the question of whether the majority of women are or aren't selfless if this could be measured and established in any way. We also don't enter into discussing how to characterize caring for someone out of selfish motives etc. Our position is that women are still – unfortunately – supposed to be selfless in virtue of their being women, i.e., our society still promotes selflessness as a cardinal women's virtue, as one of the most characteristic realizations of womanhood. Thus, for the validity of our argument, it does not matter which side of the essentialist vs. anti-essentialist debate over "women's nature" one takes. It should also be mentioned that in modern societies we can witness the phenomenon of "reversed gender roles", i.e., women become income-earners while men stay at home and care for the family. However, recent studies show that the labor force participation rates of women are still much below those of men. Thus the average labor participation rates of men 80 % and women are 64 % (Chamie, 2018). Of course, these rates differ significantly between traditional societies, such as India, where the difference between men and women is 52 %, and the Scandinavian countries where the difference is 4 %. In Italy, it is 20 %, in Japan, 17 %, and in the United States, 11 %. It is not only that parenthood has an opposite impact for men and women, as the study shows. Chamie (2018) also concludes that in all regions, women spend at least twice as much time as men on caregiving responsibilities and housework, which clearly affects women's employment rate.

The situation now is significantly better than in the past. However, it still corroborates our thesis that selflessness – here in the form of caring for family – is still, at a global level, an expected women's work. This is also supported by Gallup's survey from 2015 which shows that most women with children in the US still themselves *prefer* homemaking role (56 %, Saad, 2015).

Premise 2: Capitalism is based on selfishness.

It has been traditionally and widely accepted, as for a fact, that the main motivational factor of capitalism is selfishness (greed, egotism, etc.). Let us just take an example of one of the most classic *loca* that would testify to that. The starting point is that capitalism is a realization of human being, who is, as J. S. Mill (in)famously writes:

> (…) a being who inevitably does that by which he may obtain the greatest amount of necessaries, conveniences, and luxuries, with the smallest quantity of labor and physical self-denial with which they can be obtained in the existing state of knowledge. (Mill, 1874: V.46.)

What does it mean that capitalism is founded on human selfishness and greed? However old these ideas may be (we can find them scattered across Greek philosophy, Machiavelli, etc.), the philosopher famous for insisting on selfishness and greed as the basic human motivation for possessing private property and who is often seen as a precursor and anticipator of modern-age capitalism is Thomas Hobbes (1588–1679). Hobbes is known for a bleak vision of human nature, *homo homini deus et homo homini lupus* being his leading mottos. He argues that the state of nature is a miserable state of war and that in such a condition we cannot fully realize our ends – thus the nature has provided us with rationality as a tool to create peace so that we could realize our selfish interests. Hobbes famously writes in the "Epistle dedicatory" of his second most famous work, *Elementa philosophical de cive*, or, shortly, *On the Citizen*, explaining two postulates of human nature:

> (…) one, the postulate of human greed by which each man insists upon his own private use of common property; the other, the postulate of natural reason, by which all man strives to avoid violent death as the supreme evil in nature. (Hobbes, 1998, p.5–6).

Prima facie (i.e., putting aside more charitable interpretations of Hobbes's words) it looks rather straight forward: we all basically want two things: to avoid death and to get everything we want to get. If this is what human nature is about, then selfishness – taking care of oneself and satisfying one's own needs and desires – turns out to be the main motivating factor of human behavior. A similar thought is also expressed by Adam Smith in his *The Wealth of Nations* from 1776:

> It is not from the benevolence of the butcher, the brewer, or the baker that we expect our dinner, but from their regard of their own interest. (Smith, 1957/1776, p.13.)

It is understandable that neither butcher nor brewer nor almost any other person wants to work for free or just give away her goods out of the goodness of her heart. Economic transactions, when they function normally, presuppose that each party seeks an outcome that it considers beneficial for itself. Capitalism is based on self-interest which is justified by the recurrence to the presupposed fundamental selfishness of human nature.

Here someone may argue that self-interest and selfishness, although in contemporary, mostly political, discourse are used interchangeably, are not the same. The distinction may go along the following lines: selfishness is marked by a lack of consideration for others. For a selfish person, the self is the highest criterion. On the other hand, self-interest is looking for the best ways to promote one's welfare. In principle, this can include caring for others as a way to promote one's own welfare. So one could argue that, even though human nature might be presupposed to be selfish, capitalism itself is based on a mitigated form of selfishness, i.e., self-interest which might include also selfless acts.

If we accept this distinction, this does not really influence our argument for two reasons. First, capitalists (here: participants in the arena of capitalism), when they do selfless deeds – and obviously there are many such deeds – do them not *qua* capitalists, but *qua* good or selfless people. If a person gives money to a charity organization out of the goodness of her heart, she is doing it motivated by her goodness, she might have done the same under any socio-economic system such as communism, or feudalism, or slavery, there is nothing "capitalistic" about her act of charity. If a person gives money to a charity organization expecting some financially profitable outcome, such as tax deduction, then the welfare of the other is an instrument for one's own self-interested or selfish profit, put as a final goal of the transaction. Second, selflessness, on the one hand, and self-interest and/or selfishness, on the other hand, are opposites in *directionality*. Selflessness may be understood as an intention directed towards other people – up to the extreme point of completely neglecting oneself. Self-interest and/or selfishness may be understood as an intention directed towards oneself – either in a form that does not exclude selfless acts as a means of satisfying one's own desires and needs or in a form that excludes such acts. In either case, the directions of those intentions are opposite than the one of selflessness.

If we accept self-interest or selfishness as fuel running the machine of capitalism, it is not meant as a critique of capitalism. Even if self-interest, taken in its most negative expressions such as greed, is a motivating factor, it does not entail that the result of such a complex system must turn out bad. There is a powerful justification for capitalism that says that when individuals strive after reaching their selfish ends in the market, an overall effect of this is that goods are allocated in a socially beneficial way. As the title of Mandeville's book from 1714 suggests: private vices become public goods mediated in the arena of the open market; if true, this would mean that there is a magic in capitalist markets to turn (private) vice of greed and selfishness into a (public) virtue.

A slightly different line of defense comes from the Scottish philosopher David Hume. For him the

> if human needs and wants are successfully fulfilled only in society, and if selfishness and avidity stand in the way, that is, constitute impediments to social organization, then only a system of private property is justified because only such a system can mitigate the potentially disruptive forces of selfishness. (Panichas, 1983, p.398.)

This argument sees the role of capitalism as a socially positive factor: it is good because it somehow mitigates selfishness, by structuring it within the social rules that a capitalistic order dictates.

Here another *caveat* should be mentioned. Our argument does not rely on the *truism* that human is inexorably selfish. Even on the contrary, we believe it is not. It is about the dominant *belief* that originated in the Early Modern Era about human nature as selfish and greedy that has become generally accepted as the main explanation of a motivating factor of capitalism and as an integral part of capitalistic self-evaluation. It does not matter if one takes selfishness as a starting point of capitalism or sees capitalism as a system that mitigates the wild human nature – i.e., stands in a negative relationship to it, exists for the sake of negating it. It is important that we for traditional reasons we *perceive* and *tolerate* capitalism as an expression of human selfishness.

Conclusion: Capitalism is not a suitable "habitat" for women

There are so many different attacks on capitalism that it would be hard just to name from which perspectives they come. However, capitalism, as a system, has been relatively rarely discussed from an ethical perspective by analytic philosophers. This is especially striking given that most of the analytic political philosophers are typically "robust egalitarians" (Illy-Williamson, 2017, p.415). Capitalism not only tolerates huge social and economic inequalities which are not consequences of personal choices and gives an opportunity to a proportionally insignificant percentage of people to have an immense political influence but also in itself seems to be bound to perpetuating the inequality gap, if we are to trust Piketty's world-best-seller analysis (Piketty, 2014). From this perspective, it would seem only natural for an egalitarian to launch her attacks on such a system. Thus, all the justified and corroborated attacks on capitalism coming from these perspectives are equally applicable to men and women.

Moreover, there are also quite a few attacks on capitalism as a female-inimical system. For instance, Gimenez (2005) makes a special application of Marxist theories of production on the position of women within the capitalist mode of production, and the organization of physical and social reproduction among those who must sell their labor power to survive women make a significant part. On the other hand, there are many texts criticizing capitalism as an expression of patriarchy with all the pernicious consequences for women. In this context, one can read about male exploitation of women based on a sexual division of labor, about lack for rights and discrimination against women, different forms of harassment, representing social inequalities as natural and normal, the question of evaluation of women's domestic work, etc. The groundbreaking book in this context is the collection of seventeen texts in the book entitled *Capitalist Patriarchy and the Case for Socialist Feminism* and edited by Z. R. Eisenstein (1978).

However, in our approach, we took a different turn. Personal identity depends on social roles which some individual exhibits in a society. Personal identity also depends on the accepted and/or imposed value system which reflects itself in everyday behavior toward other individuals. In our analysis, there is an obvious conflict between the role women traditionally still take in most of the present-day societies as selfless caregivers and the supposed principle of capitalism that is care for oneself and one's own property. It is an obvious conflict of roles that is especially prominent among women: the traditional role of a businessperson is opposite to the role of a selfless caregiver. From this unfortunate standpoint, "to be a businesswomen or to be a virtuous woman/wife?" seems to be an either-or question which is hard to answer just by a distribution of a "work time" and "private time."

This conflict could be resolved – logically and rationally – either by making capitalism less selfish or making women less selfless or both. These both positions have many proponents: e.g., a trained clinical psychologist Oliver James (2008) argues, bluntly, that selfish capitalism is bad for our mental health. On the other hand, the whole movements of so-called second, and now third, feminism are concentrated around breaking the traditional roles of women in society – and thus the role of woman as a caregiver.

References

Catalyst (2018). Women in S&P 500 Companies. Retrieved from http://www.catalyst.org/knowledge/women-sp-500-companies

Chamie, J. (2018). Despite Growing Gender Equality, More Women Stay at Home Than Men. *YaleGlobal Online*. Retrieved from https://yaleglobal.yale.edu/content/despite-growing-gender-equality-more-women-stay-home-men

Davaki, K. (2016). Differences in Men's and Women's Work, Care and Leisure Time. *Directorate-General for Internal Policies, Citizens' Rights and Constitutional Affairs*. Retrieved from http://www.europarl.europa.eu/supporting-analyses

Demosthenes (1939). Against Neaera. *Orations, Volume VI: Orations 50-59: Private Cases. In Neaeram.* Translated by A. T. Murray. Loeb Classical Library 351. Cambridge, MA: Harvard University Press.

Donaldson James, S. (2008). Christians Promote Holy, Hot Sex in Marriage. *abcNEWS*, Retrieved from https://abcnews.go.com/US/story?id=4651272&page=1

Eisenstein, Z. R. (ed.) (1978). *Capitalist Patriarchy and the Case for Socialist Feminism*. New York, London: Monthly Review Press.

Eurostat (2018). Positions held by women in senior management positions. Retrieved from http://ec.europa.eu/eurostat/web/products-datasets/-/sdg_05_60

Familiaris Consortio. Apostolic Exhoration. Retrieved from http://w2.vatican.va/content/john-paul-ii/en/apost_exhortations/documents/hf_jp-ii_exh_19811122_familiaris-consortio.html

Gilligan, C. (1982). *In a different voice: Psychological theory and women's development*. Cambridge, MA: Harvard University Press.

Gimenez, M. E. (2005). Capitalism and the Oppression of Women: Marx Revisited. *Science & Society, 69*(1), 11–32.

Groarke, L. (1999). Deductivism Within Pragma-Dialectis. *Argumentation, 13*, 1–14.

Grosz, E. A. (1995). *Space, time, and perversion.* New York, London: Routledge.

Hobbes, T. (1998). *On the Citizen.* Translated and edited by R. Tuck and M. Silverthorne. Cambridge (UK): Cambridge University Press.

Illy-Williamson, D. (2017). Why Capitalism. *Political Studies Review, 15*(3), 415 –422.

James, O. (2008). *The Selfish Capitalist: The Origins of Affluenza.* London: Vermillion.

John Paul II, P. (1981). *Familiaris consortio.* Retrieved from http://w2.vatican.va/content/john-paul-ii/en/apost_exhortations/documents/hf_jp-ii_exh_19811122_familiaris-consortio.html

Kant, I. (1785/2002). *Groundwork for the Metaphysics of Morals,* A. Zweig (trans.), Oxford: Oxford University Press.

Kerber, L. K. (1986). Some Cautionary Words for Historians. *Signs, 11*(2), 304–310.

Lozada, M., D'Adamo, P., & Fuentes, M. A. (2011). Beneficial effects of human altruism. *Journal of Theoretical Biology, 289*, 12–16.

Macinnes, J. (1998). Analysing Patriarchy Capitalism and Women's Employment in Europe. *Innovation: The European Journal of Social Science Research, 11*(2), 227–248. DOI: 10.1080/13511610.1998.9968563.

Mill, J. S. (1874). On the Definition of Political Economy, and on the Method of Investigation Proper to It. *Essays on Some Unsettled Questions of Political Economy,* 2nd ed., London: Longmans, Green, Reader & Dyer.

Mikkola, M. (2017). Feminist Perspetives on Sex and Gender. *Stanford Encyclopedia of Philosophy.* Retrieved from: https://plato.stanford.edu/entries/feminism-gender/

Miller, J. B. (1976). *Toward a new psychology of women.* Boston, MA: Beacon Press.

Miriano, C. (2011). *Sposati e sii sottomessa.* [Marry him and be submissive.] Florence: Vallecchi.

Moll, J., Krueger, F., Zahn, R., Pardini, M., De Oliveira-Souza, R., & Grafman, J. (2006). Human fronto-mesolimbic networks guide decisions about charitable donation. *Proceedings of the National Academy of Sciences of the United States of America, 103*(42), 15623-15628. https://doi.org/10.1073/pnas.0604475103

Morgan, M. (1973). *The Total Woman.* New York: F.H. Revel.

Nagel, T. (1970), *The Possibility of Altruism,* Oxford: Oxford University Press.

Panichas, G. E. (1983). Hume's Theory of Property. *ARSP: Archiv für Rechts- und Sozialphilosophie / Archives for Philosophy of Law and Social Philosophy, 69*(3), 391–405.

Piketty, T. (2014), *Capital in the Twenty-First Century,* A. Goldhammer (trans.), Cambridge (Mass.), London: The Belkamp Press of Harward University Press.

Rand, A. (1964). *The Virtue of Selfishness.* New York: New American Library.

Saad, L. (2015). "Children a Key Factor in Women's Desire to Work Outside the Home", Retrieved from https://news.gallup.com/poll/186050/children-key-factor-women-desire-work-outside-home.aspx

Sherwin, B. (2014a). "Why Women Vanish As They Move Up The Career Ladder." *Business Insider.* Jan. 27, 2014. Retrieved from http://www.businessinsider.com/women-and-career-advancement-leadership-2014-1?IR=T

Sherwin, B. (2014b). "Why Women Are More Effective Leaders Than Men." *Business Insider.* Jan. 24, 2014. Retrieved from http://www.businessinsider.com/study-women-are-better-leaders-2014-1?IR=T

Smith, A. (1957/1776). *An Inquiry into the Nature and Causes of the Wealth of Nations,* Vol. 1. London: J. M. Dunt and Sons.

Soutschek, A., Burke, C.J., Raja Beharelle, A., Schreiber, R., Weber, S.C., Karipidis, I.I., ten Velden, J., Weber, B., Haker, H., Kalenscher, T., & Tobler, P.N. (2017). The dopaminergic reward system underpins gender differences in social preferences. *Nature Human Behavior, 1,* 819–827. Retrieved from https://doi.org/10.1038/s41562-017-0226-y

Statistics Canada. (2018). Labour force characteristics by occupation, annual. Retrieved from https://www150.statcan.gc.ca/t1/tbl1/en/tv.action?pid=1410029701&pickMembers%5B0%5D=1.1&pickMembers%5B1%5D=2.2&pickMembers%5B2%5D=4.3

The Workplace Gender Equality Agency. (2018). Australia's gender equality scorecard, Retrieved from https://www.wgea.gov.au/sites/default/files/2016-17-gender-equality-scorecard.pdf

Walton, D., & Gordon, Th. F. (2015). Formalizing Informal Logic. *Informal Logic,* 35 (4), 508–538. Retreived from https://scholar.uwindsor.ca/crrarpub/30

Wood, J. T. (1994). *Who cares? Women, Care, and Culture.* Carbondale, U.S.A.: Southern Illinois University Press.

Chapter 8

Prosocial Vocational Interests and Gender in the Labor Market

Dominika Ochnik,
Institute of Psychology, University of Opole, Poland

Introduction

Prosocial interests share a common ground with the selfless attitude in terms of going beyond one's objectives and focusing upon the interests/ needs of others. The literature of the subject offers findings regarding the diversity of vocational interests across gender. These indicate women as the group manifesting stronger social interests than men (Su, Rounds, & Armstrong, 2009; Thompson, Donnay, Morris, & Schaubhut, 2004). At the same time, these findings are associated with the stereotype of a social role of women linked with the involvement in interpersonal relations and with care (Wood & Eagly, 2010, 2012; Mandal, 2004). The objective of the present study is to verify the diversification of prosocial interests across gender and age.

Vocational identity and the course of the career undergo dynamic changes throughout one's lifetime, even after they reach maturity. As a consequence, it is associated with the instability of vocational interests over time (Super, Savickas, & Super, 1996). On the other hand, according to John L. Holland (1999), vocational interests constitute fixed dispositional features. The trajectory of vocational interests' stability gains an upward trend between 18 and 21 years of age. This means that vocational interests remain relatively stable and crystallize in this particular life period (Low, Yoon, Roberts, & Rounds, 2005).

Apart from the already acknowledged personality features (individual determinants) (Stoll et al., 2017), social determinants ought to be taken into account as well. These may exert an impact upon the intensity of vocational interests. Vocational clock constitutes one of the social factors. It indicates the dynamic intensity of vocational interests with regard to social expectations determined by age and gender (Ochnik & Rosmus, 2016).

Women entering the labor market (usually aged 20-24) and those in the period of a more intensive vocational activity (30-34 years of age) manifest vocational interests which go beyond gender stereotypes. This may indicate a broadened social role of women (Ochnik & Rosmus, 2016). At the same time, both women and men in their periods of peak vocational activity prefer more stereotypical vocational interests in terms of being prosocial. On the one hand, this may be associated with social roles pursued in private lives, and on the other, it acknowledges the adjustment to social stereotypical requirements present in professional environment. The requirements are labeled as the social-vocational clock (Ochnik & Rosmus, 2016).

The present paper aims to establish answers to the following questions: Do women manifest stronger prosocial vocational preferences than men? Do these interests change over different stages of the professional career. The analysis encompassed adolescents (10-14 years of age). Their results were compared with those of older age groups (20-24, 30-34, 40-44, 50-54).

Type of social vocational Interests vs. Gender

John Holland's model constitutes the key and the most frequently applied tool for measuring vocational interests. Studies based upon the model indicate that men prefer the realistic and investigative types, and women pursue the conventional, social and artistic types (Su, Rounds, & Armstrong, 2009). The meta-analysis conducted on the sample of 0.5 million confirmed that women exhibit social interests significantly more frequently than men. The social type was more characteristic for women than men in 13-59 age groups (Thompson et al., 2004).

Among young adolescents, women score higher in social interests (Murray & Hall, 2001). Other studies indicate no significant differences among adolescents (Andreea-Elena, Chraif, Vasile, & Anitei, 2014). Studies which confirm higher scores of women in the social type highlight that the compatibility of the theoretical model is more accurate with regard to men than women. Therefore, discrepancies of average scores obtained in the course of survey studies ought to be approached with caution (Proyer & Häusler, 2007).

Prediger (1982) introduced two bipolar dimensions: People-Things and Data-Ideas, into the hexagonal Holland model. Lippa (2001) emphasized that the femininity-masculinity dimension is convergent with People-Things dimension (Prediger, 1999). Women scored higher in dimensions pertaining to interpersonal dimensions (social type), and men focused upon work with objects (realistic type). The discrepancy was acknowledged as the one which diversifies gender the most from among individual differences (Lubinski, 2000) and the one which is relatively stable. Women scored higher in vocational interests in the People dimension regardless of age (Holland, Fritzsche, & Powell, 1994) and in various decades (Fouad, 1999). The results of the meta-analysis indicate that gender differences in social interests intensify along with respondents' age (Su, Rounds, & Armstrong, 2009).

Some authors observe that such a strong diversity of vocational interests ought to stimulate scholars to develop specific tools which disregard the aspect, and as a consequence, fail to reinforce gender stereotypes and reduce barriers for women developing their careers in the STEM field (Prediger & Cole, 1975). On the other hand, Gary D. Gottferdson and John L. Holland (1978) indicated that vocational interests are shaped on the basis of socializing experiences which are usually different for women and men.

Social Gender Roles in the Context of the Career

Gender roles are understood as socially determined activities suited for women and men (Mandal, 2004). The socio-structural concept explains causes of the diversification and similarities of women and men on the basis of the pursued social roles emerging from the division of tasks assigned to women and men in the society (Eagly & Wood, 1999). The division of duties in the society depends upon whether these tasks may be executed more productively by each of the genders. As a consequence, men are usually attributed with duties demanding greater physical strength and agility, and women with those emerging from childbirth and rearing. The socio-structural concept makes a premise that there exist gender roles which constitute a social construct but also are partly reflected in biological processes determining the way female and male bodies are built in. The following emerge from these biological differences: the ability to bear children only by women, along with duties associated with the division, which position women's tasks as those focused upon child rearing at home, and men on those outside it (Wood & Eagly, 2002).

The division of duties structures the perception of differences and similarities regarding gender. Beliefs associated with gender roles and particular social expectations connected with the pursuit of these roles emerge when the execution of the duties is observed (Wood & Eagly, 2012). Due to the fact that in industrialized societies women rear children more frequently than men, and men pursue high professional status more frequently than women, beliefs associated with gender roles emerge. The beliefs assume that women are more caring while men are more assertive and dominant. At the same time, women are perceived as more focused upon relationships between family members and as more effective in interpersonal relations. On the other hand, when acting in an external environment, men focus upon competitiveness and pursuit of work-related objectives, which develops the perception of the male role as instrumental and causative (Wood & Eagly, 2012).

Studies focused upon the stereotypization of gender in the work-related domain indicate that the realistic type is the one defined as masculine the most. Investigative and enterprising types are considered slightly less masculine. On the other hand, the conventional type is defined as typically feminine. Artistic and social types are considered as feminine as well, but not as clearly as the previous one (Gottefredson, 1981). It is noteworthy that both boys and girls pursue the schematically gender-determined professions since their childhoods, and girls who pursue the non-stereotypical careers are less persistent in their pursuit (Fouad, 2007).

Such a division of social roles in the work-related field is explained by evolutionary psychology as a biologically determined, divergent predisposition of women and men towards professional work (Browne, 2006). In light of the above, men will prefer professions associated with a greater risk and stress and lower social requirements. On the other hand, women are predisposed towards work with a higher level of security and demanding an involvement in interpersonal relations.

Culture vs. Gender

Cross-cultural analyses encompassing approx. 400 000 respondents from 20 countries indicate that, contrary to expectations, gender differences in terms of vocational behavior may be greater in highly egalitarian cultures than in low egalitarian-level cultures (Ott-Holland, Huang, Ryan, Elizondo, & Wadlington, 2013).

In light of Hofstede's analysis of cultural dimensions (2000), Poland constitutes a masculine culture. This denotes a clear diversification of social gender roles and pursuit of "live to work" motto. In such a context, work constitutes the primary value both for women and men. At the same time, Polish research suggests that Polish culture is defined as feminine (Boski, 1999; Mandal, 2004; Mandal, Gawor, & Buczny, 2012). Such an outlook requires good social adaptation of women in fields typically defined as masculine and high assessment of typically feminine values. It results in women clearly manifesting their femininity and in a tendency to assess behavior as extremely typical.

Methods

Research Model

In relation to Super's Life Career Rainbow model (Hornowska & Paluchowski, 2001), the Contextual model of vocational interests was offered (Ochnik, 2018; Ochnik, Stala, & Rosmus, 2018). The contextual model emphasizes the fluctuant character of vocational interests shaped by cultural, individual and social age- and gender-dependent factors.

The instability of vocational interests constituted the fundamental premise of the model. The intensity of the interests may be determined by a broad spectrum of cultural factors, such as culture's gender dimension or social expectations realized in particular social gender roles performed by women and men of various ages. The concept of the social vocational clock was linked with the intensity of vocational interests with regard to gender and age. The interests are determined by social roles and cultural factors. The dimension of individual factors (personality, values, attitudes), which will determine the reactions of individuals with regard to socio-cultural factors is also critical.

The present study verified the prosocial type of vocational interests in relation to gender and age of respondents (Fig. 8.1)

Figure 8.1. **Contextual model of vocational interests.**

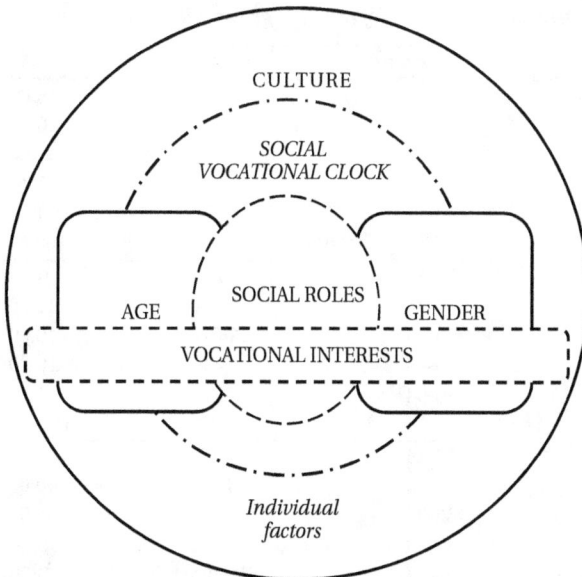

Measurements

The study applied the scale of the prosocial type of vocational interests featured in the original tool labeled Vocational Potential (Ochnik, 2018; Ochnik, Stala, & Rosmus, 2018). The scale is composed of 20 statements pertaining to the self-assessment of skills and features. The scale of the prosocial type scored the required reliability of Cronbach's alpha above 0.7, $\alpha = 0.703$.

The following constitute example skills and features of the prosocial type — skills: *advising, conflict mitigation, listening, establishing contacts*, and features: *emphatic, sensitive, friendly, helpful, cooperating*.

Research Group

The study encompassed 10 850 respondents including 6591 women (61%) and 4259 men (39%). Based upon the indexes of the Central Statistical Office of Poland (GUS) (GUS, 2015), the following age groups for the sample were established: 20-24 years of age- the group entering the labor market, and 30-34 — the group manifesting the greatest activity on the labor market. Results were analyzed in the first stage of the study (Ochnik & Rosmus, 2016). The second stage of the study incorporated further age groups: 40-44 and 50-54 (Ochnik, 2017). The third stage of the study incorporated the youngest age group of 10-14 consisting of 1491 respondents (Tab. 8.1).

Table 8.1. *Descriptive statistics of research group with regard to gender and age*

Gender	Age group		N	%
Women	10-14		1 227	19.00
	20-24		2 663	40.00
	30-34		2 030	31.00
	40-44		486	7.00
	50-54		185	3.00
		Total	6 591	100.00
Men	10-14		264	6.00
	20-24		1 756	41.00
	30-34		1 676	40.00
	40-44		444	10.00
	50-54		119	3.00
		Total	4 259	100.00
Total	10-14		1 491	14.00
	20-24		4 419	40.00
	30-34		3 706	34.00
	40-44		930	9.00
	50-54		304	3.00
		Total	10 850	100.00

It ought to be noted that the study isolated a specific group of respondents. Its size indicates that conclusions may be generalized to describe the whole Polish population. However, the participation in the study was associated with the increased motivation to learn about oneself because every respondent received feedback upon their vocational interests. Therefore, the study attracted people pursuing their work-related development. Such a high motivation may be associated with openness and intellectual curiosity, but also, may emerge from the individual not matching the professional environment.

Results

SPSS 24 was applied to conduct the statistical analysis. Variables satisfied the fundamental assumptions of normal distribution and homogeneity of variance for parametric tests.

The average intensity of prosocial interests for women and men in relation to age was established. Males aged 10-14 ($M = 66.14$, $SD = 7.64$) scored the highest and women aged 50-54 ($M = 64.16$, $SD = 7.18$) scored the lowest (Tab. 2).

Table 8.2. *Descriptive statistics of the prosocial vocational interests with regard to age and gender*

Age group	Gender	N	M	SD
10-14	Men	264	66.14	7.40
	Women	1227	65.20	7.20
	Total	1491	65.37	7.24
20-24	Men	1756	65.21	7.11
	Women	2663	64.57	7.05
	Total	4419	64.82	7.07
30-34	Men	1676	64.52	7.21
	Women	2030	64.86	6.68
	Total	3706	64.70	6.93
40-44	Men	444	64.70	7.15
	Women	486	64.81	7.87
	Total	930	64.75	7.53
50-54	Men	119	66.01	7.64
	Women	185	64.16	7.18
	Total	304	64.88	7.41
Total	Men	3995	64.89	7.18
	Women	5364	64.68	6.99
	Total	9359	64.77	7.07

The two-way analysis of variance (ANOVA) was applied in order to analyze results. Research results for individual vocational interests of the prosocial type with regard to age and gender diversity are outlined below. In order to compare the main impact of gender, age and gender-age interaction upon the prosocial type, the two-way ANOVA was conducted. Individual impact of gender and age proved insignificant. On the other hand, gender-age interaction proved to determine the intensity of the prosocial type significantly (Fig. 8.2).

Figure 8.2. **Results of the two-way ANOVA for gender-age interaction of the prosocial type of vocational interests.**

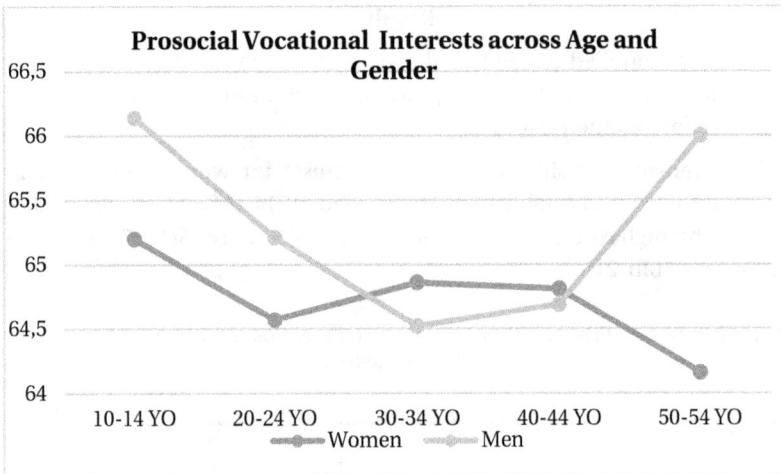

The age-gender interaction proved to be statistically significant, $F(4, 10840) = 3.90$, $p = 0.004$, $\eta^2 = 0.001$:

-   the youngest (10-14) and eldest (50-54) group of men scored higher than women in all age groups: 50-54, 40-44, 30-34, and 20-24;
-   the youngest (20-24) and eldest (50-54) group of women scored significantly lower than men in the respective age groups;
-   the lowest discrepancies were observed in groups of the highest vocational activity, among women and men aged 30-34 and 40-44.

To conclude the discussion of the gender-age interaction:

- men in the youngest (10-14) and eldest (50-54) groups scored significantly higher on the intensity of the prosocial type, and women aged 30-34 scored higher than men. Results for the 40-44 age group did not differ with regard to age (see Tab. 8.2).

The impact of age, $F(4,10840) = 3.54$, $p = 0.007$, $\eta^2 < 0.001$, proved to be statistically significant. This means that people aged 10-14 manifested the strongest prosocial vocational interests, and those aged 30-34 and 40-44 the lowest.

The impact of gender proved to be significant as well, $F(1,10849) = 7.19$, $p = 0.007$, $\eta^2 = 0.001$. However, its strength may be considered low. Men scored significantly higher in the prosocial vocational interests than women did (see Tab. 8.2).

This means that men achieved a higher level of prosocial interests than women in the assessed age groups.

Discussion

The analysis indicated that prosocial vocational interests of women and men in the period the interests are shaped in (10-14 years of age), as well as in the period of entering labor market (20-24) and in senior age (50-54) differ significantly from those for people in their peak vocational activity. Adolescents and men in the age of entering the labor market scored their prosocial vocational interests higher than women in the same age. On the other hand, women in the age of peak vocational activity scored their level of prosocial type higher than men in the same group. Among the eldest group (50-54) the tendency similar to the one observed among younger groups (10-14 and 20-24) was noted. It was men who scored their prosocial vocational interests higher.

The present scores are convergent with other studies (Su, Rounds, & Armstrong, 2009; Thompson et al., 2004; Lippa, 2001) which acknowledge higher average scores for the prosocial vocational interests among women than among men, with the exception of those in peak vocational activity, i.e. women and men aged 30-34. The discrepancies proved insignificant for the 40-year-olds. Among the 20 and 50-year-olds a reverse tendency was observed. In addition, the analysis of gender differences for the whole sample indicated that men scored higher than women. Even though the gap is marginal, it manifests a different trend and does not acknowledge the stereotypical social female roles.

As a consequence, the present results indicate that the stereotypical social roles are embraced by those in peak vocational activity. For those outside peak activity age (adolescents, those entering the labor market, seniors) the roles are non-stereotypical. Stereotypically speaking, the social gender role of women encompasses the interest in interpersonal relations, and male roles, the interest in objects (Lippa, 2001).

It may be argued that younger people may fail to establish their vocational interests correctly due to the shortage of opportunities for verifying their skills and features in work-related fields and against tangible requirements. Nevertheless, the analysis of results for the eldest age group (50+) indicates the return to the trajectory convergent with the results of the youngest group and those entering the labor market. Expanding the scope of the study to incorporate the youngest and more senior groups allowed for the conclusion to be drawn that the natural prosocial vocational predispositions depreciate during the period of peak vocational activity which calls for the stereotypical roles. It is only after the age of 50 that the intensification of these natural vocational interests returns. Therefore, a premise can be made that along with age, an individual gains work experience and functions in various interpersonal relations, and thus becomes more aware and self-confident with regard to vocational predispositions. Understanding oneself in relations with others may account for the greatest difference between women and men in the eldest group.

The present results are interpreted in the framework of the Contextual model of vocational interests. The pursued social roles constitute the key element of the model. The difference between those entering the labor market (20-24) and those in the period of peak vocational activity (30-34) may be also explained by new social roles being embraced: wife/husband and parent. The average marriage age in Poland is 27 for women and 29 for men. The median age when the first child is born is 29 (GUS, 2016). As a consequence, women manifest their prosocial features and skills the strongest when they pursue the social role of a mother and wife. For female groups older by 10 or 20 years, the intensity of the feature declines successively. Therefore, a conclusion can be drawn that stronger prosocial interests are primarily associated with the role of the mother, which in turn, is connected with elevated protectiveness. The role may "radiate" onto other spheres, and thus become reflected in work-related fields.

At the same time, the analysis of individual age groups indicates that scores of women and men in relation to prosocial vocational interests constitute mirror reflections, thus are complementary. It is only among 40-44-year-olds, when the work-related and family situation stabilizes, that the differences disappear. For the remaining age groups, women and men score results which acknowledge the fact that male and female social roles complement each other.

The cultural factor of the Contextual model of vocational interests may refer to the gender of cultural dimension, which indicates the diversification of gender roles and the perception of work as the primary value (Hofstede, 2001; Boski, 1999; Mandal, 2004). Despite barriers, Polish culture enables women to pursue diversified work-related roles, which translates into the female stereotype being broadened and becoming more diverse (Mandal et al., 2012). Male stereotypes are also expanded to incorporate features traditionally attributed with women (e.g., being gentle, emphatic, family-focused) (Mandal et al., 2012). This means that despite the evident division of roles, women and men in Poland may exhibit a tendency to go beyond their stereotypical social roles (Ochnik, 2012). This, in turn, may account for the non-stereotypical vocational interests of respondents.

It should also be noted that the subject matter of prosocial vocational interests is associated with interpersonal competencies (advising, assistance, conflict mitigation, listening, establishment of contacts). It ought to be emphasized that despite interpersonal competencies being connected with the feminine domain (Hall, & Halberstadt, 1986), studies in the general level of interpersonal competencies do not indicate a significant diversity with regard to gender (Ochnik, 2016; Kanning, 2006; Buhrmester, Furman, Wittenberg, & Reis, 1988).

Conclusions

The present study revealed significant discrepancies in prosocial interests across gender and age. The study indicated that in the period of relatively low vocational activity: early adolescence (10-14), adolescence (20-24) and in senior age (50-54), men and women prefer non-stereotypical vocational interests. On the other hand, the period of peak vocational activity, which is simultaneously the period of new social roles being embraced (e.g., transition to parenthood or marital roles), is associated with stereotypical vocational preferences with regard to prosocial vocational interests.

The development of the Contextual model of vocational interests opened the interpretation of discrepancies in the intensity of the prosocial type among women and men in their adulthood with regard to the pursued social roles and cultural factors. The adjustment to social expectations in a work-related environment, in accordance with the social role with regard to age and gender, was defined as the *social vocational clock.*

In light of the prosocial interests, it may also be acknowledged that the period of peak vocational activity is characterized by the emergence of "secondary" vocational interests in accordance with social expectations, which, decline along with age, to the benefit of "natural" vocational interests adequate to the level of interests in the adolescence and entering labor market periods.

The phenomenon of non-stereotypical vocational interests pertaining to interpersonal relations emerging in such a large sample of women and men of various ages may be significant for breaking stereotypes in the society.

References

Andreea-Elena, M., Chraif, M., Vasile, C., & Anitei, M. (2014). The role of gender in the formation of vocational interests and career orientation in adolescence. *Procedia - Social and Behavioral Sciences, 127,* 240-244.

Boski, P. (1999). Humanizm w kulturze i mentalności Polaków. [Humanism in the culture and mentality of Polish people]In B. Wojciszke, & M. Jarymowicz (Eds.). *Rozumienie zjawisk społecznych* [Understanding of social phenomena.] (pp. 79-120). Warsaw: Państwowe Wydawnictwo Naukowe.

Browne, K. R. (2006). Evolved sex differences and occupational segregation. *Journal of Organizational Behavior 27*(2), 143–162. DOI: 10.1002/job.349

Buhrmester, D., Furman, W., Wittenberg, M. T., & Reis, H. T. (1988). Five domains of interpersonal competence in peer relationships. *Journal of Personality and Social Psychology, 55*(6), 991-1008.

Fouad, N.A. (2007). Work and vocational psychology: Theory, research, and applications. *Annual Review of Psychology, 58,* 549-594.

Gottfredson, L. S. (1981). Circumscription and compromise: A developmental theory of occupational aspirations. *Journal of Counseling Psychology, 28,* 545-579.

Gottfredson, G. D., & Holland, J. L. (1996). *Dictionary of Holland Occupational Codes* (3rd ed.). Odessa, FL: Psychological Assessment Resources Gottfredson,

GUS (2016). *Central Statistical Office (GUS). Department of demographic research of the labor market. Marriage and fertility in Poland.* Retrieved from file:///C:/Users/Admin/Downloads/malzenstwa_i_dzietnosc_w_polsce.pdf

Hall, J. A., & Halberstadt, A. G. (1986). Smiling and gazing. *The psychology of gender: Advances through meta-analysis,* 136-158.

Hofstede, G. (2001) *Culture's consequences. Comparing, values, behaviors, Institutions, and organizations across nations.* Thousand Oaks, CA: Sage.

Hornowska, E., & Paluchowski, W. J. (2002). Technika badania ważności pracy D.E. Supera. In M. Strykowska (Ed.). *Współczesne organizacje. Wyzwania i zagrożenia. Perspektywa psychologiczna.* Poznań: Humaniora Press.

Holland, J. L. (1999). Why interest inventories are also personality inventories. In M. Savickas, A. Spokane (Eds.). *Vocational interests: Their meaning, measurement, and use in counseling* (pp. 87–101). Palo Alto, CA: Davies–Black.

Holland, J. L., Fritzsche, B. A., & Powell, A. B. (1994). *SDS technical manual.* Odessa, FL: Psychological Assessment Resources.

Kanning, U. W. (2006). Development and validation of a german-language version of the Interpersonal Competence Questionnaire (ICQ). *European Journal of Psychological Assessment, 22*(1), 43-51.

Lippa, R. (2001). On deconstructing and reconstructing masculinity–femininity. *Journal of Research in Personality, 35,* 168–207.

Low, K. S. D., Yoon, M., Roberts, B. W., & Rounds, J. (2005). The stability of vocational interests from early adolescence to middle adulthood: A quantitative review of longitudinal studies. *Psychological Bulletin, 131*(5), 719-737.

Lubinski, D. (2000). Scientific and social significance of assessing individual differences: "Sinking shaft at a few critical points." *AnnualReview of Psychology, 51,* 405–444.

Mandal, E. (2004). *Podmiotowe i interpersonalne konsekwencje stereotypów związanych z płcią.* [Subjective and interpersonal consequences of gender stereotypes.]2nd Edition, Katowice: University of Silesia Press.

Mandal, E., Gawor, A., & Buczny, J. (2012), The stereotypes of man and woman in Poland – content and factor structures. In E. Mandal (Ed.). *Masculinity and femininity in everyday life.* Katowice: University of Silesia.

Murray, J. L., & Hall, P.M. (2001). Gender Differences in Undergraduate Holland Personality Types: Vocational and Cocurricular Implications. *NASPA Journal, 39,*1, 14-21.

Ochnik, D. (2012). Przedsiębiorczość i wartości cenione w pracy w kontekście płci psychologicznej [Entrepreneurship, work values and gender identity./]. In Z. Ratajczak (Ed.). *Przedsiębiorczość. Źródła i uwarunkowania psychologiczne [Entrepreneurship.Its sources and psychological conditioning.*] (pp. 82-106). Warsaw: Difin.

Ochnik, D. (2016). *Życie w pojedynkę – psychospołeczne konsekwencje bycia singlem u kobiet i mężczyzn.* [Singlehood – psychocial consequences of being single in women and men] (*doctoral thesis*), http://www.sbc.org.pl/publication/246942

Ochnik, D. (2018). Entrepreneurial Attitude and Personality as predictors of Leadership Vocational Interests in Men and Women. *Innovation Management, Entrepreneurship and Sustainability (IMES 2018) – Proceedings of the 6th International Conference,* 857-866.

Ochnik, D., & Rosmus, R. (2016). Vocational preferences of young Polish men and women. *Human Recource Management, 6*(113), 43-56.

Ochnik, D., Stala, M., & Rosmus, R. (2018). Skala prospołecznych preferencji zawodowych.[Prosocial scale of vocational interests.] *Czasopismo Psychologiczne — Psychological Journal, 24(1), 151-158.* DOI: 10.14691/CPPJ.24.1.151

Ott-Holland, C. J., Huang, J. L., Ryan, A. M., Elizondo, F., & Wadlington, P.L. (2013). Culture and vocational interests: the moderating role of collectivism and gender egalitarianism. *Journal of Counseling Psychology, 60*(4), 569-81.

Prediger, D. J. (1982). Dimensions underlying Holland's hexagon: Missing link between interests and occupations? *Journal of Vocational Behavior,* 21, 259–287.

Prediger, D. J. (1999). Basic structure of work-relevant abilities. *Journal of Counseling Psychology,* 42, 178-184.

Prediger, D. J., & Cole, N. S. (1975). Sex-role socialization and employment realities: Implications for vocational interest measures. *Journal of Vocational Behavior,* 7, 239–251.

Proyer, R., & Häusler, J. (2007). Gender differences in vocational interests and their stability across different assessment methods. *Swiss Journal of Psychology / Schweizerische Zeitschrift für Psychologie / Revue Suisse de Psychologie, 66*(4), 243-247. DOI: 10.1024/1421-0185.66.4.243

Stoll, G, Rieger, S., Lüdtke, O., Nagengast, B., Trautwein, U., & Roberts, B. W. (2017). Vocational interests assessed at the end of high school predict life outcomes assessed 10 years later over and above IQ and Big Five personality traits. *Journal of Personality and Social Psychology,* 113(1), 167-184. DOI: 10.1037/pspp0000117.

Su, R., Rounds J., & Armstrong, P. (2009). Men and things, women and people: A meta-analysis of sex differences in interests, *Psychological Bulletin,* 135(6), 859-884. DOI:10.1037/a0017364

Super, D. E., Savickas, M. L., & Super, C. M. (1996). A Life-Span, Life-Space Approach to Career Development. In: Brown D., & Brooks L (Eds.). *Career choice and development.* San Francisco: Jossey-Bass.

Thompson, R. C., Donnay, D. A. C., Morris, M. L., & Schaubhut, N. A. (2004). Exploring age and gender differences and vocational interests, Retrieved from http://www.cppasiapacific.com/content/Research%20and%20White%20Papers/Strong/Strong_Age_and_Gender.pdf

Wood, W., & Eagly, A. H. (2002). A cross-cultural analysis of the behavior of women and men: Implications for the origin of sex differences. *Psychological Bulletin, 128,* 699-727.

Wood, W., & Eagly, A. H. (2012). Biosocial construction of sex differences and similarities in behavior. In M.P.Zanna, J.M. Olson, (Eds.). *Advances in experimental social psychology,* Vol.46 (pp. 55-123). Burlington: Academic Press.

Part IV:
Selflessness in Practice

Chapter 9

Selflessness in Business
– Theory vs. Practice

Monika Jakubiak,
Institute of Management,
Maria Curie Sklodowska University in Lublin, Poland

Introduction

Globalization, research and technological progress along with accompanying global socio-economic changes pose significant challenges for modern organizations. Companies' competitiveness and profits they gain acquire new meanings. This is due to the fact that these terms are increasingly analyzed in light of a broader application of profits than a mere multiplication of capital by owners. In order to achieve a permanent competitive advantage, non-material resources, especially company reputation, are applied more frequently. It is a unique resource and one which is difficult to duplicate. Moreover it enables companies to establish a market position and maintain it in long-term (Szwajca, 2014).

The subject matter in the literature of the subject

Modern business practice discusses the operations of contemporary organizations in light of Corporate Social Responsibility (CSR). Modern enterprises have begun to recognize the relationship between a proper attitude towards clients, employees, and local communities, and profits gained and development achieved (Adamik & Nowicki, 2012; Sładkiewicz & Wanicki, 2016).

The literature of the subject offers several definitions of CSR and approaches to the concept. The following constitute the most significant features of responsible businesses:

- sensitivity of companies, their owners and managers to social problems;
- establishment of moral principles of organizations' operations, inclusion of ethical values in business operations;
- balancing needs of various stakeholder groups as well as environmental and social spheres;
- honest satisfaction of duties and application of transparent business practices.

As a consequence, corporate social responsibility may be understood as companies' pursuit of actions whose primary objective consists of maintaining balance between productivity, search for sources of permanent competitive advantage, and at the same time, social interest in a broad sense (Gajda, 2015). CSR revolves around the capability of the organization, its owners and employees, to shape relations with its social environment (Adamik & Nowicki, 2012; Żychlewicz, 2014).

At present, CSR is discussed in light of the definition offered in the ISO 26000 standard. It approaches corporate responsibility holistically as a correlation of seven areas: (1) social involvement and development of local communities, (2) consumer issues, (3) honest operational practices, (4) human rights, (5) work-related practices, (6) environment (International Organization ..., 2012).

Depending upon the field entrepreneurs' actions are focused on, the literature of the subject offers several types of CSR. Selfless actions in business practice constitute the subject matter of the present paper. Selflessness is defined in the Polish Language Dictionary as "an action undertaken on the basis of noble motives, without the pursuit of private profits, especially material in character." Terms charity, altruism, and philanthropy are offered as synonyms.

In light of the subject matter of the present study, philanthropic activity, understood as donating a part of profits, material resources, or contributing free-of-charge services for public benefit or to the operation of non-profit organizations, deserves particular attention (Teneta-Skwiercz, 2011). The following are undertaken in the framework of the philanthropic activity (Adamczyk, 2009; Teneta-Skwiercz, 2011):

- programs supporting the public (especially in education);
- involvement in local community affairs;
- charity initiatives;
- corporate volunteering.

Social education undertaken by responsible companies may pertain to the development of awareness and essence of CSR or its practical aspects, as well as more general issues, e.g., promotion of education or healthy lifestyles. Companies organize various types of meetings, conferences, trainings, debates, and participate in significant events and public campaigns.

On the other hand, undertaking local community actions encompasses initiation and long-term execution of activities organized by members of the local community. The following include fields enterprises are interested in the most: education, unemployment, healthcare, environment protection. Companies which pursue such activities often aim to boost the acceptance of operations conducted by them and to improve the company's public image (Adamik & Nowicki, 2012; Szwajca, 2014).

Other popular forms of actions undertaken by companies include charity initiatives manifested in contributing donations or other forms of assistance (e.g., food collections, donations in kind, etc.) to the benefit of individuals or people in care of public institutions. Such initiatives are driven by altruism. Therefore, they encompass, discreet, unobtrusive assistance with the logo of a particular brand concealed. The supported is by no means obliged to reciprocate (lack of mutual services) (Adamik & Nowicki, 2012).

Corporate volunteering has gained significance in recent years. It constitutes a form of business volunteering, i.e., unpaid, voluntary and conscious activity undertaken to the benefit of others, which goes beyond the circle of family and friends. Upon employers' consent, in their work time, employees become volunteers and remain employed in the company at the same time. Responsibility for actions and attitudes of volunteers is embraced by the company (Lorecka, 2011). Employees may undertake several charity-related initiatives depending on social needs (Klimek-Michno, 2012). In order for these actions to bring desired outcomes, not only the creativity of individual people is required, but also the support of the management, and the presence of a proper strategy (Bsoul, 2014).

Due to the fact that people are usually driven by egoism, altruism poses specific challenges, especially for owners and managers of companies. It is because it is they who are motivated to achieve a competitive advantage. They are competition-focused and pursue their own interests and those of the organization. However, the literature of the subject offers examples of leadership based upon values which have selflessness at the core (Brookes, 2014). This is especially valid for managers interested in acquiring the trust of their subordinates, but also for those whose actions regarding employees ought to be characterized by selflessness, care for safety, support of employees and manifesting personal involvement (Dame, 2014).

CSR and cooperation with stakeholders broadly, constitute the fields the Responsible Business Forum operates in (abbrev. FOB in Polish). It is a „think-and-do-tank" type of organization. It initiated and partnered in several key Polish CSR initiatives. The Forum is active in sustainable development via research, analyses and publications pertaining to corporate social responsibility in Poland and worldwide. The Forum has been operating for over 16 years. It grants open access to all its materials via the following website http://odpowiedzialnybiznes.pl/.

The concept of corporate social responsibility has become increasingly popular not only in large international enterprises but also in businesses acting locally and employing few. The fact that a growing interest of companies in CSR-related initiatives has emerged proves the necessity of actions serving the benefit of organizations' surrounding environment in broad terms being undertaken.

Methodology

The objective of the present paper is to identify the motivation behind and types of philanthropic initiatives undertaken by the employees of the studied companies representing the financial sector. The analysis encompassed the drive behind the selfless initiatives serving various types of stakeholders of the companies, as well as the impact of these actions upon the operations of the studied companies themselves.

The following research questions were posed:

1.   What type of philanthropic actions serving stakeholders are undertaken by the studied companies?
2.   What are the motives behind these initiatives?
3.   What are the outcomes of these actions?

When searching for answers to these questions, both empirical studies and the review of literature were conducted. The case study method was applied in the empirical study. The method constitutes the fundamental tool in qualitative studies. The case study evaluates a selected object (or objects) which manifests considerable internal complexity and extensive relations with the surrounding environment. The method uses various sources of information such as documents, observations, interviews, and takes the context of the studied object into consideration (Creswell, 2007; Baxter & Jack, 2008). The term "case" denotes a single research object examined with regard to the particular purpose, situated in a specific time and place, with the object's specific circumstances being taken into consideration (Czakon, 2013).

The compilation of an extensive collection of information pertaining to complex relationships is possible with the application of the case study method. This enables the hitherto unexplained issues to be described and assessed. When examining the research object, a premise is made that the results of the study will be influenced by situational determinants, immediate and indirect surrounding of the studied object, its internal and other features. As a consequence, the case study method is applied when the research problem encompasses a considerable number of inter-related variables and the scholar has little control over the object. The method is preferable for cases when cause-effect relationships, which are too complex for a survey study, are to be examined, when actions or outcomes of a program are to be analyzed from the perspective of their productivity, and when outcomes of initiatives whose results are difficult to predict are to be comprehensively assessed (Czakon, 2013).

This particular research approach was applied in the present paper. A premise was made that the application of a strongly standardized questionnaire may lead to extensive simplifications and result in an outcome which merely scratches the surface of the issue

The following methods were applied in order to conduct the case study: the review of literature and CSR reports, analysis of documentation, observations.

Unstructured material encompassing verbal (documents, reports) and visual data (videos, photos) was analyzed in order to extract information regarding the following matters:

- Types of philanthropic initiatives,
- Addressees of the initiatives,
- Joint initiatives for all the surveyed organizations,
- Innovative initiatives, original projects executed by the surveyed financial institutions,
- Motives behind the responsibility-related initiatives (including those pertaining to bottom-up activities initiated by employees and propositions of the managing cadre)
- Outcomes of the initiatives:
    - Support of the addressees (financial, material, psychological),
    - Outcomes for employees of companies involved in the philanthropic initiatives,
    - Outcomes for organizations (including brand building, recognition, building positive PR).

Open coding was applied when seeking to determine joint and differentiating features of the philanthropic initiatives undertaken in the surveyed companies.

Selflessness in Business in the Practice of Financial Institutions

Charity and philanthropic initiatives undertaken by the employees of companies representing the financial sector and operating in Poland constituted the subject matter of the present study.

Among several branches of economy, the analysis examined financial institutions. The sector was selected due to specific aspects of its operation. It consists of business entities whose main objective is to offer financial services to their clients. Financial institutions are particularly active in accumulating and spending financial resources and offering financial agency services. Such a purely economic and business-like character of their operation seems to exclude selfless initiatives. As a consequence, the present study aimed to identify and assess these types of activities undertaken by the board or employees of financial institutions.

The analysis of philanthropic and charity initiatives encompassed five financial institutions whose actions were outlined in the FOB report titled „2017 Responsible Business in Poland. Good Practices" (available online: http://odpowiedzialnybiznes.pl/wp-content/uploads/2018/04/Raport2017.pdf). The institutions include:

-   Eurobank;
-   ING Bank Śląski;
-   ANG Spółdzielnia;
-   Bank BGŻ BNP Paribas;
-   Bank Zachodni WBK.

Based upon the review of literature, reports and observations, the following catalogue of philanthropic initiatives undertaken by these institutions can be offered (Tab. 9.1).

Apart from the initiatives outlined in Tab. 9.1, each of the studied institutions undertakes other initiatives which may constitute examples of innovative good practices in philanthropic activities.

Table 9.1. *Philanthropic initiatives executed by the studied companies*

No.	Type of initiative	Example activities undertaken by the organizations
1.	Programs supporting the public (education)	• free-of-charge classes for pupils and students and for the public in general. The subject matter involved operations of financial institutions; • awareness-raising in terms of money saving, financing, impact of credits, etc.; • managing social media profiles, websites with advice on financing, blogs with articles and advice; • promotion of various types of activities, including physical activities and team-working in the framework of sports events, competitions and tournaments (including the sponsorship of awards).
2.	Involvement in local community affairs	• organization of workshops in kindergartens, schools, educational institutions, both for the faculty, children and students regarding education, therapy via sports, as well as the promotion of an active lifestyle and healthy nutrition; • organization of meetings for certain groups and people, especially those in difficult situation, e.g. youth from troubled communities, women, the unemployed or ill (sponsorship of meetings and awards).
3.	Charity initiatives	• support for the needy (e.g. participation in nationwide initiatives such as Świąteczna Paczka, sponsoring Christmas presents for specific people and families in need in the company's environment); • collections of financial resources for the needy and public benefit organizations (e.g. hospices, foundations, animal shelters, etc.).
4.	Corporate volunteering	• various types of activities serving the benefit of those in a difficult situation (e.g. classes for children and the youth organized in community centers, tutoring, holidays events, etc.) organized by employees of financial institutions and on their initiative, often undertaken in their working hours with the agreement and support of the employer; • employees undertake activities they have experience and competences in.

In 2017, the employees of Eurobank realized *Our People Round The World* campaign. The initiative revolved around the bank's employees covering the distance of the equator (40 075 km) over the period of 4 weeks. The employees were to complete the objective by any physical activity of choice. The distance was measured by a dedicated application. The initiative aimed to collect the amount equal to the distance covered

(1km=1PLN). Money was to be donated to a foundation selected in a general bank selection. In 2017, the amount was donated to Fundacja Mam Marzenie.

The *Our People Round The World* campaign was very well planned and prepared. A dedicated webpage was launched (www.ourpeople.pl). The website featured an interactive globe indicating the distance covered by the employees. The campaign was promoted by a video featuring the bank's employees — ambassadors of the campaign. The video featured a relay race and promoted the idea of physical fitness. The activity was promoted among employees of the bank via batons circulating around Poland, by a competition for employees, by photos or videos symbolizing passing the baton, by internal mailing, sportswear, participation in tournaments, gadgets bearing the hashtag of the campaign, etc. (http://www.ourpeople.pl). In total, 505 Eurobank's employees in Poland became actively involved in the campaign. Fundacja Mam Marzenie received the sum exceeding the originally planned amount (55 412 PLN were collected). The *Our People Round The World* campaign was awarded the Brown Paper Clip award in CSR.

Employees of BGŻ BNP Paribas bank also undertook an interesting philanthropic initiative. The activity is titled "Wspieram cały rok" ("I support year round"). It constitutes a simple, voluntary tool for systematic individual philanthropy realized by the bank's employees. The activity was launched in September 2017. It revolves around making a declaration of an individually selected monthly deduction on the employees' salaries which will be subsequently donated to a social purpose. Donations are given to the "Klasa"("Class") stipend program for wards of the BGŻ BNP Paribas Foundation, as well as to a public benefit organization selected by the bank's employees on an annual basis. Every donor decides whether their donations help both organizations or just a single one. In 2017, employees decided to support association "Stowarzyszenie mali bracia Ubogich" assisting the senior and elderly.

ING Bank Śląski constitutes another financial institution whose employees undertook initiatives to help those in need. In partnership with ING Dzieciom Foundation and the organizers of Biegnij Warszawo initiative, they undertook to start in and complete a 10 km run and 5 km march. The bank donated money to the ING Dzieciom Foundation for every participant who completed the run. The bank's employees trained for participation in the framework of trainings organized by the bank in 16 cities in Poland. In 2017, 1017 employees decided to participate in the Biegnij Warszawo ("Run Warsaw") initiative, and 266 in Maszeruję-Kibicuję (Marching-Cheering). The run was completed by 833. In total, 93

600 PLN were donated to the foundation. It will finance sports and education activities for children and the youth to promote healthy lifestyles and being active in leisure time.

Another notable initiative was undertaken by ANG Spółdzielnia in 2017. So far, the institution has held annual events for business partners titled Smocza Impreza. However, in 2017, instead of organizing the event, it was decided that the money usually spent would be donated to charity. ANG Spółdzielnia encouraged business partners who were to attend the event to donate their contribution to three charity organizations. In this way, 30 000 PLN was donated to Stowarzyszenie "mali bracia Ubogich", Fundacja Hospicjum Onkologiczne, and Zwierzochron. To commemorate the participation in the initiative, a poster was designed and printed for every participant (more information on http://blog.angkredyty.pl/dobroczynnosc-nowym-trendem-wsrod-pracodawcow-przed-swietami.php).

Bank Zachodni WBK also supports philanthropic initiatives of its employees and clients. A public gamification-based project was implemented in 2017. When a player reached a certain score in the game, money was donated to a public benefit organization. The initiative enabled Karkonoskie Stowarzyszenie Pomocy Dzieciom i Rodzinie „Nadzieja" facilities to be renovated. The institution houses 100 wards. The renovation was conducted by a team of professionals with volunteers originating from the WBK western macro-region assisting in the works. They were tasked with conducting simple works, which in general, contributed to a better functioning of the institution.

The above-mentioned initiatives were conducted by the institutions in 2017. Their outcome was so successful that the continuation in the coming years is expected.

Example initiatives undertaken by the employees of financial institutions, as well as examples of innovative good practices outlined in Tab. 1, constitute a mere section of selfless activities conducted by the board and employees of the studied companies. The following initiatives executed by the financial institutions in the field of CSR can be enumerated:

1.   Clients assisting initiatives:
     -   pursuit of the Good Practice Code at work,
     -   tailor-made approach towards clients, reacting to needs voiced, listening to opinions and improvement of work methods in accordance with feedback received,

-   offering clients reliable information regarding opportunities associated with financial services and consequences of their decisions,
-   offering clients made-to-measure products or services while pursing the benefit of the institution and long-term relations with clients,
-   ensuring discretion, availability and involvement.

2. Employees assisting initiatives:
    -   ethics-promoting programs for employees (ethical code, information flow and communications structure, transparency of behavior, involvement in the undertaken initiatives, promotion of ethical behavior, care for compliance with norms),
    -   care for physical and mental state of employees, encouragement of being active,
    -   numerous trainings, team-working events, conferences (including those fitting the needs and interests of employees),
    -   pursuit of CSR in recruitment and selection (selection of candidates, recruitment, motivating, development, promotion, relocation, etc.),
    -   establishment of kindergartens or nurseries for children of employees,
    -   establishment of on-site facilities employees may spend their breaks in,
    -   flexible working hours or partly remote work for employees raising small children.

3. Cooperation with schools, educational institutions, universities:
    -   organization of joint events, conferences, trainings,
    -   compilation of BA and MA papers, projects to solve practical problems of a given organization,
    -   open days,
    -   transferring information regarding competence profiles of candidates for specific positions,
    -   classes conducted by practitioners,
    -   organizing student internships, etc.

4. Sponsorship of sports, educational events, etc.

5. Care for environment:
    -   by energy efficient equipment used at work,
    -   limiting unnecessary pollution (e.g., replacement of paper correspondence with e-correspondence).

Motivation behind responsible Initiatives

The fundamental motivation behind philanthropic initiatives undertaken by the employees of the studied companies is to offer assistance to the needy, those in a difficult situation, in troublesome predicament.

Philanthropic initiatives undertaken by the studied companies were frequently initiated by the employees of the organizations. It was the case with, e.g. "Wspieramy cały rok" program, which was introduced in response to BGŻ BNP Paribas employees' needs. Some of them, for various reasons, did not have an opportunity to devote time to volunteering or participation in public actions. However, they wanted to become involved in initiatives benefiting local communities.

Employees of other organizations offer similar motivation as far as CSR-related initiatives are concerned. They would like to support the needy on frequent occasions, but they believe that the actions of individuals are not effective enough. However, if a greater number of people are successfully involved in such activities, significantly better outcomes can be achieved. Such bottom-up initiatives are supported by the management of the organizations due to the fact that they are considered not only as benefiting the public, but also as a tool for integrating employees and tightening the bond with the organization.

Outcomes of Initiatives

The analysis of documentation, published reports, and outcomes of philanthropic initiatives undertaken by the employees of the studied organizations acknowledged the fact that each of the actions was successful. Participants managed to achieve, and frequently, overachieve their objectives.

When assessing the outcomes of the philanthropic initiatives, the tangible assistance offered to the needy ought to be highlighted. This is due to the fact that the participation of a particular organization in the supportive program supplies concrete financing for the supported public benefit organizations. The support usually takes the form of financing or in-kind contribution. However, the psychological support is no less important as it convinces the needy that they are not left to themselves in dire situations and can hope for their conditions to improve.

Positive outcomes of these actions can be observed among employees of the studied institutions as well. Owing to a shared objective, they become more integrated as a group contributing to a social purpose. In this way, the philanthropic initiative becomes a tool tightening employees' bond with the organization, and as a consequence, contributes to the growth of engagement in the company.

If the initiative was associated with the support of an employee-selected public benefit organization, the involvement was even greater. People who exert an impact upon the selection of the organization they identify with the most are usually even more involved in the initiative. An additional outcome can be observed in a greater care for a healthy lifestyle and physical activity of people whose daily routine usually involves several hours spent in the office in front of a computer screen. Moreover, a greater credibility and recognition of the enterprise and its perception as a responsible company on the market, can also be considered as benefits of such actions.

Results of studies in the subject matter confirm the need for perceiving benefits of philanthropic initiatives in the long-term with the improved loyalty of internal and external stakeholders taken into consideration. The growth of public awareness of recipients of services results in the fact that, when making decisions, they are often motivated by the image of the company, its renown and values it pursues. As a consequence, social responsibility exerts an impact upon the lasting presence of the company in the awareness of the surrounding environment, which in the long-term, translates into tangible benefits for the organization itself. The consolidation of ethical norms of functioning exerts an impact upon employees and constitutes a significant element of extra-financial motivation and development of involvement. The ethical code and care for various aspects of sustainable functioning of the company improve its image and growth of credibility in the eyes of employees.

Discussion and Conclusions

The subject matter of the present paper pertains to motives and outcomes of actions undertaken by the employees of financial institutions. Results of the present study are not convergent with the results of studies featured in the literature of the subject, especially as far as the presence of the issue of CSR in the awareness of owners of Polish companies is concerned. The literature presents the view that entrepreneurs do not identify CSR with undertaking initiatives serving local communities and with the development of positive relations with stakeholders of organizations (Gajda, 2015). In addition, the study titled "CSR Audit of Polish Companies" compiled in 2014 indicates that businesses had problems with defining CSR. Only half of the large companies (54%) and every fifth SME (19%) implemented a CSR strategy. As far as the remaining companies are concerned, even if they did become involved in such initiatives, they did it ad-hoc. According to the studied business owners, financial limitations and formal and legal obstructions constituted barriers in this respect. As a consequence, several businesses view CSR primarily as a cost instead of an investment and a source of innovation (Bartnik, 2015).

Meanwhile, the results of the present case study indicate a strong awareness of employees of the financial sector regarding needs and benefits emerging from the application of CSR principles in practice. This may be motivated by their high education and competencies of employees of financial institutions, who, due to their position and duties, may be characterized by a high awareness of social problems as well as by the familiarity with the wants of the needy.

This high awareness regarding the need for selfless assistance to the needy may also stem from values pursued by companies and a suitable internal organizational culture. The studied companies implemented Good Practice Code and guidelines on ethical behavior. The undertaken initiatives are characterized by a specific care for both internal and external stakeholders.

As far as this field is concerned, the results of the present study are convergent with those offered in the literature and the practical implementation of CSR principles declared by Polish entrepreneurs. This is especially valid with regard to relations with employees, cooperation with the surrounding environment of the organization, and the pursuit of fair market practices (Gajda, 2015; Filipp, 2012).

Results of the present study confirm the existence of benefits emerging from the application of CSR-related practices. The following constitute the most significant of these: development of the organization, achievement and retention of a lasting competitive advantage, greater creativity, and development of organizational competencies such as risk-management skills.

Not all managers of Polish companies are able to manage their businesses on the basis of ethical norms. The literature offers numerous examples of abuse and transgression of these rules and regulations. Such an approach may offer short-term tangible benefits. However, in the long-term, it inevitably leads to the decline of trust and renown, and to financial losses (Glinka & Gudkova, 2011). As a consequence, the need for a proper development and training of prospective managers is highlighted, especially as far as moral aspects are concerned (Sułkowski & Ignatowski, 2016). Undoubtedly, the stimulation of moral sensitivity of managers translates into the application of ethical behavior, which in turn, exerts an impact upon the growth of organizational value.

The present paper discusses only selected aspects of selflessness in business practice. As a consequence, it ought to be considered as a voice in the discussion of philanthropic initiatives of employees of modern businesses. In order to become familiar with the rationale behind their activity and outcomes of the initiatives, further empirical studies ought to be conducted. Opinions of employees and their superiors regarding the motivation ought to be collected. Their views ought to be compared with those of the supported.

References

Adamczyk, J. (2009). *Społeczna odpowiedzialność przedsiębiorstw.* [Corporate Social Responsibility]. Warsaw: PWE.

Adamik, A., & Nowicki, M. (2012). *Etyka i społeczna odpowiedzialność biznesu.* [The ethics and corporate social responsibility]. In Zakrzewska-Bielawska, A. (ed.). *Podstawy zarządzania* [Fundamentals of management], Warsaw: Wolters Kluwer Business, 492-532.

Bartnik, J. (2015). CSR po polsku – czy działamy wspólnie? [CSR in Polish — do we work together?]. *Personel i Zarządzanie, 5(302),* 16-18.

Baxter, P., & Jack, S. (2008). Qualitative Case Study Methodology: Study Design and Implementation for Novice Researchers. *The Qualitative Report, 13*(4), 544-559.

Brookes, S. (2014). Is selfless leadership an impossible ideal for public leaders? *International Journal of Leadership in Public Services, 10*(4), 200-216.

Bsoul, M. (2014). Wolontariat pracowniczy jako przejaw działań z zakresu społecznie odpowiedzialnego biznesu (CSR). [Employee volunteering as a manifestation of activities in the field of socially responsible business (CSR).]. *Rynek-Społeczeństwo-Kultura, 3*(11), 10-15.

Creswell, J. W. (2007). *Qualitative Inquiry and Research Design: Choosing among Five Approaches.* Second Edition. California: SAGE Publications, Inc.

Czakon, W. (ed.). (2013). *Podstawy metodologii badań w naukach o zarządzaniu.* Warsaw: Wolters Kluwer Business.

Dame, J. (2014). The Four Keys to Being a Trusted Leader. *Harvard Business Review Digital Articles, 3*(10), 2-3.

Filipp, E. (2012). *Społeczna odpowiedzialność organizacji.* [Social responsibility of the organization]. In Glinka, B., & Kostera, M. (eds.). Nowe kierunki w organizacji i zarządzaniu. [New directions in organization and management.] Warsaw: Wolters Kluwer Business, 95-113.

Gajda, J. (2015). Rola i znaczenie efektywnego zarządzania społeczną sferą biznesu dla przedsiębiorców w świetle badań autorskich. [The role and importance of effective social management of the business sphere for entrepreneurs in the light of author's research]. *Organizacja i Kierowanie*, 4(169), 71-83.

Glinka, B., & Gudkova, S. (2011). *Przedsiębiorczość*. [Entrepreneurship]. Warsaw: Wolters Kluwer business.

International Organization for Standarization (2012). ISO 26000:2010 Wytyczne dotyczące społecznej odpowiedzialności. [Guidelines on social responsibility]. Warsaw: PKN.

Klimek-Michno, K. (2012). Więcej dajesz, więcej masz: wolontariat pracowniczy sposobem na budowanie kultury organizacji i kształtowanie postaw prospołecznych. [You give more, you have more: employee volunteering is a way to build organizational culture and shape pro-social attitudes]. *Personel i Zarządzanie*, 1, 58-62.

Lorecka, K. (2011). *Wolontariat pracowniczy w praktyce*. [Employee volontary in practice.] Warsaw: Wydawnictwo Naukowe Instytutu Technologii Eksploracji – PIB.

Sładkiewicz, D., & Wanicki, P. (2016). Istota społecznej odpowiedzialności biznesu w procesie kreowania wartości przedsiębiorstwa. [The essence of corporate social responsibility in the process of creating enterprise value]. *Prace Naukowe Uniwersytetu Ekonomicznego we Wrocławiu*, 436, 253-260.

Sułkowski, Ł., & Ignatowski, G. (2016). Zagadnienia etyczne a edukacja polskich menedżerów. [Ethical issues and education of Polish managers]. *Horyzonty Wychowania*, 15(34), 283-295.

Szwajca, D. (2014). Rola społecznej odpowiedzialności przedsiębiorstwa w budowaniu jego reputacji. [The role of corporate social responsibility in building its reputation]. *Prace Naukowe Akademii im. Jana Długosza w Częstochowie, Pragmata Tes Oikonomias*, 1(8), 341-361.

Teneta-Skwiercz, D. (2011). Filantropia korporacyjna–istota, formy i motywy dobroczynności przedsiębiorstwa. [Corporate philanthropy-the essence, forms and motives of the charity of the enterprise]. *Prace Naukowe Uniwersytetu Ekonomicznego we Wrocławiu*, 222, 297-305.

Żychlewicz, M. (2014). Dobre praktyki społecznej odpowiedzialności biznesu w Polsce. [Good practices of corporate social responsibility in Poland]. *Studia Ekonomiczne Regionu Łódzkiego*, 14, 35-45.

Chapter 10

Donations from Ecuadorian Firms:

A quantitative Analysis

Hector Alberto Botello Peñaloza,
Department of Economics,
Industrial University of Santander, Colombia

Introduction

Corporate Social Responsibility (CSR) has been understood as a subset of philanthropic activities in society. This is undertaken not only because of the good image it generates in society, but also because of the capacity to return part of the resources that the company uses to the same, as well as to reverse the economic, social and environmental deterioration that business activity causes in society and the environment. For this reason, Corporate Social Responsibility (CSR) has become a medium and long-term objective of companies, international organizations, trade unions and governments.

The notion of this concept has been documented for some time; Bowen (1953, 69–106) related CSR to business ethics, but clarified that they are not equivalent (Araque and Montero, 2006). To explain the above, we understand a unidirectional relationship that the social commitment of the company responds to an ethics and therefore to human values but not inversely. Dejo (2005) states that the company's social commitment is a way of compensating and becoming aware of the productive consequences of companies and their commitment to the social development of society. The Mexican Center for Philanthropy of Mexico (CEMEFI), defines CSR as the conscious and congruent commitment to fully fulfill the company's purpose, taking into account the economic, social and environmental expectations of all its participants, demonstrating respect for people and communities, thus contributing to the construction of the common good (Cajiga, 2009).

The ISO international certification guide defines social responsibility as "the responsibility of an organization for the impacts of its decisions and activities on society and the environment through ethical and transparent behavior that contributes to sustainable development" (ISO, 2010). According to ISO it includes the health and well-being of society; takes into account the expectations of its stakeholders; complies with applicable legislation and is consistent with international standards of behavior; and is integrated throughout the organization and implemented in its relationships.

Various researches have been carried out to characterize the companies that have carried out different forms of social commitment. In this sense, Mercado and García (2007), García and Hernández (2010), and Blasco and Zølner (2010) analyzed the factors that drive greater social responsibility in different countries. They found that there is resistance from companies to CSR because of the cost of undertaking activities. There is also a lack of awareness of companies for their social commitment due to the lack of promotion of this practice. Mukiur (2010) analyzed the perception of entrepreneurs of CSR according to the size of the companies, finding significant differences between SMEs and large companies. These focused on internal practices and the ethics of entrepreneurs.

Another group of works has been to characterize the propensity of companies by type of characteristics. They have found that the size and dimension of the companies is directly related to the total donation amounts, with the medium and large ones being the ones with the greatest relative and absolute contribution. On the other hand, micro and small enterprises apply good practices in a scarce way and without a defined objective of CSR (Demirdjian, Izaguirre, Sotelo, & Durán, 2010). In line with the above, companies committed to CSR are led by value-inspired leaders with clear objectives and goals.

Balabanis, Stables & Phillips (1997) measure the orientation of British charities to donations. To gather information, they sent 200 forms to the UK's leading charities and obtained a response rate of 29%. Although the orientation of charities towards their donor market remains relatively low, it has increased significantly over the last five years. The orientation was negatively correlated with the size of the organization. A lag effect was detected between donor market orientation and performance.

For developing countries, the most interesting and longest-developed case study is that of India. In 2014, companies with an annual income of more than 105 million pounds sterling were required to earmark 2% of their profits after taxable charities. However, an analysis of the policy shows that two years later the overall charity spending of companies has increased. This rose from £357.5 million in 2013 to £2.63 billion after the enactment of the law. Nevertheless, a survey by the accounting firm KPMG found that 52 of the country's 100 largest companies did not spend the required 2% last year. The Guardian's and KPMG's research showed that large charities are the ones that get the most funding. This is because small organizations lack the capacity to cope with the bureaucratic and operational demands of business. As a result, states with higher levels of development are getting more funds, ahead of the most vulnerable where aid is most needed.

In Ecuador, the main resource for CSR has been donations. For Ecuador's corporate regulation, donations are free acts where one person, natural or legal, freely gives something to another person who accepts it without any consideration for the other. All kinds of goods can be donated, movable goods can be donated by means of a written or verbal acceptance, while the donation of real estate must be made by means of a public deed that has been certified in a notary's office. Donations may come with or without conditions, provided that this is legal and possible. Once accepted, donations cannot be returned, but there may be circumstances that justify the cancellation of the donation. Such reasons would be non-compliance with the conditions of the transfer of the property, offences or other facts.

Ecuadorian law provides for exceptions for all donations made to state entities, but does not provide for exceptions in the case of donations made through private bodies. In tax terms, only deliveries to the State and non-profit institutions are tax-free. This aspect is important when considering the motivation of companies to undertake social commitment actions with their employees or non-profit organizations.

Currently, the income received by non-profit institutions is exempt from income tax, in accordance with article 9.5 of the Internal Tax Regime Law. However, Article 8.9 of this Law mentions that donations to individuals or private companies are taxed when the amount exceeds 71,220 dollars. This is responsible for the value-added tax (VAT), which is located at 12% in the national customs territory. Under this scheme, the company that donates the goods must file the declaration of the goods and in case of failure to do so is subject to a pecuniary sanction in case of non-compliance, in addition to the interest on tax arrears.

In the analysis of existing literature, Ecuador has not conducted quantitative research on the issue of corporate donations, their distribution and importance to the economy. Therefore, the objective of this work is to contribute to this gap in the literature by being part of an investigation of the economic census of the year 2010-2011 conducted in this country to quantify what companies do as a non-market activity. This work seeks to quantify the donations of companies in Ecuador, discretizing by size and volume of sales, economic sectors, location among other factors. For the above, the work is distributed in 4 additional sections not including this one. The following section presents the form of Quantitative Analysis used in the work together with the data source. The results of the exercise are shown below and then the conclusions and the bibliography used are shown.

Methodology

Methodological Design

A descriptive methodological design is followed. In this sense, the units of analysis are the Ecuadorian companies registered in the economic census. The analysis is cross-sectional for the year 2010. The descriptive analysis uses the SPSS software to make contingency tables representing variables related to size, location and economic sector. The number of employees determines the size of the companies. The administrative provinces defined by the government define location. The Statistics Institution of Ecuador defines the type of economic sector using the Uniform Industrial Classification revision 4 carried out by the United Nations and implemented.

Source

This work uses the exhaustive survey derived from the economic census carried out by the National Statistics Institute of Ecuador in 2011 (INEC, 2011). In this research, a descriptive quantitative analysis of 12,753 companies is carried out, which discriminates the volume of donations made by type of economic sector, location, size of companies and sales. The following table shows the distribution in the number of companies by size and economic sector. Medium and small enterprises make up 90% of the sample of enterprises. The sector with the smallest companies is the service sector with 78% of companies with less than 10 people. The commerce sector was the one that presented the highest number of large companies with 624 (20%) of the total.

Table10. 1. *Distribution in the number of companies by size and economic sector*

Economic Sector	Small	Medium	Large	Total
Manufacturing	1.439	819	455	2.713
Commerce	693	1.868	624	3.186
Services	5.373	1.210	271	6.855
Total	7.506	3.897	1.350	12.753

Source: Economic census of Ecuador

In relation to the distribution by economic sectors, the service sector employs 54% of the companies, followed by trade with 24% and industry with 21%. Small firms account for 72 per cent of the services sector, while large firms are concentrated in the trade sector with 46%.

Results

The results of the economic census are shown in table 2, showing that the number of donor companies in Ecuador is significantly low. Of the 12,753 companies surveyed, only 34 were donors in 2011, equivalent to 0.26%. The industrial sector contributed the largest number of companies with 31, of which 18 were large, 10 medium and 3 small companies.

Table 10. 2. *Numbers of companies by size and economic sector between non donors and donors*

Economic sector	Size	Non-donors	Donors
Manufacturing	Small	1.436	3
	Medium	809	10
	Large	437	18
Trade	Small	693	0
	Medium	1.868	0
	Large	624	0
Service	Small	5.372	1
	Medium	1.209	1
	Large	270	1

Note. Calculations based on the Ecuadorian economic census.

The distribution of companies by region is shown in Table 3, with companies from regions other than the capital (Guayas) and the main industrial center (Pichincha) contributing 17 of the 34 companies out of the total number of donor companies. In this territory, donor companies accounted for 0.34% of the 4,934.

Table 10.3. *Donor company data by region*

Region	Non-donors	Donors	%
Pichincha	4238	7	0.17
Guayas	3547	10	0.29
Other regions	4934	17	0.34

Note. Calculations based on the Ecuadorian economic census.

Donations in 2011 totaled $37 million. According to Table 4, total sales of $62.5 billion were 0.06% of total sales. By region, in Guayas, donations totaled 28.6 million dollars, representing 77% of the total. Within the total sales of this region, donations had a share of 0.13%. In other regions, donations totaled $6.6 million, 0.05% of total sales.

Table 10.3. *Importance of corporate donations by region*

Region	Total Revenue ($ millons)	Donations ($ millons)	Donations as a percentage of sales (%)
Guayas	20 998.4	28.6	0.14
Pichincha	29 078.6	1.7	0.01
Other regions	12 472.9	6.6	0.05
Total	62.5	37	0.06

Note. Calculations based on the Ecuadorian economic census.

In relation to the size of the companies, table 5 shows that donations from large companies accounted for 98% of total donations. Within its sales, the percentage was 0.07%. The remaining types of companies submitted donations of less than US$ one million and a share of sales of less than 0.004%.

Table 10.4. *Importance of corporate donations by size of the firms*

Size	Total Revenue ($ millons)	Donations ($ millons)	Donations as a percentage of sales (%)
Small	2.60	0.79	0.003
Medium	9.84	0.38	0.003
Large	50.07	36.5	0.072

Note. Calculations based on the Ecuadorian economic census.

The age distribution of the companies is shown in table 6; donations from companies between the ages of 16 and 20 accounted for $29.7 million, representing 79% of the total. Within the total sales of this region, donations had a share of 0.33%. Table 6 shows that young and older companies are less likely to donate than middle-aged companies. This situation is repeated in an absolute and relative way.

Table 10.5. *Importance of corporate donations by age*

Years	Total Revenue ($ millions)	Donations ($ millions)	Donations as a percentage of sales (%)
Between 1 and 5 years	4.75	0.00	0.00
Between 11 and 15 years	7.73	1.30	0.02
Between 16 and 20 years	8.95	29.70	0.33
Between 21 and 25 years	4.32	3.00	0.07
Between 6 and 10 years	5.65	0.00	0.00
More than 25 years	31.15	2.90	0.01

Note. Calculations based on the Ecuadorian economic census.

In relation to donations by sector, table 7 shows that the industrial sector contributes 95% of the companies that donate with 36.9 million in 2011. This represented 0.18% of total sales for the year. Secondly, there is the service sector with a hundred thousand dollars.

Table 10.6. *Importance of corporate donations by economic sector*

Sector	Total Revenue ($ millons)	Donations ($ millons)	Donations as a percentage of sales (%)
Manufacturing	20.69	36.90	0.18
Commerce	28.18	0.00	0.00
Services	13.67	0.10	0.00
Total	62.55	37.00	0.06

Note. Calculations based on the Ecuadorian economic census.

Figure 1 shows the distribution of the volume of donations by type of goods, machines and equipment accounted for 35% of total donations, especially in large companies. Secondly, there is transport equipment (20%) and computer equipment (15%). It shows that larger companies are diversified in their donations as they occupy the full spectrum of available assets. In the case of medium and small enterprises, they concentrate on a smaller number of goods. This is the case of furniture that takes up 40% of its transfers without any counterpart.

Figure 10.1. Percentage of physical goods donated by size of companies.

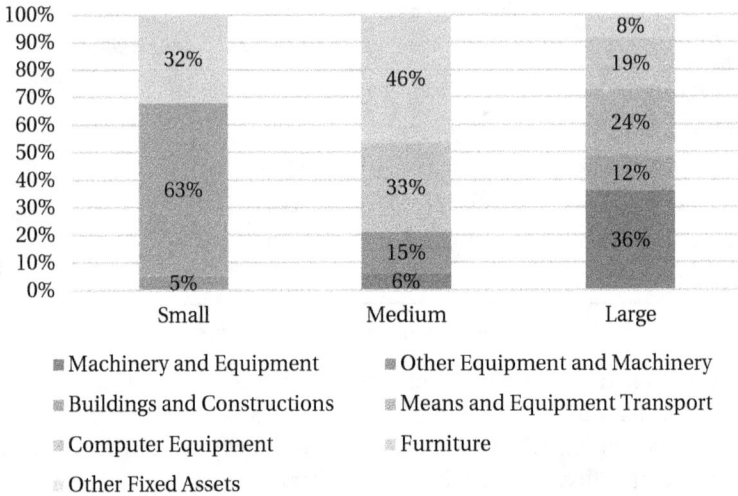

Note. Calculations based on the Ecuadorian economic census.

Conclusions

The results show that the propensity of companies to donate in Ecuador is significantly low. Only 37 of the 12 753 companies analyzed made donations in the period of time analyzed. The industrial companies located in the capital city of the country with more than 100 employees (large) and with an age between 16 and 20 years old donated nearly 90% of the total. In terms of the physical assets donated, transportation, furniture and information equipment accounted for nearly 80% of the total.

In terms of public policy, it is considered to modify the tax benefits obtained by companies by donating to motivate a greater number of companies to exercise corporate social responsibility in an optimal way and with impact.

This should ensure that donations and corporate social responsibility are no longer fortuitous and scarce events that occur at specific times, such as natural disasters. A situation that frequently occurs in developing countries. They must be practices that go hand in hand with the set of missionary values that the signatures have been drawn up to return part of the profits they acquire through the use of the tangible and intangible resources they obtain from society.

In future analyses, it is possible to follow up on the economic surveys and censuses that continue to be carried out in Ecuador where changes in the patterns detected in this research can be exposed. However, the most promising line of research is to establish causal links between donations and the firm's performance (financial, productive, in sales, etc).

Wang & Qian (2011) with their Empirical analyses using data on Chinese firms listed on stock exchanges from 2001 to 2006 support these arguments. Corporate philanthropy is expected to positively affect firm financial performance because it helps firms gain social recognition and impact products sales. In their paper, the authors find that positive philanthropy performance relationship is stronger for large firms with greater public visibility. Firms that are not government-owned or politically connected were shown to benefit more from philanthropy, as gaining political resources is more critical for such firms.

In Latin America and the equator, the relationship between the firm's performance and its ability to donate. In this sense, with the 2010 economic census, it is possible to carry out matching exercises and check between firms that have donated and those that have not. Likewise, case study methodologies can be followed to try to respond to this hypothesis.

References

Araque, R., & Montero, M. J. (2006). *La responsabilidad social de la empresa a debate.* Barcelona: Icaria.

Balabanis, G., Stables, R. E., & Phillips, H. C. (1997). Market orientation in the top 200 British charity organizations and its impact on their performance. *European Journal of Marketing, 31*(8), 583-603.

Blasco, M., & Zølner, M. (2010). Corporate social responsibility in Mexico and France: Exploring the role of normative institutions. *Business & Society, 49*(2), 216-251.

Bowen, H. R. (1953). *Social Responsibilities of a Businessman.* New York: Harper & Row.

Cajiga, J. (2009). El concepto de responsabilidad social empresarial. *México: Cemefi.*

Dejo, F. (2005). Las empresas ante su desafío histórico: De la acumulación egoísta a la responsabilidad social. *The bi-annual academic publication of Universidad ESAN, 10*(18-19).

Demirdjian, M. H., Izaguirre, F., Sotelo, H., & García, D. (2010). Implicaciones socioeconómicas de la responsabilidad social empresarial en México, casos: Televisa y TV Azteca. Observatorio de la Economía Latinoamericana, (131). Recuperado de http://www.eumed.net/cursecon/ecolat/mx/2010/plsu.htm

García, A., & Hernández, J. (2010). Responsabilidad Social Corporativa: el caso de algunas empresas de la industria del calzado en Guanajuato. In *Memorias del Congreso SINNCO*.

INEC (2011). National Statistics Institute and Censuses (Ecuador). Retrieved from http://www.ecuadorencifras.gob.ec/institucional/home/

International Organization for Standarization (2010). *ISO 26000:2010. Guidance on social responsibility*. U.S.A.: American National Standards Institute (ANSI).

Mababu Mukiur, R. (2010). Actitudes de los empresarios y directivos hacia la responsabilidad social corporativa. *Revista de Psicología del Trabajo y de las Organizaciones, 26*(2), 101-114.

Mercado Salgado, P., & García Hernández, P. (2007). La responsabilidad social en empresas del Valle de Toluca (México): un estudio exploratorio. *Estudios gerenciales, 23*(102), 119-135.

Wang, H., & Qian, C. (2011). Corporate philanthropy and corporate financial performance: The roles of stakeholder response and political access. *Academy of Management Journal, 54*(6), 1159-1181.

Chapter 11

Prosocial Motivation and Selflessness in Cultural Institutions. A Case Study of CAC Málaga

Lucía Pérez-Pérez,
Cultural Management,
International University of Catalonia, Barcelona, Spain

Miquel Banstons Prat,
School of Economics and Social Sciences,
International University of Catalonia, Barcelona, Spain

Introduction

The technological revolution deeply affects the world of business and institutions. This revolution calls for new ways to operate, meaning by "operation" the set of activities that are responsible for providing service to the public. Although much has been done in the last thirty years in regards to service management, now a new management approach is required (Muñoz-Seca & Riverola, 2011). Traditional management or "by function" has gone to the management "by objectives", which has returned to the individual their freedom and their initiative. This new concept is much more real than the previous one, but achieving goals remains insufficient to manage organizations in modern societies. What is needed, therefore, is a new management system capable of enriching and making sense of the objectives. Objectives have no value in themselves but only as a means to fulfill the mission. After the "management by objectives" the "management by missions" is needed. This new management approach is much richer and better able to persuade people to identify with the museum they work for and so ensure superior performance at all levels of the organization (Cardona & Rey, 2008). XXI century institutions raised the need for a new management model that considers the person in their ability to contribute. Current organizations, including the museums, require "management by missions". Both, academicians and practitioners consider that the mission statement is more and more a crucial element in the strategic planning of any business organization (Rajasekar, 2013).

The International Council of Museums defines the museum as a permanent institution, non-profit, serving the society and open to the public, which acquires, conserves, researches, communicates and exhibits the tangible and intangible heritage of humanity for study, education and recreation (ICOM, 2007). Communication plays a special role here. However, communication often arises in a unilateral way, that means, as a *system for reporting* without possibility of receptor response by the public, which results in its excessive passivity. In this context, we note that cultural institutions are more *informative* than *participatory*. The public management through the Network in cultural institutions is a unidirectional model, which aims to inform data or services of the institution but does not open it to new forms of communication. However, we observe a tendency to change, which suggests that in the coming years this situation will be much more collaborative and participatory (Viñarás, 2010). Furthermore, there is no doubt that the traditional relationships between museums and their publics have been modified (Bantimaroudis, Zyglidopoulos, & Symeou, 2010). In fact, Museums´ growing integration of Web 2.0 techniques is indicative of their readiness to redefine their relationship with their audience. While visitors were traditionally kept at arm´s length, the use of these techniques now allows involvement (Pulh & Mencarelli, 2015). In this sense the challenge for arts managers is to embrace the possibilities of participatory decision-making and, rather than replicating existing models, try to find their own way to implementing it within their organizations and to break down a fourth wall, which often acts as a barrier between the organization and its public, whoever they might be (Jancovich, 2015). Research by Camarero, Garrido and San José (2016) reveals that the success of a museum´s online communication strategy depends on the organization´s ability to construct a website that sparks the public´s interest and attracts visitors.

Advancing a step forward in this article we therefore analyze a management model that allows us to get two concepts closer: communication and service ("prosocial motivation") and aligns communication with the fulfillment of the mission (the meeting of people needs).

According to this model, the institution develops its communication strategy based, not on the information the institution is interested in giving but in the information oriented to what interests the public. It will be seen that this change in approach is a key to using social networks as a bidirectional communication channel. We will demonstrate that when management and communication focus on service, communication between the museum and the public is reinforced.

Theoretical Framework

Mission–based Management

Using the classical concept of organization proposed by authors such as Barnard (1971) or Simon (1976), it can be stated that *an organization is* (a) *a system of interactions between persons (employees) who cooperate together* (b) *to achieve a common objective (in an environment), even if* (c) *this takes place for different motives (provided by a control system)* (Pérez-López, 1994). According to this model (see Figure 1), the coordinated actions of an organization taken together is called its **operating system**. The *operating system* encompasses everything relating to the way of acting, including both formalized aspects (governed by regulations, organization charts, timetables, etc.) and non-formalized behavior. In organizational theory this is what is called *programs* or "*standard operating procedures*" (March & Simon, 1958; Cyert & March, 1963). The results produced through the *operating system* in any given environment is what can be called the organization's *mission* (Drucker, 1974). The mission expresses the ensemble of people's (i.e. consumer or public) necessities that an organization satisfies. The compensations (salaries, prestige, recognition, etc.) provided by the control system (management) according to the achievement of the results (the mission) by the employees constitutes the *motivation system* (Simon, 1976). The motivation system encompasses the *personal goals* that incite individuals to participate through their actions in the achievement of the *mission*.

Taking the previous model as a starting point, it can be seen what "managing" an organization means: it means establishing a flow of interactions between those participating in an organization by being *(1) able to motivate members of the organization* (i.e., by defining its *motivation systems) so that (2) they carry out a series of actions* (i.e., by defining its *operating systems) in such a way that (3) certain objectives or results are achieved, within a given environment* (i.e., by defining its *mission)*.

There are different styles, approaches or models in organizations management. Scott (1981) identified three main organizational patterns depending on whether the organization is understood as "rational", "natural" or an "open" system. While other authors have identified three basic paradigms: "mechanical", "psychosocial" and "anthropological"

(Pérez-López, 1994; Rosanas, 2008). In any case, the model of organization and the management system depend largely on the conception of the person and their motivations that the company has formulated (Barnard, 1971; Pérez-López, 1994; Chinchilla, 2001).

Human motivations have been studied for many years in Social Psychology and in Organizational Theory. Their study has been addressed from different perspectives: the hierarchy of human needs (Maslow, 1954), distinguishing between hygienic and non-hygienic factors (Herzberg, 1966) as well as the intrinsic or extrinsic character of the motivation (McGregor, 1966). This last perspective has had a great influence, so that the concepts of "extrinsic motivation" and "intrinsic motivation" are an essential mindset both in theoretical research and practice management (Deci & Ryan, 1985; Ryan & Deci, 2000; Gagné & Deci, 2005; Çınar, Bektas, & Aslan, 2011). Extrinsic motivation is understood as the impulse that drives people to take an action for what you get in return: salary, bonuses, rewards, prizes. The first organizational models were built on an idea of the behavior that focused exclusively on two of the elements of an interface: actions and results. Both elements operate as stimulus and response, to which the agent would respond mechanically (March & Simon, 1958). Therefore, this type of approach is included under the general heading of "mechanistic model" of the organization (Pérez-López, 1994). Instead, intrinsic motivation would be the impulse that moves an agent to perform an action by the value it has for him the action itself: learning, self-realization, etc. (Ryan & Deci, 2000). In this case, what drives the agent to act is the satisfaction of psychosocial needs. In this case it is drawn from a model of organizational behavior different from the previous one. It is the "psychosocial model" (Perez-Lopez, 1994).

Along with those studies focusing on the role of extrinsic and intrinsic motivation in organizational behavior, there is a line of research that analyzes another type of motivation: prosocial motivation (Batson, 1987; Brief & Motowidlo, 1986; Grant, 2008). In general, people are not only interested in what benefits themselves; it also satisfies them when what they do benefits others. Contributing to something that is good for others also motivates, it is also a *value*; in this case a *social value*. For example, what makes car sellers consider the sale of a car, as well as producing an economic incentive or for it to be a job that satisfies or gives them professional prestige is that it is something *suitable* for the client. Or what makes sellers reluctant to sell a product (even though they are capable of doing so) is if they know that it is of poor quality and is bad for the client. One can say that prosocial values express the "weight" that the *real* welfare of others (the environment) has in the decisions of members of the organization. Grant (2008) has showed in different studies how *serving* others also motivates. It generates a special form of motivation which he calls *prosocial motivation*, which arises when we put ourselves in the perspective of others and can "feel" our contribution to the welfare of others. Other researchers (Pérez-López, 1994; Rosanas, 2008; Bastons, 2000; Melé, 2003; Guillen, Ferrero, & Hoffman, 2014) have shown in different ways that to serve others also motivates. It generates a special form of motivation, prosocial motivation, which arises when we put ourselves in the place of another and we feel our contribution to the welfare of others. All of them refer to motivation at work that takes into account the needs of others and gives a sense of contribution to actions.

In organizational contexts prosocial motivation plays an important role in relation to the mission of an institution. In fact, the motivation of employees is one of the main reasons why many organizations define a mission (Bart, Bontis & Tagar, 2001; Ireland & Hitt, 1992; Campbell & Yeung, 1991; Klemm, Sanderson, & Luffman, 1991). There are many studies that show that the mission, when it is actually implemented in everyday life and the philosophy of the company, has a strong ability to awaken in people the sense of contribution and a source of prosocial motivation (Cardona & Rey, 2009; Wang, 2011). Thus, depending on the model of behavior and motivation on which they rest, they can differentiate three basic models of management: mechanic, prosocial, and anthropological (Pérez-Pérez, Bastons, & Berlanga, 2015).

The Mission of the Museum and the Role of Communication

To carry out the mission of the museum, communication can arise: according to the criterion of effectiveness (achieving my goals: information); according to attractiveness (emotional communication approach, seeking to persuade an adherence to the institution, but not of service to the public), and according to the prosocial criteria: the "mission-based motivation" communication aimed at satisfying real public needs (the mission). The International Council of Museums (ICOM) in its paper on key concepts of museology (2009) describes the communication process according to the logic of the PRC system (Preservation-Research-Communication) proposed by the Reinhardt Academy, which involves functions of exhibition, publication and education carried out in the museum. This document, in its latest version, stops to describe the significant changes that the Internet and social networks have caused in the traditional conception of communication, and therefore in carrying out the mission of the museum institution. Yet, surprisingly concludes with the following statement: "It seems, however, that the real task of the museum is closer to a transmission understood as unilateral communication" (p.30).

Parallel to and with regard to the transmission of culture in today's society we find a particular phenomenon: the growing generational divorce. To reach the younger population becomes an absolute necessity that leads to integral questioning of current forms. This generation is a new type of public and requires appropriate actions to capture it (Muñoz-Seca & Riverola, 2007). We do not try to reach many with quantitative parameters but to approach, listen and respond to specific needs of each person. At this point the correct use of ICTs gets to redirect the communicative activity to this goal.

Recent research on the communicative management of Spanish Museums recognize the efforts of institutions to incorporate the services of the social web (ICOM Digital, 2012), but also show gaps in the results of its use. Thus, Baraybar and Ibañez (2012) warn that the dream of full interactivity with the general public, beyond scientific slogans, is still in its initial stage, and that to some extent, the realities that new technologies can bring to the present are not being fully incorporated except in experimental exceptions. Becerra and Dominguez (2014), in an exploratory study on museums, communication and youth, conclude that there is a need for staff to work in communicative aspects in order to "cover the deficiency of not knowing well their public, and therefore, they do not cleave in order to carry out their actions of communication" (p.609). Meanwhile, Gomez-Vilchez (2012) talks about a communication program structured to establish a role and a function to each social environment, so that they get "user loyalty; build community and be community; speaking and listening; energize, engage, feedback, evaluate and ultimately, grow and improve" (p.85). As recent studies show mobile technologies have opened up new venues for cultural appreciation and cultural participation has become multiplatform (Chen, 2014).

These and other studies claim new models of work and denounce the lack of further research on organization and management models (Gómez-Vilches, 2012; Sloep & Berlanga, 2012). Definitely, a museum communication model that has the focus on the person is required. A model designed to cover the real needs of the audience, that is, the mission of the institution.

The CAC Málaga Mission

For the director of the CAC, the museum has many missions, but the main one is to spread the contemporary art, the current world art and not only the local one. To this end, exhibitions and cultural interrelation programs are held: Cinema, music, dance, literary actions, any type of performance, action or event. The objective is very much focused towards citizens, especially Malaga's neighbours and also shows how culture, and especially art, can change the structure of society. With this main idea they look for artists from a global context to see how they can serve to the local. The opposite route is also made: look for artists whose local discourse has a lot to say in the international scene. This is done not only with temporary exhibitions but also with permanent exhibition. They design a collection that tries to be permeable to the problems and sensitivities that are dealing with contemporary art in the world, well with international artists, good with local artists. Both for temporary exhibitions as for the permanent, works that serve the general discourse of the Museum. He cannot conceive that a museum has a closed collection, as it is a collector of stamps, with a beginning and an end. The museum collection has to be unique, and the works they buy should be acquired according to the principles of the museum. That's why sometimes, from an artist you can have 50 works and from another none, because his speech does not serve for the development of the objectives. The collection is conceived as an organic, living element that can go in one direction based on a conceptual thesis. They are very concerned about the issues border (and in this sense the location of Malaga is not casual: it is in the southern limit of a continent, is between two seas, it is between two continents, it is between two cultures, and it is between two religions). All those circumstances are important for them. Reflection on the concept of the South or on the concept of frontier, appears systematically in the program and artists are invited to reflect on those subjects. The issue of language is another recurring theme, as well as the issue of painting's concern. He considers that painting is not present in Spanish museums — yes in Germany — and he understands that this fact is due to the fact that in Spain painting is not consider modern, but in his opinion it is. That's why the CAC is the museum that exhibits the most of paintings, just because they consider themselves the most modern, not on the contrary: there is more painting than, for example, in the Reina Sofía that they have more documents, due to another way of understanding the matter, than in his opinion is wrong, because a museum of national character should have a global vision and not exclusive. Unlike, the CAC can have it because it is not a national museum. In his opinion, a museum must have its own idiosyncrasy, and the more unique it is, the more different, the more identifiable and it is better what it does. Summarizing the mission in one sentence, this would be: make citizens free. Undoubtedly, the mission affects the motivation of workers, it is considered something essential. And he thinks that this is the reason why public museums can never work—or they rarely work—from the parameter of the CAC. Despite he is an official service worker himself, he declares against the public administration public and does not believe that it works in a general way. He thinks that it is fundamental to involve the team in the objective — something that is not done in the administration, and therefore neither in public museums, rather, exclusively public. The CAC demonstrates how with a team of 20, six times more exhibitions than in other museums, can be done, without leaving the same region, whereas when the team is not involved even if they have more budget they cannot.

The public of the CAC knows the mission better and better, and progressively because it is something that has a lot of difficulty to transmit. What is true is that when the years go by the public, especially the local public gets special sensitivity. And in the opinion of its director, it is an incredible achievement the fact that the public get to detect a kind of sensitivity. If there is not a coherent program, it is very difficult to identify the museum's objective; and on the contrary, if one is very faithful to the program itself, to the objectives, overtime people come to detect it. Citizens get to interpret in what museum are recognized and what not. There are museums in which the citizen feels special when he gets into it, he feels care, singular, and the citizen detects it.

CAC Málaga Communication

They have a strategic plan of communication and it is a plan that changes to the sound of the problems of a changing society that evolves rapidly. It adapts and changes whenever a need arises. At the same time, they have control of the museum's quality methodology, so that when a singularity arises in any of the work processes -including that of communication— a solution is sought to correct the problem, which already implies a change of the strategic plan. There is no department that has a stable norm; all the rules are established or modified according to the daily experience of the museum. A concrete example is the modification of the weighting criterion, two years ago of social networks for the objectives of the institution, a fact that led to granting 265 analysis and interpretation of data the priority to the Instagram network: when a new social network appeared that gave its Top priority to the image, they were echoed and given primacy over Twitter. They believe that it is very difficult to transmit values or maintain a debate in 140 characters, because the nuances in art are fundamental, as they are in the culture, in society. This is the reason why in 2014 the CAC was the Spanish museum with more influence on

Instagram in Spain, above the Prado, of Reina Sofía, of Thyssen. It was an achievement fruit of an enormous dedication of attention and time.

Methodology

This research takes as its starting point the definition of a museum that offers ICOM (2007), as it has been defined in the introduction. This presented us with the following research questions: Does society really have involvement and prominence in the museum that is attributed to it? Is technology fully exploited to make the service a reality to society and are they open to the public as they say they are? Are audiences heard to manage the museum and to organize the activities? Does the museum have a strategic planning of communication? and if so is it based on the mission of the institution?

The most usual experience leads us to affirm that the prevailing model of communication management in Spanish museums is unidirectional, despite having introduced the use of social networks to communicate with the public. One of the main causes is the lack of education in media literacy of managers and employees who have incorporated them more like fashion than as authentic social service. We suspect that a management model based on the mission provides institutions that include among its main purposes the educational and communicative, necessary tools to achieve successfully those purposes. We set as research objectives:

1. Study in depth the prosocial management model (Muñoz-Seca & Riverola, 2011) that receives its impulse of the technological revolution and its profound effects on the world of the company and the institutions;
2. Contextualize two fundamental concepts to carry out the research: communication and mission;
3. Identify a representative museum;
4. Do an in-depth interview with the director;
5. Assess the results of the research and propose applications both theoretical as practices.

The methodological technique is the case study, which is recommended for underdeveloped areas of knowledge, in which they have to create new research theories and hypotheses inductively that further studies will try to confirm (Stake, 1995). Museum bidirectional communication for the development of museum strategy is still very recent and a little studied practice. So we set out first an approach to the CAC museum, its management and the way new technologies are used as communication tools, and, from there, to offer interpretations applicable to other entities. CAC Málaga selection responds to its preeminence in the areas that are the subject of our study. As for communication management, it is an innovative museum. For them, communication with the public is considered absolutely bi-directional. They created the first web 2.0 of Spanish museums. And actually, they are considering designing another. Their web allows you to have a conversation with the viewer in each service: in the specific information, in the blog, in the pedagogical aspect. As a data, the only document that is always in the entrance and never change is: "What do you think?". The TICs they use in this bi-directional communication are Instagram, Facebook, Twitter, Ninja, Pinterest, YouTube, with its own video channel, Google+, Friend Feed, Flickr, Picassa, Delicious, Foursquare and LinkedIn.

Results

About the management model, the CAC Málaga has a novel and unique system in Spain, it is an Art Center in which private management is linked (limited company), with the public objectives set by the Public Administration. It is a model of service concession (Francés, 2007).

Regarding the mission, the CAC Málaga has a fairly defined mission: to spread among citizens contemporary local and international art. They also do it from a concrete form that consists of inserting current social issues into the museum. For example, to attract young audiences, they put the Museum in "ArtStreet". They say they are not aware of working on a mission statement. But the fact is that they have it very defined. The mission affects completely the staff of the museum as a whole, and their permanence in the museum depends on the identification they have with the mission. Regarding the communication of the mission, although the director told us that the mission is communicated with conferences or social networks, after the study of the museum as a whole we have detected that the mission is communicated more than what is has been said, unconsciously, both formally and informally. In reference to whether it has been heard the public for the elaboration of the mission, it must be said that, although on the part of the director the answer is negative, we think that implicitly yes, the audience has been heard, especially the potential audience, as there is a clear determination to cover a need for cultural training on art contemporary existing in the diverse public.

The communication of the CAC Málaga is completely based on the mission of the museum, it has no other meaning. They have a strategic communication plan flexible, since they are adapting it to all technological innovations that come up. It is a totally bidirectional communication, even the website was the first that gave the possibility to interact in all the aspects. They use a great variety of Tics: Web 2.0, Blog, social networks like Instagram, Twitter, Ninja, Pinterest, YouTube Channel and Google+. With the information received from the public there is a dialogue and active listening is done.

With the data collected we will try to answer the research questions that we set out initially and that respond to how the management of the museums is studied, and if this corresponds to the characteristics of a prosocial management model.

Regarding to the question about society implication and involvement with the museum, we think that as far as the mission is concerned, there is no such prominence. The mission is unidirectional, it comes exclusively from the museum, the public is not involved at all and, far from being a protagonist, it is treated as a mere spectator. With regard to communication however, the approach is different. We have discovered that, occasionally, It is the public who approach the museum on the subject of social networks, as they are incorporated into society as something natural, while institutions still do not know how to treat the information that is received. In fact, the CAC Malaga has had and maintains initiatives to attract potential publics, giving them certain importance, as it is the case of the youth, when introducing the "Art Street" in the Museum.

The second research question is about maximum utilization of technology to make service to society a reality and open to the public that these institutions postulate. We have been struck by the ability to adaptation of the CAC Málaga to ICTs; the fact that they have a strategic plan of communication that continually adapts to the latest trends is quite symptomatic.

With regard to the third research question on whether the museum listen to the audiences for the management and for the organization of activities, we have observed that in general the answer has been negative. But on the other hand, we realize that they do not do it explicitly. For example, the director told us that planning starts directly from the museum, without taking into account the tastes of the public at all. And that if they took into account the tastes of the public they would lose their mission, because what the public requests is an aesthetically pleasing art. The proof is that the most numerous exhibition that they have had has been that of Sorolla. But one thing is taste and another is necessity. Not giving the audience what they like does not mean that they do not know their needs. They think that to cover those needs you have to listen to the public, at least know their shortcomings. To show contemporary art is a necessity, since — as Kandinsky said — "each work of art is the daughter of its time "and to know the man of today we have to know what he reflects through art. So we can say that the CAC, definitely "listens" to the publics implicitly and plan accordingly.

Regarding the last question raised about whether the museum has a strategic plan of communication and if it is based on the mission of the institution. We think that the CAC Málaga works with a strategy of communication based on the mission.

Discussion & Contribution

We make a critical and contextualized review of the results and conclusions. In the first place, it is noted that the general methodology established for the object of study has been a valid instrument since it has allowed us to know how a museum is managed and how would this management be with the parameters of the prosocial model. As we described in the section on the method chosen for this research the transfer of the prosocial model in general to museum management in particular is a new and necessary point to address the object of study in depth and without bias. And being this something that we have not found in the approaches of the investigations carried out regarding museum management, we consider it is the strongest point of the work.

The case study together with the focused interview to the director of the museum is proposed as an effective method that allows us to know in depth what a unique conception of mission is, the role that it occupies in the configuration of the institution and the particular concretions of the management and communication. For these reasons, we believe that this general methodology can be extrapolated to other researches that intend to analyse the management of cultural-museum communication in other contexts.

However, it seems to us that the reflection of the particular management of museums and the communication could be more valuable if you complete the results of a concrete empirical application. Taking into account the novelty and interest of this translation because it was not done previously, and due to the high component humanistic and by the new perspectives that it offers us, this empirical research remains pending for the near future. We believe that the investigation it is neither finished nor final. The evolution of the object of study demands a constant updating and methodological reformulation. We leave by so open the debate on all the issues that emerge from this investigation.

Theoretical and Practical Applications

The theoretical applications are mainly adjusted to the development of knowledge in itself and the generation of new conceptual research tools. So we hope that this study serves to provide innovative ideas to future researchers who apply to his works the exposed anthropological management model applied to the communication in museums in other contexts, or at least that they use it as a starting point.

In terms of practical applications remember that the final result we were pursuing in this research was to perform work that could serve as a model and inspiration in the management of museum communication. And also, that this model can be an open proposal to subsequent contributions and new ways of reflection among museum management professionals and in particular on communication.

References

Bantimaroudis, P., Zyglidopoulos, S., & Symeou, P. C. (2010). Greek Museum Media Visibility and Museum Visitation: An Exploration of Cultural Agenda Setting. *Journal of Communication, 60*, 743-757.

Baraybar, A., & Ibañez, J. A. (2012). La gestión de la comunicación museística. Hábitos y usos profesionales. *Revista Telos, 93*, 127-135.

Barnard, C. (1971). *The Functions of the Executive*. Massachusetts: Harvard University Press.

Bart, C., Bontis, N., & Taggar, S. (2001). A model of the impact of mission statements on firm performance. *Management Decision, 39*(1), 19-35.

Bastons, M. (2000). *La toma de decisiones en la organización*. Barcelona: Ariel.

Batson, D. (1987). Prosocial motivation: It is ever truly altruistic? *Advances in Experimental Social Psychology, 20*, 65-122. New York: Academic Press.

Becerra, E., & Domínguez, B. (2014). Museos, comunicación y jóvenes: la comunicación y sus efectos en la población de referencia del museo. *Historia y Comunicación Social,19*, 603-611. DOI: http://dx.doi.org/10.5209/rev_HICS.2014.v19.44988.

Brief, A., & Motowidlo, S. (1986). Prosocial Organizational Behaviors. *Academy of Management Review, 11*(4), 710 - 725.

Camarero, C., Garrido, M. J., & San José, R. (2016). Efficiency of Web Communication Strategies: The Case of Art Museums. *International Journal of Arts Management, 18*(2), 42-62.

Campbell, A., & Yeung, S. (1991). Creating a sense of mission. *Long Range Planning, 24*(4), 10-20.

Cardona, P., & Rey, C. (2008). *Management by Missions*. New York: Palgrave.

Chen, W. (2015). A Moveable Feast: Do Mobile Media Technologies Mobilize or Normalize Cultural Participation? *Human Communication Research, 41*,82-101.

Çinar, O., Bektas, Ç., & Aslan, I. (2011). A motivation study on the effectiveness of intrinsic and extrinsic factors. *Economics & Management, 16,* 690-695.

Chinchilla, N. (2001). *Paradigmas del Liderazgo. Distintos enfoques para la dirección de personas en las organizaciones.* Madrid: Mcgraw-Hill.

Cyert, R., &March, J. (1963). *A behavioral Theory of the Firm.* New Jersey: Prentice-Hall.

Deci, E., & Ryan, R. (1985). *Intrinsic motivation and Self-Determination in human behavior.* New York: Plenum Press.

Drucker, P. (1974/1993). *Management: Tasks, responsabilities, practices.* New Brunswick: Harper & Row.

Frances, F. (2007). Modelos públicos de gestión privada. *Museos,12.*

Gagné, M., & Deci, E. (2005). Self-determination theory and work motivation. *Journal of Organizational Behavior, 26,* 331-362.

Gómez Vilchez, S. (2012). Evaluación de preferencia y participación. Museos españoles y redes sociales. *Revista Telos, 90,* 79-86.

Grant, A. (2008). Does Intrinsic Motivation Fuel the Prosocial Fire? Motivational Synergy in Predicting Persistence, Performance and Productivity. *Journal of Applied Psychology, 93*(1), 48-58.

Guillen, M., Ferrero I., & Hoffman, M. (2014). The Neglected Ethical and Spiritual Motivations in the Workplace. *Journal of Business Ethics,128,* 803–816 DOI 10.1007/s10551-013-1985-7.

Herzberg, F. (1966). *Work and the nature of man.* New York: Crowell.

ICOM (2007). Museum definition. Retrieved from http://icom.museum/the-vision/museum-definition/

ICOM (2009). Key Concepts of Museology. Retrieved from http://icom.museum/fileadmin/user_upload/pdf/Key_Concepts_of_M useology/Museologie_Anglais_BD.pdf

ICOM Digital (2012). Museos y redes sociales. Revista del Comité Español del ICOM. No. 5. Retrieved from http://goo.gl/fR3p1c.

Ireland, D., & Hitt, M. (1992). Mission statements: Importance, challenge, and recommendations for development. *Business Horizons, 35*(3), 34-42.

Klemm, M., Sanderson, S., & Luffman, G. (1991). Mission statements: selling corporate values to employees. *Long Range Planning, 24*(3),73-78.

Jancovich, L. (2015). Breaking Downs the Fourth Wall in Arts Management: The Implications of Engaging Users in Decision-Making. *International Journal of Arts Management, 18*(1),14-28.

March, J., & Simon, H. (1958/1993). *Organizations.* Cambridge: Blackwell.

Maslow, A. (1954). *Motivation and Personality.* New York: Harper and Row.

McGregor, D. (1966). *Leadership and Motivation.* Massachusetts: The MIT Press.

Melé, D. (2003). The Challenge of Humanistic Management. *Journal of Business Ethics, 44,* 77-88.

Muñoz-Seca, B., & Riverola. J. (2007). *Opera Operaciones*. Madrid: Pearson Educación.

Muñoz-Seca, B., & Riverola, J. (Eds.) (2011). *Arte y eficiencia: el sector de la cultura visto desde la empresa*. Pamplona: Ediciones Universidad de Navarra.

Pulh, M., & Mencarelli, R. (2015). Web 2.0: Is the Museum-Visitor Relationship Being Redefined?, *International Journal of Arts Management, 18*(1), 43-51.

Pérez-López, L. (1994/2018). *Fundamentos de la Dirección de Empresas*. Madrid: Ediciones Rialp.

Pérez-Pérez, L., Bastons, M., & Berlanga, I. (2015). Modelo prosocial de comunicación de museos. El caso Thyssen Bornemisza. *Opción, 31*(31), 1008-1026.

Rajasekar, J. (2013). A Comparative Analysis of Mission Statement Content an Readability. *Journal of Management Policy and Practice, 14*(6), 131-147.

Rosanas, J. (2008). Beyond Economic Criteria: A Humanistic Approach to Organizational Survival. *Journal of Business Ethics, 78*, 447-462.

Ryan, R., & Deci, E. (2000). Intrinsic and Extrinsic Motivations: Classic Definitions and New Directions. *Contemporary Educational Psychology, 25*, 54-67.

Scott, W. (1981). *Organizations: Rational, Natural and Open Systems*. New Jersey: Prentice-Hall.

Sloep, P.& Berlanga, A. (2011). Redes de aprendizaje, aprendizaje en red. *Revista Comunicar, 19*(37), 55-64. Accessed 15 April 2016 at DOI: http://dx.doi.org/10.3916/C37-2011-02-05.

Simon, H. (1976). *Administrative Behavior*. New York: The Free Press.

Stake, R. (1995). *The Art of Case Study Research*. SAGE Publications. London.

Viñarás, M. (2010). Acciones bidireccionales en la Red. Herramientas de la Web 2. London 0 en la gestión de la comunicación de las instituciones culturales. *Revista Telos, 82*, 1-9.

Wang, Y. (2011). Mission-Driven Organizations in Japan: Management Philosophy and Individual Outcomes. *Journal of Business Ethics, 101*,111-126.

Contributors

Claudia Nelly Berrones-Flemmig is currently lecturer, postdoctoral researcher and consultant in International SEPT Program – Small Enterprise Promotion and Training at Leipzig University, Germany. She has a PhD in Small Enterprise Development from Leipzig University, Germany. She has been Lecturer at ITESM University, Mexico and Friedrich-Schiller-University Jena, Germany. She is also international business consultant, particularly for Mexican SMEs and German Start-ups. Her research interests are SME finance and SME financial management, social entrepreneurship and immigrant entrepreneurship.

Francoise Contreras is full professor and director of research in the School of Administration at the Universidad del Rosario in Bogotá, Colombia. She is psychologist, Master in Education and PhD in Psychology from Universidad Autónoma de Madrid in Spain. Her research area of interest is leadership and organizational behaviour. She is the author of several articles, which have been published in important journals such as International Journal of Entrepreneurial Behaviour and Research (UK), Asian Social Science (Canada), Journal of Human Values (India), among others.

Utz Dornberger is the Director of the International SEPT Program and has a Professorship in Development economics at Leipzig University (Germany). He is also Director of Start-up initiative Self-Management Initiative Leipzig (SMILE) at Leipzig University (Germany), Director of MBA Program at Hanoi University of Science and Technology (HUST) and Vietnamese-German University (VGU) and Lecturer on innovation management and entrepreneurship promotion, and head of the unit of Entrepreneurship and Innovation for Development Cooperation at Fraunhofer Center for International Management and Knowledge Economy (IMW) (Leipzig, Germany).
His academic and professional focus is especially on innovation in SMEs, innovation policy, entrepreneurship promotion and internationalization processes.

Yonni Angel Cuero Acosta has a PhD in Small Enterprises Development (Leipzig University, Germany). Currently, he is a postdoctoral researcher and lecturer in International SEPT Program at Leipzig University. His research interests include international entrepreneurship, the development of technology-intensive suppliers in emerging economies, and the analysis of natural resources-based value chains.

Andreana Drencheva is a Lecturer (Assistant Professor) in Entrepreneurship at the University of Sheffield, UK. Her research explores the microfoundations of (social) entrepreneurship and social change, recognising the influence of culture. She holds a PhD from the Institute of Work Psychology, University of Sheffield. She collaborates with support organisations to co-create services, programmes, and tools for (potential) social entrepreneurs – particularly focusing on catalysing social change, leading and scaling social ventures, and avoiding mission drift.

Edward J. O'Boyle earned his doctorate in economics at Saint Louis University. He is Senior Research Associate with Mayo Research Institute, specializing in personalist economics that focuses on economic agency in which *homo economicus* and the individualism of orthodox economics are replaced by the *person of action* and personalism. He has published in the *Monthly Labor Review, Review of Social Economy, Forum for Social Economics, Pediatrics, The Linacre Quarterly, International Journal of Social Economics, Business Insights, Journal of Business Ethics, Quarterly Journal of Ideology, Ethics and Information Technology, Journal of Markets and Morality, Storia del Pensiero Economico, Corporate Governance,* and others. Dr. O'Boyle has authored or edited books on economics, edited journal issues, contributed chapters in several books, and written an e-text for use in teaching principles of economics. He has taught economics in Poland, Ireland, and Italy. Dr. O'Boyle is a past president of the Association for Social Economics and a recipient of its *Thomas Divine Award* for lifetime contributions to social economics and the social economy.

Joanna M. Szulc is a Lecturer in Department of Management in Huddersfield Business School, Behavioral Research Centre, UK. Her research interests focus broadly on workplace relationships and the overriding aim of Joanna's work is to enhance a range of organizational outcomes including its effectiveness, competitiveness, and employee morale. Joanna is a an Associate member of the Chartered Institute of Personnel and Development and a member of the European Academy of Management.

Michael A. Piel, D.M., is a retired aerospace information technology project manager and university professor in leadership, philosophy, ethics, and critical thinking. Mike as a consultant to international organizations helps leaders achieve higher levels of performance excellence through focused reflection on the management pillars of emotional intelligence, critical thinking, ethics, and project management. In addition to having published papers in academic journals and book chapters, Mike has pen-name written the novel *The Cambrian Rod.*

Karen Putnam, ABD., works as an international contractor supporting the Unites States military and State Department. Working in the US, Afghanistan, and Iraq on a variety of Information Technology contracts, Karen earned several technology certifications from various global organizations. Working in Kabul since February 2017, and in support of a doctorate in management at the University of Phoenix, Karen is writing her dissertation- *ICT Usage Among Afghan Women Business Leaders: A Descriptive Case Study.* Karen can be contacted at *kp5487@cox.net.*

Karen K. Johnson, Ed.D., is a state, regional, and internationally recognized leader, innovator, coach, and mentor. After four decades of coaching leaders on how to sustain and grow organizations, her work in professional organizations, businesses, manufacturing firms, universities, and charter schools has earned her regional, state, and international awards. Dr. Johnson mentors doctoral students at the University of Phoenix through their dissertation research. She has mentored over 30 students to successful completion since 2007. Karen can be contacted at *kkayj@comcast.net.*

Renata Rosmus, PhD. Specializations: psychology of adults and psychology of work, preparing for study exams on psychological functioning of an individual and human groups (diagnosing and giving help). Didactic abilities gained from formal education (graduating from postgraduate study of methodology of psychology of teaching) and professional experience (giving lectures, conversations, plans, training sessions). Professional experience gained from work with patients thanks to employment in GZOZ in Bytom. Staff member of Katowice School of Economics. Cooperation: University of Silesia, Silesian University of Technology, University of Economics in Katowice, Medical University o Silesia. Interests: matter of justice in an interpersonal relationship, attachment and loyalty, process of appraising, conflicts and ways of solving them, trust and manipulation, social abilities, management.

Luka Boršić is senior scientific associate at the Institute of Philosophy in Zagreb and a lecturer at Rochester Institute of Technology (USA, Croatia). His areas of specialization are the following: ancient philosophy (particularly Plato and Platonic tradition), Early Modern philosophy, philosophical foundation of science, history of science and gender philosophy. He is author of 3 books, editor of 8 books, author of 10 book chapters and 15 journal articles.

Ivana Skuhala Karasman is senior scientific associate at the Institute of Philosophy in Zagreb. Her areas of specialization are the following: Early Modern philosophy and gender philosophy. Skuhala Karasman authored 3 books, edited 6 books, wrote 8 book chapters and 26 journal articles.
Boršić and Skuhala Karasman have been collaborating for many years on various publications regarding gender philosophy and presently are leading the 5-year project "Women Philosophers in the European Context". For their work they received the Excellence Award in Scientific Work at the Institute of Philosophy two years in a row (2016 and 2017).

Dominika Ochnik, PhD, doctor of social science, psychologist and trainer, Assistant Professor in Department of Psychology at University of Opole, Poland. Certificated coach (Centre for Coaching, ILM, London). Experienced consultant in Talent Management area. Author of honored PhD dissertation and articles as well as chapters in books on entrepreneurship. Co-editor of a book: 'Psychology in business. New perspectives.' Organizer of a conference cycle: Psychology and Business, dedicated to the theme of Selflessness and Business. Presenter on international conferences. Research interests focus on psychology of work: vocational interests, entrepreneurial attitude, and psychological aspects of singlehood. Research project manager in grant on Internet Addiction funded by Ministry of Health, Republic of Poland. Member of Association for Psychological Science (APS), and American Psychological Association (APA).

Monika Jakubiak, PhD, since 2014 Assistant Professor at the Faculty of Economics Maria Curie-Sklodowska University, Lublin, Poland. Between 2002-2014 Lublin University of Technology Career Services Office Coordinator, author and coordinator of 4 Higher Education and Training projects co-financed by the European Social Fund (EFS) in the domains: internships and professional career counselling for engineering students, development of the university's didactic potential. She is the author of over 50 reviewed scientific papers in fields of competencies, entrepreneurship and university-business cooperation.

Hector Alberto Botello Peñaloza gained master's degree in economics. Member of the Research Group on Regional Development and Spatial Planning at the Industrial University of Santander.

Lucía Pérez-Pérez has a Ph.D. in Communication (Culture and Museum) at the University of Málaga. She is an associate professor at the Cultural Management Master of the International University of Catalonia (Barcelona, Spain) and at the International University of la Rioja. Her research focuses on cultural management through missions. She is a research member of the Chair in Mission Leadership and Corporate Governance at the Catalonian International University.

Miquel Bastons has a Ph.D. in Philosophy and a Ph.D. in Management. He is an associate professor of organizational behavior and ethics at the School of Economics and Social Sciences of the International University of Catalonia (Barcelona, Spain). His research focuses on organizational decision-making and business ethics. He has published books and articles on organizational behavior, decision-making in organizations and business ethics.

Index

www.ingramcontent.com/pod-product-compliance
Lightning Source LLC
Chambersburg PA
CBHW061218220326
41599CB00025B/4677